't Jo

D0301592

Design for Inclusivity

Design for Social Responsibility Series

Series Editor: Rachel Cooper

Social responsibility, in various disguises, has been a recurring theme in design for many years. Since the 1960s several more or less commercial approaches have evolved. In the 1970s designers were encouraged to abandon 'design for profit' in favour of a more compassionate approach inspired by Papanek.

In the 1980s and 1990s profit and ethical issues were no longer considered mutually exclusive and more market-oriented concepts emerged, such as the 'green consumer' and ethical investment. The purchase of socially responsible, 'ethical' products and services has been stimulated by the dissemination of research into sustainability issues in consumer publications. Accessibility and inclusivity have also attracted a great deal of design interest and recently designers have turned to solving social and crime-related problems.

Organisations supporting and funding such projects have recently included the NHS (research into design for patient safety); the Home Office has (design against crime); Engineering and Physical Sciences Research Council (design decision-making for urban sustainability). Businesses are encouraged (and increasingly forced by legislation) to set their own socially responsible agendas that depend on design to be realised.

Design decisions all have environmental, social and ethical impacts, so there is a pressing need to provide guidelines for designers and design students within an overarching framework that takes a holistic approach to socially responsible design.

This edited series of guides is aimed at students of design, product development, architecture and marketing, and design and management professionals working in the sectors covered by each title. Each volume includes:

- The background and history of the topic, its significance in social and commercial contexts and trends in the field.

- Exemplar design case studies.

- Guidelines for the designer and advice on tools, techniques and resources available.

Design for Inclusivity

A Practical Guide to Accessible, Innovative and User-Centred Design

ROGER COLEMAN, JOHN CLARKSON, HUA DONG and JULIA CASSIM

GOWER

Published by
Gower Publishing Limited
Gower House
Croft Road
Aldershot
Hampshire GU11 3HR
England

Ashgate Publishing Company
Suite 420
101 Cherry Street
Burlington, VT 05401-4405
USA

Roger Coleman, John Clarkson, Hua Dong and Julia Cassim have asserted their moral right under the Copyright, Designs and Patents Act, 1988, to be identified as the authors of this work.

British Library Cataloguing in Publication Data
Design for inclusivity : a practical guide to accessible,
    innovative and user-centered design. - (Design for social
    responsibility)
    1. Design, Industrial - Social aspects 2. Design -
    Philosophy 3. Social responsibility of business
    I. Coleman, Roger
    745.2

    ISBN-13: 9780566087073

Library of Congress Cataloging-in-Publication Data
Design for inclusivity : a practical guide to accessible, innovative and user-centred design / by Roger Coleman ... [et al.].
        p. cm. -- (Design for social responsibility)
    Includes bibliographical references and index.
    ISBN-13: 978-0-566-08707-3
    1. Design, Industrial. 2. Engineering design--Technological innovations. I. Coleman, Roger.
    TS171.D4638 2007
    745.2--dc22

                                                                                    2007035656

Printed and bound in Great Britain by TJ International Ltd, Padstow, Cornwall.

Contents

List of Figures

List of Contributors

Maria Benktzon, Partner, Ergonomidesign, Stockholm. Professor and partner of Ergonomidesign, one of Scandinavia's largest and best-renowned industrial design consultancies, and active inclusive design practitioner.

Olle Bobjer, Partner, Ergonomidesign, Stockholm. Dr Bobjer worked as a researcher at the National Swedish Institute for Occupational Safety and Health and became a partner in Ergonomidesign in 1980, developing products whose performance and ease-of-use have resulted in measurable gains for the users.

Robert Brown, Director and Co-founder, Sprout Design Ltd. Sprout Design specialises in developing inclusive and environment-friendly products and packaging for commercial clients in manufacturing and retail. Robert has also developed inclusive design assessment methodologies with colleagues at Cambridge and the RCA.

Carlos Cardoso, Assistant Professor of Design Theory and Methodology, Delft University of Technology. Trained as an industrial designer at the Faculty of Architecture, Technical University of Lisbon, Carlos is currently investigating ways to improve design usability and accessibility of products, services and environments for all users.

Julia Cassim, Senior Research Fellow, Helen Hamlyn Centre, Royal College of Art, London. Julia is leader of the HHCs Inclusive Business Programme and organiser of the DBA Inclusive Design Challenge. Her expertise encompasses visual and cognitive impairment, museum and exhibition design and interpretation, inclusive design and design education.

John Clarkson, Engineering Design Centre, University of Cambridge. Professor of Engineering Design and Director of the Cambridge Engineering Design Centre. He returned to the University after 7 years with PA Consulting Group. His research interests are focused on the areas of design process improvement, healthcare design and inclusive design.

Roger Coleman, Helen Hamlyn Centre, Royal College of Art, London. Roger is Research Professor in Inclusive design and Patient Safety at the RCA, where he established the award-winning DesignAge programme in 1991, followed by the Helen Hamlyn Centre in 1999. He is active in promoting inclusive design practice to business and industry and introducing an evidence-based approach to healthcare design.

Hua Dong, Lecturer in Design, Brunel University. Dr Hua Dong was a Research Associate at the Cambridge Engineering Design Centre. She has a first degree in Industrial Design, a masters in Architectural Design and Theory (Tongji University) and her PhD (University of Cambridge) focused on barriers to inclusive design.

Susan Hewer, Head of Design, Royal Society for the Encouragement of Arts, Manufactures and Commerce. Susan has had a special interest in inclusive design since running the first student project in this area in 1986. She has been involved with many European Commission funded projects, networks, workshops and conferences on inclusive design.

Ian Hosking, Managing Consultant, Sagentia Ltd, Cambridge. Ian has 18 years of experience in applying usability in business. He is currently focusing on the application of leading academic research to help companies design more inclusive products and services. This work has included the development of an on-line Inclusive Design Toolkit in conjunction with the inclusive design research programme and BT plc.

Cherie Lebbon, Senior Lecturer in Design Theory at the University of Coventry. Cherie Lebbon is a lecturer, researcher and designer and has been a major contributor in the field of inclusive design over the past 10 years; first as a Research Fellow at the Helen Hamlyn Centre and later a senior lecturer at the South Bank University and Coventry.

Andrew Monk, Department of Psychology, University of York. Professor of Psychology and Fellow of the British Computer Society. His research interests include requirements for the home use of information and communication technology and formative evaluation of prototypes, especially communication systems.

Jeremy Myerson, Director of the Helen Hamlyn Centre at the Royal College of Art. Jeremy Myerson is Professor of Design Studies at the RCA, where he is a member of the Senior Management Group and leads the College's innovation network for business. He was the founding editor of Design Week and has authored many books on design.

Alan Newell, School of Computing, University of Dundee. Professor Newell was Head of the Applied Computing Department until 2002. His major research interests are in computer systems to assist people with disabilities, computer systems in areas of high social impact, and Human Computer Interaction.

Colette Nicolle, Ergonomics and Safety Research Institute, Loughborough University. Research Fellow at ESRI, contributing to both research and teaching in ergonomics and inclusive design. She is Secretary to IFIP WG 13.3 on Human Computer Interaction and Disability and a Fellow of the Ergonomics Society.

Ingelise Nielsen, Head of Human Resources (Europe), IDEO, London. While leading the Marketing Communications at IDEO in Europe, she contributed to many publications that tell the story of IDEO's unique user-focused approach to design and innovation.

Graham Pullin, IDEO, London. An interaction designer with experience of designing for people with severe disabilities, Graham has designed award-winning furniture for children with cerebral palsy and led the project 'Social Mobiles' at IDEO. He is particularly interested in verbal communication.

Barry Tanner, Applied Energy Product Ltd. Barry is the New Product Introduction Manager of the Applied Energy Product Ltd. He led the award-winning Redring's Selectronic shower project in partnership with the RNIB for use by vulnerable members of the public and visually impaired users.

Alan Topalian, Director, Alto Design Management, London. Acknowledged pioneer in developing design management into a rigorous discipline in business. With research interests in design and innovation management, he is co-author of several British Standards on managing design and innovation and inclusive design.

David Yelding, Research Institute for Consumer Affairs (Ricability). Director of Ricability, a national research charity dedicated to providing independent information of value to disabled and older consumers, David's expertise includes consumer education, ergonomics, information provision and dissemination, and research methods.

Acknowledgements

Design for Inclusivity is the latest in a series of publications on the subject from a collaborative team at the University of Cambridge and the Royal College of Art, London, working with an extensive network of designers, engineers and researchers, many of whom have contributed to this and earlier books. Inclusive design has evolved over the past 10 years in the UK as a way of helping and supporting business and industry to meet the needs of older people and those with disabilities, and working towards a more inclusive society where all people can participate and contribute on an equal footing.

The work presented in the book has been generously supported by the UK Engineering and Physical Sciences Research Council (EPSRC), and championed by the Design Council, the DTI and Scope, the disability organisation whose focus is cerebral palsy. Many companies have been involved with it, in particular technology management and product development consultancy Sagentia, DIY leader B&Q through new product development, and BT, especially through its Age and Disability Action Programme and by making the Inclusive Design Toolkit it developed with the editorial team available to the general public at www.inclusivedesigntoolkit.com.

Much of the other work illustrated has come from two main sources, the Design Business Association Inclusive Design Challenge and the Helen Hamlyn Research Associates Programme, and the authors owe a considerable debt to all the design consultancies and the young designers who have participated in both programmes.

Coordinating the work of 20 authors has not been easy and the editors wish to thank Mari Hutala of the Cambridge Engineering Design Centre Cambridge, and Margaret Durkan of the Helen Hamlyn Centre at the Royal College of Art for all their help and support, in particular with sourcing images.

Finally the editors would like to thank Professor Peter Lansley, Director of the EPSRC EQUAL Network and the BBSRC / EPSRC SPARC Network, who has been an indomitable promoter and supporter of inclusive design in the UK and of the editorial team and its work; Fiona Miller and David Barret of BT who collaborated with the editorial team over 3 years on promoting inclusive design to industry; David Alcock of Scope for championing inclusive design through the CITD initiative; and Alan Topalian for leading the work on the British Standard in inclusive design management, BS 7000-6.

The Editors

Preface

Concern for society has often been a theme amongst designers and craftsworkers. Indeed in the UK, Ruskin and Morris at the turn of the 20th century actively pursued design and production in the material world in a manner consistent with moral and ethical values for the benefit of the wider society. During that century the design profession grew, becoming divorced from both art and crafts and production, first with the commercial designer, then the product designer, interior designer and so on, whilst architecture continued to remain an independent profession outside the broader domains of design. During that period too, the economies of the West, consumption and the use of the world's resources continued to grow at an alarming rate, contributing to the ongoing fragility of society and planet earth.

By the 1960s designers began to actively consider the wider implications of design for society. Several approaches emerged, including green design and consumerism; responsible design and ethical consuming; ecodesign and sustainability; and feminist design. In the 1970s Papanek, amongst others, encouraged designers to abandon 'design for profit' in favour of a more compassionate approach. In the 1980s and 1990s profit and ethical issues were no longer considered mutually exclusive and more market-oriented approaches emerged, such as the 'green consumer' and ethical investment. The purchase of socially responsible, 'ethical' products and services was facilitated by the dissemination of research into sustainability in consumer publications and the emergence of retail entrepreneurs such as the late Anita Roddick of The Body Shop. Accessibility and inclusivity also saw a great deal of design interest and activity and, more recently, designers have turned to resolving issues related to crime.

At the same time governments, businesses and individuals have become increasingly aware of what we are doing, not only to the world, but also to each other. Human rights, sustainability and ethics are all issues of concern, whilst the relationship between national economies and poverty struggles to be resolved. Global businesses have recognised the changing environment and are setting their own corporate social responsibility (CSR) agendas. The World Business Council for Sustainable Development proposes that 'CSR is the continuing commitment by business to behave ethically and contribute to economic development while improving the quality of life of the workforce and their families as well as of the local community and society at large' (Moir, 2001). If businesses and organisations are to turn these ideas into reality, 'design' is an essential ingredient.

Designers make daily decisions with regard to the use of resources, and to the lifestyle and use of products, places and communications. In order to achieve the needs of businesses, the desires of the consumer and improvement of the world, the designer in making decisions must embrace dimensions of social responsibility. However, there is now a need to shift from focusing on a single issue towards taking a more holistic approach to socially responsible design. This book is part of a series that brings together the leading authors and researchers to provide texts on each of the major socially responsible dimensions. Each book in the series provides a background to the history and emergence of the topic, provides case study exemplars and indicates where the reader can access further information and help.

Professor Rachel Cooper
Lancaster University, UK

Introduction

Julia Cassim, Roger Coleman,
John Clarkson and Hua Dong

> 'We believe that applying an inclusive design approach is good for business as well as for customers. We are proud of our reputation for developing products which can be used by all our customers, regardless of age or ability.'
>
> BT Inclusive Design Toolkit (www.inclusivedesigntoolkit.com)

About This Book

By the time you read this introduction there will be more people living in urban areas than rural, and 60 per cent projected to live in urban areas by 2030 (United Nations, 2005), we can no longer claim to live in a world shaped primarily by nature, but in a designed and constructed environment, shaped by human beings. There is little doubt that as a consequence we are changing the climate, reducing species diversity and consuming natural resources above and beyond replacement rates. We have to think and act at a global level if we are to meet the challenges posed by our success as a species, and ask questions about the role and responsibilities of design and designers in shaping the future. Importantly, we have to recognise that we share the planet with over 6 billion other human beings, and we are not all the same.

Thinking globally means recognising and celebrating human diversity. It means embracing difference, be it physical, intellectual, cultural, aspirational, or of lifestyle. And in an increasingly global marketplace, understanding and catering for difference is crucial to business success. The design challenge is to include, and not to exclude unknowingly. Design for inclusivity, like the other forms of socially responsive design featured in this series, has its origins in the 1960s when a small number of designers, engineers and scientists began to grapple with the implications of a global society. They questioned the assumptions and consequences of modern design and production, and began to make the case for a more socially responsive and responsible approach to design.

Since then, inclusivity has moved from the margins of design thinking to the mainstream. It is increasingly embraced by major companies and there is a British Standard in inclusive design management that gives practical guidance for business leaders, design managers and design teams.

This book comes from an established research team in inclusive design, that brings together the Engineering Design Centre at the University of Cambridge and the Helen Hamlyn Centre at the Royal College of Art, London. The research has been funded in three phases by the Engineering and Physical Sciences Research Council as part of its EQUAL/SPARC programme on extending quality life, and this book is an important outcome from the second phase of that research. It builds on an earlier book that was the result of the first research phase published by Springer-Verlag under the title *Inclusive Design, Design for the Whole Population*. It is divided into three parts, the first exploring the background and significance of the subject, the second presenting a series of exemplar case studies and initiatives, and the third introducing a range of tools, techniques, resources and guidance. Other books have been published covering the theory, background, history and international aspects of inclusive design, whereas this is very much a practical handbook on the subject. The intention is to cover more of the 'how' rather than the 'why', and to offer a multiplicity of practical starting points for readers from industry, design, engineering and management, and in particular students of design and business, and their tutors.

Inclusive design grew out of and builds on earlier approaches to design for primarily disabled people that focused very much on access to the built environment. The drive for 'barrier-free' and 'universal' design in particular in the US, which culminated in the Americans with Disabilities Act (ADA), focused on the right of universal access to buildings and public places. In the UK, through the Disability Discrimination Act (DDA) those rights have been extended to access to services, while in Europe the 'Design for All' movement has campaigned for and promoted similar objectives in terms of universal access, extending this concept to include access to information and related services via the Internet and telecommunications media (ICT). This work is well documented and referenced in *Inclusive Design, Design for the Whole Population* – and also in the *Universal Design Handbook* (Ostroff and Preiser, 2001) published by McGraw-Hill, New York. There is, however, far less literature dealing with the practicalities of product design, manufacturing and business management with regard to the inclusion of older, disabled and other marginalised groups. The purpose of this book is to redress that balance, and look beyond the changing requirements of legislation towards the business and commercial advantages that flow from an inclusive approach to design and innovation, along with the considerable social and economic benefits that come with social inclusion.

Background and Significance

The first part of the book, Chapters 2 to 4, presents inclusive design as a reaction to the tendency of mass production to exclude significant groups of consumers as it developed over the twentieth century. In Chapter 2, 'Why Inclusive Design?', the editors present a brief overview of the origins and development of the subject, and key drivers for it, such as population ageing and the growth of the international disability movement. They discuss how rapid technology development has the potential of including large numbers of people through increased functionality and embedded intelligence, and why this is not being realised. The major failure has been that functionality and accessibility have been addressed separately rather than together. As a consequence, consumer dissatisfaction with technology-driven products has been high.

These challenges can only be properly tackled at the systems level and through better design management and processes, which in turn require high-level management commitment to an inclusive design approach. How this understanding came about is discussed in Chapter 3, 'A Growing Movement', where Jeremy Myerson surveys the work and influence of key individuals and organisations. This gives us an understanding of the growth and dynamism of thinking and practice on a global basis, and introduces important considerations for the future, in particular the need for people to remain economically active for longer as the ratio of young to old shifts dramatically with an ageing workforce. Solving the associated design challenges will be a major task for design and industry in the future.

Much progress has been made in recent years in understanding the business case for inclusive design and the management task of delivering more inclusive products and services. Considerable progress has also been made in developing the tools, techniques and resources to support and facilitate an appropriate business response. This is the focus of Chapter 4, 'The Business Case', where Roger Coleman, Alan Topalian, John Clarkson and Hua Dong present an exemplar case study of a highly successful US company whose core business strategy is based on an inclusive approach to design and innovation.

This is followed by a discussion of research into industry barriers, drivers and initiatives aimed at encouraging and supporting industry uptake of inclusive design, the most significant of these being the 2005 British Standard guide to managing inclusive design, BS 7000-6. The purpose, structure and key process diagrams of the Standard are introduced, along with other resources for industry developed by the research community. Future design challenges are presented, for example the need to fuse functionality and desirability in more user-aware products and services, and the pressing need to support design management with relevant research into the practicalities of implementing, evaluating and promoting inclusive design. The desired outcome is a better understood and fully professional approach to inclusive design, the importance of which can be seen in the progress made by Japanese companies and the market potential of resulting consumer products.

Case Studies of Inclusive Design Practice

The second part of the book, Chapters 5 to 8, shifts the focus away from broader, contextual factors, and takes an in-depth look at examples of inclusive design in action. Chapter 5, 'Market Advantage: Practitioners' Viewpoints', features a conversation between Hua Dong and design practitioners from the UK and Sweden: Graham Pullin, formerly Senior Interaction Designer at IDEO; Ingelise Nielsen, Head of Public Relations at IDEO in London; Maria Benktzon and Olle Bobjer, partners of Ergonomidesign, Sweden; and Barry Tanner, New Product Introduction Manager of Applied Energy Products Ltd, a UK-based manufacturer of water, heating and ventilation products.

The conversation was centred on four inclusive design projects, their development processes and the market value through practitioners' eyes. It provides a vivid insight into the motivations and practices of leading design consultancies and their perception of the business case for an inclusive approach to design.

This is followed by Chapter 6, 'Designer Education: Case Studies from Graduate Partnerships with Industry', where Julia Cassim and Hua Dong present a series of inclusive design projects undertaken by new graduates of the Royal College of Art with private and voluntary sector partners. Working with disabled and older users who are often excluded from design consideration helped young designers understand the needs of people who are very different from them, and that insight has inspired innovative, user-centred design solutions with mainstream appeal.

Chapter 7, 'Empowering Designers and Users: Case Studies from the DBA Inclusive Design Challenge', also by Julia Cassim and Hua Dong, describes how partnerships between designers and severely disabled people can shift the emphasis from the user as passive subject to a more equal interaction between designer and user. Through six case studies from the Design Business Association (DBA) Inclusive Design Challenge, they demonstrate that such partnerships can be both liberating and inspirational for designers, and lead them in new directions towards genuine innovations that reframe design for disability as a driver for new applications, products, services and environments.

The DBA Challenge is an annual design competition organised since 2000 by the Helen Hamlyn Centre at the Royal College of Art, that is gaining international currency. Importantly it facilitates team building and motivates young designers to think out of the box in ways that have real commercial potential; hence the interest of major Japanese and European companies in this model of innovation through design collaboration with disabled and older users.

Chapter 8, 'Involving Older People in Design', by Alan Newell and Andrew Monk not only explores ways of understanding the needs of older people, in particular with regard to IT applications; but also tackles the difficult subject of communicating those insights to designers who are on the whole very much younger. Service design is another important subject covered in this chapter, and arguably the most effective way of supporting independence in later life. We have heard much about 'Smart Home' technology, yet seen little in the way of concrete results and applications. This chapter demonstrates how a more holistic approach built around enabling support rather than remote monitoring can deliver real benefits to older people.

Tools, Techniques and Resources

The concluding section of this book, Chapters 9 to 14, focuses on practical aspects of delivering inclusive design solutions, and introduces the key issue of design exclusion, how it impacts on both users and business, and how to counter it. Designing for inclusion is not a trivial challenge. On the contrary, it places a high level of demand on both designers and those who commission, manage and implement design and production within industry. In order to ensure that a product or service is genuinely inclusive, user research and understanding is required at the outset, to ensure a level of inclusion that matches the requirements of the target consumer. Design solutions must be evaluated with regard to accessibility and usability, as well as technical fitness for purpose. In taking the design through to production it is important that changes to the specification do not compromise inclusivity in the final realisation, and that advertising, sales, promotion and after sales service all support the inclusive intent of the project.

This approach is set out in BS 7000-6, and covered in detail in Chapter 4. However, in order to fully implement the standard, a range of tools, techniques and other resources is necessary to support the whole design, development and commercialisation process. Much work has already gone into developing such resources, but more remains to be done. This section is therefore more of a work in progress, and readers are encouraged to develop, refine and add to the material described here, and in particular adapt it to their own purposes and disciplines.

The section starts with the rapidly growing field of user research. In Chapter 9, 'Designer-oriented User Research Methods', Hua Dong, Colette Nicolle, Robert Brown and John Clarkson first classify the primary types of user-research methods and then discuss how they have been adapted by and for the design community. Examples are cited and guidance is given on how to apply these methods and how to gather data and utilise results. Task analysis is featured as an important way of understanding user demand, while techniques which help designers understand consumer motivations, preferences and lifestyles, such as the use of personas, are outlined. A combination of such techniques can help designers approach the Holy Grail of uniting accessibility and desirability in the form of inclusive, 'must have' products and services, that appeal to and can be enjoyed by the widest possible audience.

Chapter 10, 'Practicalities of Working with Users', by David Yelding and Julia Cassim, 'does exactly what it says on the tin'. It offers a practical guide to working with users, not just for designers, but for market researchers, business planning and product/service evaluation. It also covers recruitment, research techniques, costs and ethical considerations and is in itself a mini handbook and essential reference on the subject.

A central tenet in the inclusive design approach is 'design exclusion': what happens when we get things wrong. Design exclusion can arise for many reasons. Designers may be unaware of or take a cavalier view of the needs and capabilities of users less able than themselves; they may focus on technology first and usability second, or the product development budget may not stretch to proper user evaluation and assessment. However it arises, design exclusion can damage both reputation and profitability. And in an era of increasing discrimination and equality legislation, it can lead to costly litigation and product withdrawal or modification.

A far better and more cost effective approach is to consider these factors from the outset, in the earliest design thinking and decision making, when investment levels are low, rather than post market, when change is extremely costly. In Chapter 11, John Clarkson tackles these issues head on, with a theoretical analysis of the context, implications, impact and potential for design exclusion, and a very clear exposition of the practical steps we can take to minimise it. Understanding the distribution of capabilities across the population is an important beginning, but the subject is not easy or readily comprehensible, particularly since there is an insufficiency of available high quality data. Clarkson steers the reader through this maze and offers practical guidance with clear and insightful case studies that demonstrate the benefits of exclusion audits and other techniques to help us maximise design inclusion.

So far so good. We have learnt how to work with and understand users and how to consider and counter design exclusion, but how do we know we have achieved a successful and inclusive design? And if we have, how do we communicate that fact? How do we prove to ourselves and others that we have got it right? Evaluation plays an important part in the product development and introduction process, and is a well-understood concept in engineering and industry.

In Chapter 12, 'Product Evaluation: Practical Approaches', John Clarkson, along with Ian Hosking of technology development consultancy Sagentia, build on the existing knowledge base in evaluation theory and technique to demonstrate how this can be extended to the evaluation of inclusivity. Importantly they demonstrate that we do not have to reinvent any wheels in this regard, but simply to refocus well-understood processes and techniques, such as the stage-gate approach to product development, on the evaluation of design inclusion and exclusion. Like the new British Standard BS 7000-6, what they outline is an extension of existing good practice, rather than a radical departure from it; an added level of quality that will ensure a better and more successful outcome in new product and service development, a better return on investment, and higher levels of customer satisfaction and brand value.

Chapter 13, 'Using Simulation in Product Evaluation', by Carlos Cardoso and John Clarkson, takes us deeper into the territory of product evaluation, to discuss recently developed tools and techniques that assist in product evaluation, and can inform earlier stages of the product development process. User testing is expensive, which is one reason why it is not performed as extensively as it should be, to the detriment of many technology-based products. Simulation offers a short cut; not one that should replace user research and testing in its entirety – there is nothing like the real thing after all – but an expedient and insightful way of getting closer to the truth.

Indeed, the closer designers and design students can get to experiencing the world and their designs through the eyes and skin of people who are different from them in age or capability, the more they are likely to empathise with and wish to problem solve for those less able than themselves. The benefits and limitations of simulation are weighed, and a practical user-simulation toolkit is described, along with a discussion of its application and evaluation as a design tool.

The third section concludes with a survey of available resources and exemplars. In Chapter 14, 'Where Do We Find Out?', Susan Hewer and Cherie Lebbon present a series of 'top ten' websites, books, conferences and journals, and suggest routes through and starting points for three key information-user communities, in business, design and education. The chapter concludes with an overview of the work and influence of the Royal Society for the encouragement of Arts, Manufactures and Commerce, through its Student Design Awards programmes and more recent Design Directions competition. The education benefit of this is demonstrated by the impact these schemes have had on the careers of winners such as Jeremy Lindley, who went on to become design director at Tesco, and introduced several age- and ability-friendly innovations to the stores nationwide. Since this book went into production and important new web resource sponsored by BT has been launched at www.inclusivedesigntoolkit.com and is proving invaluable to students entering the RSA Design Directions competition.

The book concludes with a state of the subject survey. Looking back to the first set of targets established for inclusive design, Chapter 15, 'Towards Inclusion: Future Challenges', teases out progress and leaves us with a set of future challenges and suggestions for how they might be addressed.

Inclusive design is now a well-established but still young discipline. Early pioneers mapped out the broad territory for the subject, and we now have good exemplars of best practice, both for design and industry, along with tools and techniques to support practitioners. However, there is still much work to be done, and a great opportunity for a new generation of young and committed designers to complete the transition from margins to mainstream and deliver a genuinely inclusive and considerate environment for the predominantly urban society of the twenty-first century. Extending that user-centred and accessible design approach to deliver equivalent benefits to rural communities, in particular in the Developing World, is a further challenge that has yet to be undertaken. If we are to see radical new developments in the more mature era of inclusive design that we are now entering, it will be in those less advantaged and resourced communities. And it is in those areas where we perhaps have the greatest opportunities for delivering products and services that are both inclusive and sustainable.

References

ADA (1990), *Americans with Disabilities Act*, US Public Law, pp. 101–336.

Clarkson, J., Coleman, R., Keates, S. and Lebbon C, (eds.) (2003), *Inclusive Design: Design for the Whole Population* (London: Springer-Verlag).

BS 7000-6 (2005), *Guide to Managing Inclusive Design* (London: British Standards Institution).

DDA (1995), *Disability Discrimination Act* (London: Department for Education and Employment).

Ostroff, E. and Preiser, W. (eds.) (2001), *Universal Design Handbook* (New York, NY: McGraw-Hill).

United Nations (2005), *World Urbanization Prospects: The 2005 Revision* (New York, NY: Department of Economic and Social Affairs, Population Division).

Why Inclusive Design?

Julia Cassim, Roger Coleman,
John Clarkson and Hua Dong

CHAPTER

2

The Origins of Inclusive Design

Inclusive design can be seen as a response to the shortcomings of design for mass production, in particular in the second half of the 20th century. In that era of rapid economic expansion, architects, and professional designers working on product and service development tended to treat people as 'universal types' rather than individuals. An important text of the period for designers, *The Measure of Man* by the American industrial designer Henry Dreyfuss, established the study of anthropometrics – the dimensions of scale including arm and leg reach – as an essential tool for designers (Dreyfuss, 1960). The impact of *The Measure of Man* was profound, and its thinking influenced the design of everything from workplaces, homes and public buildings to furniture, appliances and transport.

Dreyfuss measured hundreds of men, women and children and calculated mean averages and dimensional ranges, intended to underpin design decision-making for mass production. This gave rise to a one-size-fits-all approach, which allowed for the volume production of affordable goods that fuelled the growth of consumerism. Great social and economic benefits ensued for the majority of people, but those who did not conform in terms of height, weight, cognitive or sensory capacity or physical strength became vulnerable to design exclusion. They did not measure up to assumptions about what is 'average' or 'normal', and as a consequence their needs were not addressed through mainstream mass production.

A growing mismatch arose between significant groups of consumers and the design assumptions underpinning products, services and environments. Initially this seemed of little relevance, as older and disabled people were considered outside the workforce, outside consumer society and economically dependent on state, charitable or family provision. However, as the consumer society expanded across the Developed World, this mismatch became less and less acceptable at a social and economic level, and even more so at a personal level (Czaja, 2001). In particular, people who grew up with consumerism developed very different expectations and aspirations to their parents. They rejected assumptions about dependency and exclusion due to age and disability, and insisted increasingly on equal rights in society and in the market place.

Until recently, older and disabled people, who clearly did not fit the carefully calculated norms of mass production, have been treated as special cases or groups falling outside the mainstream and requiring special design solutions. In many instances they still are. As a consequence, a whole movement arose around the development of 'special needs' design to bridge the widening gap, outside the mainstream late 20th century design discourse about lifestyle, aesthetics and consumer needs.

Special needs design, though well intentioned, was blighted by limited markets and small production runs, and the results were all too often more akin to hospital aids and appliances than consumer-based products and services. Many products and environments for older and disabled people stigmatised their users through ugly, inappropriate and often ineffective design (Gardner et al., 1993). The message given out by these designs to the people obliged to use them was clear: you are in the shadows, outside the normal patterns of production and consumption in society (Audit Commission, 2000; DTI, 2000a).

Gradually, however, a powerful reaction grew up against this stigmatising approach in the design profession. It began slowly at first, catalysed by a few charismatic individuals, but built up into a vocal movement to integrate older and disabled people into the mainstream of everyday life through a more inclusive approach to the design of products, services and environments. A new message was proclaimed: these groups were not special cases with special needs but people whose requirements should be considered and incorporated at every stage of the design process. Significantly, there was also a shift towards a more enlightened view that people are not disabled by their own impairments, irrespective of the shortcomings of design, but included or excluded by social attitudes, and the quality of design, irrespective of their capabilities (DTI, 2000b; DTI, 2000c; DTI, 2002).

Whose Disability is it Anyway?

Terminology such as 'design for disability' and 'barrier-free design' began to give way to more egalitarian concepts. Some of these, such as 'design-for-all' and 'universal design', reflected the aspirations of campaigning disability

Figure 2.1 Foresight Ageing Population Panel, Executive Summary (UK, Department of Trade and Industry)

groups in Europe and the US. Others, such as 'inclusive design' and 'transgenerational design' reflected the social, economic and demographic factors that were impacting on markets and governments and driving a reassessment of design goals and approaches among the design management, education and research communities (Pirkl, 1993; Clarkson et al., 2003).

With the emergence of inclusive design came a transference of responsibility from the user of design – be it product, service or environment – to the design process itself. If designers – and the organisations that commissioned them – did not accept responsibility for what happens when people try to use their designs, the outcome would be exclusion by design, and the fault would lie not with the user or consumer, but with the producer, provider, supplier or building manager.

Increasingly this transference of responsibility is being enshrined in laws, building codes, standards and guidance documents that regulate the provision and delivery of goods, services and environments (for example ADA, DDA, BS 8300; BS 7000-6). In particular, this new regulatory structure has established rights of access to such goods, services and environments, irrespective of age and ability, and gives consumers the power to seek redress under law if they believe they are subject to discrimination. This legislation is part of a profound shift in attitudes and expectations and will have a long-lasting effect on business and design.

> *In the UK, the number of people under 50 has barely changed over the course of the past century, while the number over 50 has increased dramatically.*

These trends have been reinforced by significant demographic and market shifts. Over the course of the 20th century, life spans increased significantly, with life expectation at birth in the Developed World rising by close to 25 years and that in developing countries following suit as the century progressed. Over the same period, and particularly in the second half of the century, birth rates fell significantly on a global basis.

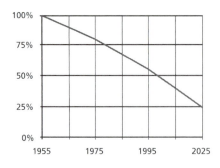

Figure 2.2   World fertility rates 1955–2025 (WHO Report, 1998)

As a consequence, in the UK, the number of people under 50 has barely changed over the course of the past century, while the number over 50 has increased dramatically. Effectively, every additional consumer on the street has been an older person, and in the latter part of the 20th century we have seen a growth in disposable income in later life that makes the older consumer a very attractive target market for goods and services (Laslett, 1989; Coleman, 1993).

Tapping into the opportunities offered by an ageing market requires an in-depth understanding of the changing aspirations of older people and the ageing process itself. Longer life spans mean the almost certain experience of age-related capability loss. Reductions in eyesight, hearing, mobility, dexterity and cognition will come to us all, and disability will be a common experience, but older people do not wish to be stigmatised or singled out as a special needs group. The result is a profound shift in consumer attitudes, market realities and design requirements.

Technological Development and Design Response

Rapid technological change during the late 20th century has brought many benefits, but has itself also led to increasing design exclusion, as new products and services are introduced that are not readily understandable or intuitive

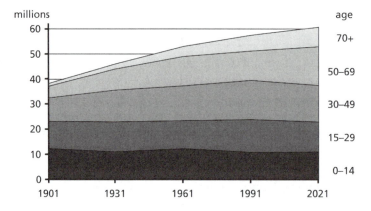

Figure 2.3   Population ageing in the UK (1901–2021) (Coleman, 1993)

to use. The public has become frustrated and disillusioned with technology products like the video recorder, which offer much but prove excessively complex to set up and operate (Microsoft, 2003, 2004; Philips, 2004).

We all know of the frustration, annoyance and anger that can follow a long-anticipated purchase the moment the box is opened and we start to grapple with overly complex interfaces and inadequate instructions; or the long wait on an automated system to register a new mobile phone, only to discover that we do not have the right information, or number, or code, and need to speak to a human being but do not know how to get hold of one. What is so often evident is that no one in the design, engineering or production chain has actually tried the new product or service as a naive consumer, because if they had, then the consumer would not have to experience such problems and frustrations. Those are things we remember, and they have a big impact on brand perception and loyalty. So getting the user experience right for the 'average' consumer is a huge commercial step forward.

Understanding that the 'average' user probably does not match marketing and design assumptions – for instance products and services are used as much, if not more, by families as by individuals – can help broaden the consumer base. Also, design improvements that include older and disabled people can offer real benefits to young able-bodied users. For example, remote controls, foot-operated flip top bins and hands-free interfaces were first developed as 'aids' for people with special needs and are now ubiquitous, while mobile phones and computers have given disabled people a wide range of new opportunities – as long as they can use them (Goldsmith, 1997, 2001).

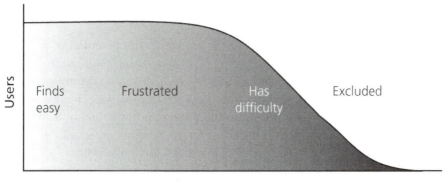

Figure 2.4   Increasing frustration with technology-based products

In an era of rapid technological development, products and services are becoming more complex, more global and more integrated. As a consequence, there is an urgent need to ensure that they function effectively at the systems level, in terms of both engineering and usability. Each component of a mobile phone system, for instance, has to achieve the same level of usability and customer-friendliness, or it will negatively impact the overall perception of the service. If the handset, the manual, the customer support line, or the sales advice and service given in the shop fail to impress, then the whole consumer offer suffers.

In essence, each component is a potential weak link, which could exclude or antagonise a significant number of customers. The consequences will not just be reflected in sales but will inflate help-line costs, returns and refunds, and lead to negative perceptions being passed virus-like by a word of mouth and via the Internet, to undermine brand value and position. This is why inclusive design and design management are closely linked, because it is only through careful management of the whole design process that we can ensure that the complete consumer offer – product, packaging, instructions, after sales service, upgrades and add-ons, and sales staff training – will deliver a consistent level of simplicity, intuitiveness and accessibility.

There is therefore a powerful, common sense business case for the inclusive design approach, the core of which is understanding and prioritising the user experience. It is also about understanding that the less tangible human factors – identity, emotion, delight, self-expression – are common to us all, and that getting these right for users who are vulnerable to exclusion is an effective way of ensuring that what we design really does enhance life quality, simply and intuitively, for as many people as possible; a mission to which any modern company can and should subscribe (BS 7000-6, 2005).

The design and business challenge is to exploit the potential of new and existing technologies to reduce and eventually eliminate exclusion, and to harness emerging design and manufacturing trends to enable mass-customisation and user-specific product and service offers for the same reason. However, what we must avoid is an overemphasis on the power and potential of technology alone, and recognise that it is just part of an overarching consumer offer that includes packaging, interface, controls, manuals, pre-sales advice, after-sales service, and all the other points at which the consumer interacts with both the product or service and the brand and company behind it.

Figure 2.5   BS 7000-6 (February 2005)

Accessibility is a key criterion, but so is desirability, and although it is not possible to make all products accessible to all people, there are strategies, such as a modular design, or a portfolio approach, that can extend the usability of mainstream products and services. We take remote controls for granted, and now expect hands-free and wireless earpieces for mobile phones. With inclusive design management there is no reason why such special and multifunctional add-ons and range extensions should not be developed to maximise the number of potential users. Doing so within the styling and brand identity of the core product or service will ensure that functionality is not separated from desirability, and thereby include rather than exclude currently marginalised groups.

This inclusive design approach is likely to deliver better thought-out products with a wider and longer lasting appeal, which are accessible and usable by as many people as reasonably possible. However, it would be wrong to see inclusive design as a panacea, since there is a danger that complacency could result in a small, but important group of people finding themselves excluded because they cannot be accommodated by mainstream design. What we need is to focus on the role of assistive technology and design as a precursor to inclusive design, to plug the gaps where the mainstream market fails to provide, and to work towards a continuum of the two through the integration of assistive technology solutions with mainstream products and services.

Inclusive Design at the Systems Level

Inclusive design is not a new design genre or fashion, it is a logical response to changing social realities and an approach to design that places the user at the heart of the design process. In essence this is simply better design, but without conscious effort, it is very easy to exclude by design. Until the necessary understanding and processes are thoroughly embedded across the range of people who practice, commission or manage design, there will be a need for the conscious adoption and application of inclusive design principles. However, the benefits are considerable. Inclusive design offers commercial advantage at

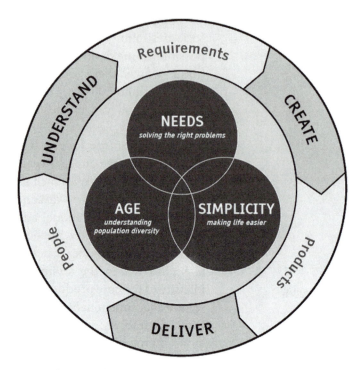

Figure 2.6   Inclusive design strategy as developed by the Centre for Inclusive Design and Technology (CITD)

'Inclusive design is an approach to the design of mainstream products and services that are "accessible to and usable by as many people as reasonably possible, without the need for adaptation or specialist design.'

[BS 7000-6]

each stage of the business cycle, by adding insight and user understanding to market positioning, helping to prioritise and focus sales and exploitation strategy, inspiring innovation and development processes, and validating and evaluating the product offer.

Meeting the needs of the whole population through the mechanism of the consumer market requires thinking at the systems level, about how products, services and environments are integrated, and how they are delivered. It requires understanding and designing for carers and companions, who are integral to the life quality of people with more severely limited capabilities. It also requires the development of assistive technologies and interfaces and their progressive integration into mainstream products. We already have some good evidence of how this can be done through the incorporation of accessibility features into computer operating system software, and the computer mouse itself, which makes many operations easier and more intuitive.

Without continuous work at the remaining margins, there is unlikely to be the stream of innovations that will deliver the highest level of usability in the future. It is also important to understand how the accessibility of products and services can be extended by making them more customisable, and by ensuring that accessibility aids are thought of in the original design and, even if provided by third-party manufacturers, integrated in their design and appearance to reduce costs and eliminate stigma, as does the hands-free mobile phone interface.

Design exclusion does not come about by chance, it comes about through neglect, ignorance, and a lack of adequate information and data. There is much work that needs to be done in this direction, but already good evidence from some of the UK's leading design consultancies demonstrates that by working with older and disabled people they can be inspired and motivated to arrive at truly innovative solutions with mainstream appeal and commercial value. It is imperative that we develop and nurture a cadre of young designers and researchers to advance practice, develop methodology and provide exemplars of good practice. It is these young people who will seed much of the theory and practice of inclusive design into industry and the business community and ensure that the world of the future is truly inclusive.

References

ADA (1990), *Americans with Disabilities Act*, US Public Law, pp. 101–336.

Audit Commission (2000), *Fully Equipped: The Provision of Equipment to Older or Disabled People by the NHS and Social Services in England and Wales* (London: Audit Commission).

BS 7000-6 (2005), *Guide to Managing Inclusive Design* (London: British Standards Institution).

BS 8300 (2001), *Design of Buildings and their Approaches to Meet the Needs of Disabled People. Code of Practice* (London: British Standards Institution).

Clarkson, J., Coleman, R., Keates, S. and Lebbon, C. (2003), 'From margins to mainstream' In *Inclusive Design: Design for the Whole Population*, Clarkson, P.J., Coleman, R., Keates, S. and Lebbon, C. (eds.) (London: Springer-Verlag).

Coleman, R. (1993), 'A Demographic Overview of the Ageing of First World Populations', *Applied Ergonomics*, 24(1), pp. 5–8. [PubMed: 15676889] [DOI: 10.1016/0003-6870%2893%2990152-Y]

Czaja, S.J. (2001), 'Technological change and the older worker', *Handbook of the Psychology of Aging* (San Diego, CA: Academic Press), pp. 547–555.

DDA (1995), *Disability Discrimination Act* (London: Department for Education and Employment).

Dreyfuss, H. (1960), *The Measure of Man: Human Factors in Design* (New York, NY: Whitney Library of Design).

DTI (2000a), *A Study on the Difficulties Disabled People Have When Using Everyday Consumer Products* (London: Department of Trade and Industry).

DTI (2000b), *Design for Living Taskforce Report*, DTI Foresight Ageing Population Panel (London: Department of Trade and Industry).

DTI (2000c), *The Age Shift: Priorities for Action*, DTI Foresight Ageing Population Panel (London: Department of Trade and Industry).

DTI (2002), *Equality and Diversity: The Way Ahead* (London: Department of Trade and Industry).

Gardner, I., Powell, L. and Page, M. (1993), 'An Appraisal of a Selection of Products Currently Available to Older Consumers', *Applied Ergonomics*, 24(1), pp. 35-39. [DOI: 10.1016/0003-6870%2893%2990158-6].

Goldsmith, S. (1997), *Designing for the Disabled: The New Paradigm* (London: Architectural Press).

Goldsmith, S. (2001), 'The bottom-up methodology of universal design' In *Universal Design Handbook*, Ostroff, E. and Preiser, W. (eds.) (New York, NY: McGraw-Hill).

Laslett, P. (1989), *A Fresh Map of Life: The Emergence of the Third Age* (London: Weidenfeld & Nicolson).

Microsoft (2003), *The Wide Range of Abilities and Its Impact on Computer Technology* (Redmond, WA: Microsoft Corporation). Research conducted by Forrester

Research, Inc. www.microsoft.com.

Microsoft (2004), *Accessible Technology in Computing – Examining Awareness, Use, and Future Potential* (Redmond, WA: Microsoft Corporation). Research conducted by Forrester Research, Inc. www.microsoft.com.

Philips (2004), *The Philips Index: Calibrating the Convergence of Healthcare, Lifestyle and Technology* (New York, NY: Philips Electronics North America). Study administered by Taylor Nelson Sofres. www.designcouncil.org.uk/ Documents/About design/Design techniques/ Inclusive design/Philips Index (US version).pdf.

Pirkl, J. (1993), *Transgenerational Design: Products for an Ageing Population* (New York, NY: Van Nostrand Reinhold).

WHO (1998), *The World Health Report Report 1998 – Life in the 21st Century: A Vision for All* (Geneva, Switzerland: World Health Organization).

A Growing Movement

Jeremy Myerson

Pioneering Individuals

Special needs equipment and assistive products – from bath chairs to simple gadgets – have been manufactured over a long period of time with the intention to 'fit' so-called disabled people to their environment. Many of these meet a need, but little or no design input has gone into their development. As a consequence, a significant proportion of aids and assistive products prescribed by Occupational Therapists and other professionals are rejected as stigmatising. Such products have become increasingly sophisticated in technical terms, but the problem of desirability and acceptability remains.

Two World Wars, and later the Vietnam War, prompted the development of prosthetics and aids and equipment for disabled combatants, in particular wheelchairs. Assistive products were also developed to aid independence, such as stair lifts and jar openers. Advances in technology led to innovations in assistive technology, such as voice synthesisers and electric wheelchairs, while new materials and manufacturing techniques were harnessed in the development of contact and varifocal lenses.

Surgical advances, such as cochlear implants, today offer new treatments for disabling conditions; developments in replacement joints, and so on are ameliorating some age-related conditions; and cosmetic surgery can reverse some of the signs of ageing. Genetic science offers considerable potential to modify and manipulate bodily processes, while intelligent technologies have the potential to make environments, products and services significantly more responsive to individual needs and preferences. These developments raise important social and ethical issues to which there are no simple answers.

But while broader trends and legislative moves undoubtedly helped to shape the emergence of inclusive design, individual designers in a variety of disciplines and circumstances were instrumental in driving these ideas forward. In 1963, for example, British architect Selwyn Goldsmith published the first comprehensive set of building guidelines on the subject of designing for disability (Goldsmith, 1963), while in the US, the work of architect, designer and educational pioneer Ron Mace effectively defined the concept of universal design, which was further advanced through the Adaptive Environments Centre, Boston, founded in 1978 by Elaine Ostroff and Cora Beth Abel (Ostroff, 2001).

Like Goldsmith, Ron Mace was a wheelchair user who realised that accessibility and equal opportunities depended not just on better ramps or more accessible toilets but on the detail of all our interactions with the designed world. It was Mace, a key figure in establishing a Center for Universal Design at North Carolina State University, who shifted the debate beyond accessibility – which continues to be perceived in terms of adapting buildings or products to disabled users – and towards designs which are usable by people of all ages and abilities, and therefore more universal or inclusive.

The Center for Universal Design would go on, under Mace's leadership, to develop and refine a set of seven principles or criteria against which designs could be judged (Story, Mueller and Mace, 1998):

Equitable use	the design is useful and marketable to people with diverse abilities.
Flexibility in use	the design accommodates a wide range of individual preferences and abilities.
Simple and intuitive to use	use of the design is easy to understand, regardless of the user's experience, knowledge, language skill or current concentration level.
Perceptible information	the design communicates necessary information effectively to the user, regardless of ambient conditions or the user's sensory abilities.
Tolerance for error	the design minimises hazards and the adverse consequences of accidental or unintended actions.
Low physical effort	the design can be used efficiently and effectively with a minimum of fatigue.
Size and space for approach and use	appropriate size and space is provided for approach, reach, manipulation, and use regardless of user's body size, posture or mobility.

Today, these principles may seem somewhat prescriptive in the context of thinking about design supporting lifestyle goals and aspirations, the importance of desirability and other aesthetic factors, and the shift in focus from products to services. But in the narrow design orthodoxy of the time, these principles were genuinely mould-breaking and a challenge to the status quo. They were also eminently practical and could be implemented both as individual design criteria and as an aid to design evaluation.

As new thinking on excluded groups began to emerge in the late 1970s, one research experiment in particular caught the imagination. Between 1979 and 1982, Patricia Moore, a young industrial designer in her twenties, toured North America disguised as an old woman. She used the skills of a leading Hollywood make up artist to radically 'age' her appearance as she visited several cities, not only dressed as an old woman but also with artificial restrictions to her joints, her hearing, her vision and so on (Moore, 1985).

Moore was frequently abused and marginalised and subjected to discrimination. On one occasion she was attacked in the street; on a flight, an air hostess poured coffee down her without apology. The discoveries she made were hugely influential on the growing universal design movement in America. The impact of her work, which pioneered an empathic research

approach to user needs, was also felt in Japan, Australia and elsewhere. The fact that at the time she was employed in the New York office of Raymond Loewy, a high-profile contemporary of Henry Dreyfuss, added to the growing sense of unease about the human limitations of commercial US design practice.

Figures 3.1, 3.2 and 3.3 Patricia Moore in and out of disguise (© Moore Design Inc.)

Moore's experiment also triggered the development of 'age suits' for use by designers in the UK, Germany and other countries in training and product development programmes to simulate the effects of ageing. Automotive giants such as Ford and Fiat started to take a particular interest in the subject, triggered by an awareness of population ageing and the relative seniority of the average new car purchaser.

Earlier, another seminal figure in America's universal design movement, Victor Papanek, published *Design for the Real World*, which challenged the dominant market-led approach to industrial design and called for more social responsibility from designers (Papanek, 1971). Papanek's stance meant that he was effectively blackballed by the Industrial Designers Society of America. But many of his assertions about the moral dangers of America's mono-dimensional design approach were backed up by Moore's role-playing research.

Such ideas were bound to filter through to European designers. In Sweden, for example, working within a strong tradition of democratic Scandinavian design, Maria Benktzon and Sven-Eric Juhlins of Ergonomi Design Gruppen were inspired by Papanek's writing and teaching to develop new tools for older and disabled people. These combined functionality, performance and aesthetic appeal in a way that positioned them within the mainstream of consumer products rather than as disability aids or equipment (see Ergonomi Design website).

In 1976, Victor Papanek was among the keynote speakers at a landmark international conference called Design for Need at the Royal College of Art in London (Bicknell and McQuiston, 1977). This explored many social aspects of design, including the idea of 'designing out disability'. Later, the Royal College of Art would become a hub of activity in the area of inclusive design. In 1991, the DesignAge action research programme was established at the RCA under the direction of Roger Coleman to explore the design effects of ageing populations. This was supported by the Helen Hamlyn Foundation, a charity set up in 1985 to improve the homes and lives of older people through design.

DesignAge put one of the central themes of inclusive design on the map: the right to freedom of choice, independence and dignity of older people. After all, ageing is a universal experience – we will all get older. What Coleman and his team managed to do was to make the issue of ageing a hot topic for young designers – by reframing it as an area of self-interest, as 'design for our future selves'. DesignAge also established a Europe-wide network called DAN (Design for Ageing Network) to pursue the agenda. In 1999, DesignAge was subsumed into the Helen Hamlyn Centre, a new centre for inclusive design at the Royal College of Art, with a programme of industry collaborations for young designers.

Pioneers like Goldsmith, Mace, Ostroff, Benktzon and Coleman are names which recur in the inclusive design literature. In particular, Elaine Ostroff's work with Wolfgang Preiser on the *Universal Design Handbook* (Ostroff and Prieser, 2001), and Roger Coleman's work with John Clarkson, director of the Engineering Design Centre at the University of Cambridge, on *Inclusive Design: Design for the Whole Population* (Clarkson et al., 2003) represent key texts on the entire movement and offer extensive design guidance to professionals in the field.

The work of commercial design firms such as IDEO and Smart Design on high-profile design projects in the medical and home wares sectors has further reinforced a focus on user-centred design methods, in which scenario building or story telling with diverse design users has evolved over the past 15 years into an extensive methodology.

More recently, in Japan, a major international conference in Yokohama in 2002 led directly to the establishment of an industry network. Despite being set up as recently as November 2003, the Japanese International Association for Universal Design (IAUD) today boasts over 130 corporate members, including such household names as Sony, NEC, Toyota, Honda, Matsushita, Panasonic, Toshiba, Hitachi and Mitsubishi. The IAUD network is now having a powerful impact on Japanese corporate thinking, and already new, inclusive products, such as the Toyota Raum and Porte are appearing in the market (see Chapter 4). The current mission of IAUD members is to engage in 'conversations with consumers', in other words, prioritising the user experience (see IAUD website).

Social Drivers

Two major social trends are evident at the international level as drivers of inclusive design: population ageing and the recognition of the rights of disabled people. However, the picture is much more complicated at the micro or local level. Some countries and continents have high levels of immigration within their populations, relating social inclusion to ethnic and cultural diversity; others are more homogenous. Levels of personal wealth and economic development vary widely, while factors like AIDS and the move from rural to city dwelling, which impact directly on adults and indirectly on children and older people, are radically reshaping populations and changing the way people live.

What this means is that we should not make blanket assumptions, but look at and understand the local and cultural context as well as the big picture. Although inclusive design has developed in the context of social and technological change in the Developed World, and the growth of consumer societies, the focus on understanding user needs and aspirations can be applied in many other situations.

Inclusive design and other people-centered approaches have arisen in the context of a major change in the way we view different people in society. The tendency to refer to 'the elderly' and 'the disabled' as if they form distinct groups outside the mainstream is today being challenged by a growing trend to recognise age and disability as something we will all experience as part of the normal course of life.

Personal computers, the Internet and email, mobile phones and broadband media connections, are providing the technology push, while consumer pull is coming not just from older people, but younger people who are looking for a better work-life balance. Young disabled people constitute an important group that is finding these new technologies liberating and enabling. Not only can they offer access to work, they can do so on equal terms. When we talk to someone, say, on a help line, guiding us through setting up computer access to a new service, or via a computer chat line, we have no real way of telling whether they are young or old, able-bodied or disabled, or on the chat line, male or female. We meet as equals through new media, in new spaces where the old rules and assumptions do not apply. Such possibilities can introduce new dangers, for children, but disabled people can find them truly liberating.

Increasingly, both older and disabled people aspire to active participation within the mainstream of society, reject the dependency and institutionalisation that were the norm for much of the last century, and are beginning to assert themselves as consumers who control significant amounts of disposable income and as participants in the knowledge economy who have valuable expertise and experience to offer in the workplace. Such new expectations offer a rationale for inclusive design that extends beyond the home and public buildings to embrace the workplace and more closely align personal and communications products to contemporary social expectations.

Access to Work

Much of the debate – whether in design practice, industry or academia – has inescapably centred on gaining independence in the home or access to the built environment. Older and disabled people have been largely defined as having consumer or civil rights; they have not been seen as active economic contributors, other than when exercising their rights as purchasers. As a result, there has been little active or detailed consideration of a multi-generational workplace. It must also be said that in the more extensive literature of workplace design research, the focus on meeting user needs rarely strays from the 'average' worker in the 20–45 age range; there is little debate on learning from seniors or the inter-generational workplace.

Part of the problem for the inclusive design lobby is that it is constantly fighting a tendency to associate age and disability with deficit, decline and incompetence, all of which militate against paid employment. The first frontiers to be pushed back are therefore domestic and public ones, to make life more liveable for older and disabled people. Access to work, it appears, is in a second wave.

However, some pioneering work from the 1990s suggests how this second wave could take shape. James Pirkl and his colleagues at the University of Syracuse developed the concept of 'transgenerational design' to describe products, services and environments that meet the needs of people across a wide range of age and ability. They also evolved a series of guidelines and strategies for applying this concept, and similar methods for approaching journalism, advertising, marketing, retailing, and employment policy (Pirkl and Babic, 1988; Pirkl, 1991, 1993).

Transgenerational design is framed as a market-aware response to population ageing and the need for products and environments that can be used by both young and old people living and, importantly, working in the same environment. Pirkl's book on the subject outlines practical strategies in response to population ageing, along with case study examples based on applying a better understanding of age-related capabilities in tandem with a recognition of the needs and preferences of younger people, in particular where they live in the same house, share the same facilities or use the same products.

Some of the stereotypes that have barred older people from the workplace in the past are now outdated. For example, older people are now far more active than previous generations. Sporting activities, exercise and fitness classes feature as part of the new lifestyles of older people, who are not only healthier but more experimental and flexible than before. Increasingly, part of that vision of a dynamic, participatory later life depends on maintaining economic independence by remaining at work, especially as pension funds fail to bridge the gap.

Moving beyond barrier-free design and the specialist access advisers and specialist architecture practices it has given rise to – such as Buro Happold

Disability Design Consultancy (see Buro Happold website), which was a major force in ensuring maximum accessibility in the new Scottish Parliament Building – to guarantee the same level of access to work and the workplace for older and disabled people is one of the new challenges facing inclusive design. Another area is healthcare design, where the new and much desired patient-centred focus will require an equivalent patient and carer-centred design process if it is to become a reality. Many of the tools and techniques developed so far are readily transferable, but new ones will be needed to meet these new challenges.

References

Bicknell, J. and McQuiston, L. (eds.) (1977), 'Design for Need: The Social Contribution of Design', Proceedings of the International Conference held at the Royal College of Art, London (London: Pergamon Press and Royal College of Art).

Buro Happold. Available at: www.burohappold.com.

Clarkson, J., Coleman, R., Keates, S. and Lebbon, C. (eds.) (2003), *Inclusive Design: Design for the Whole Population* (London: Springer-Verlag).

Ergonomi Design. Available at: www.ergonomidesign.com.

Goldsmith, S. (1963), *Designing for the Disabled* (London: Royal Institute of British Architects).

Helen Hamlyn Centre. Available at www.hhc.rca.ac.uk.

International Association for Universal Design (Japan). Available at: www. iaud.net/en.

Moore, P. (1985), *Disguised* (Waco, TX: Word Books).

Ostroff, E. (2001), 'Universal Design Practice in the United States' In *Universal Design Handbook*, Ostroff, E. and Preiser, W. (eds.) (New York, NY: McGraw-Hill).

Ostroff, E. and Preiser, W. (eds.) (2001), *Universal Design Handbook* (New York, NY: McGraw-Hill).

Papanek, V. (1971), *Design for the Real World: Human Ecology and Social Change* (New York, NY: Pantheon Books).

Pirkl, J. (1991), 'Transgenerational Design: A Design Strategy Whose Time Has Arrived', *Design Management Journal*, Fall, pp. 55–60.

Pirkl, J. (1993), *Transgenerational Design: Products for an Ageing Population* (New York, NY: Van Nostrand Reinhold).

Pirkl, J. and Babic, A. (1988), *Guidelines and Strategies for Designing Transgenerational Products: An Instructors Manual* (Acton, MA: Copley Publishing Group).

Story, M.F., Mueller, J. and Mace, R.L. (1998), *The Universal Design File: Designing for People of All Ages and Abilities* (Raleigh, NC: Center for Universal Design, North Carolina State University).

The Business Case

Roger Coleman, Alan Topalian,
John Clarkson and Hua Dong

Figure 4.1   Good Grips salad spinner (©OXO Inc.)

Creating Commercial Value Through Inclusive Design: An Exemplary Case

Inclusive design can create considerable value for businesses especially when managed effectively. Progressive organisations are adopting this approach, and one stands out as a business built on inclusive design principles. OXO Good Grips (not to be confused with the UK gravy brand) was launched in 1990 at the Gourmet Show in San Francisco with a range of 15 products. It was the brainchild of Sam Farber, a serial entrepreneur who had made one fortune already by building up then selling cookware company, Copco. He and his wife, Betsy, enjoyed entertaining, but she suffered from arthritis and found cooking utensils increasingly difficult to use. Sam recognised a business opportunity as a result of a gap in the market and sought to capitalise on his experience in the kitchen goods market.

Sam did several clever things which set OXO on the road to success. First, he commissioned top New York consultancy, Smart Design, to develop a new, user-friendly range of kitchen utensils. Second, he briefed them to create mainstream products with high design values, *not* special needs products: this would help to attract press coverage and propel the range into the market. Third, instead of a fee, Sam offered Smart a small advance plus a 3 per cent royalty share of the profits generated.

Figure 4.2   Good Grips serving utensils (©OXO Inc.)

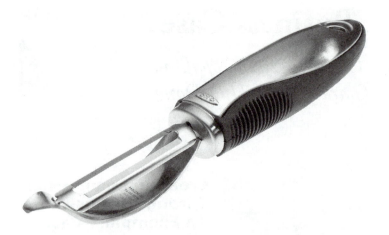

Figure 4.3   Good Grips potato peeler – second iteration (©OXO Inc.)

Smart Design were also clever in their response. They realised that new utensils in a crowded, mature market had to work exceptionally well and offer distinctive features that were valued by customers. User research confirmed that the sharpest of blades were needed for the potato peeler, the first product in the range. The blades were eventually sourced from Japan which has a long history of superb sharp tools and swords. Next, they looked for the right material to enhance and cushion the grip to make the product more comfortable for those suffering from arthritis. Then they worked through hundreds of handle shapes before settling on one that worked well and looked good. Finally, they added unique 'fins' near the top of the handle which offered a natural resting place for a thumb, and created a talking point that communicated the functional benefits of the product. This patentable feature became a signature detail for the range.

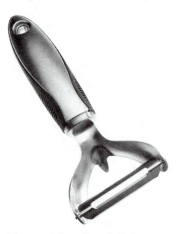

User understanding and research was at the heart of this process – and Patricia Moore (see Chapter 3) contributed her experience and expertise to the team – ensuring an age-friendly focus throughout design development. The rest is history. Good Grips has been a remarkable success: it achieved a turnover of US$3 million in 1991 and over 100 international design awards, including the distinction of being exhibited in New York's Museum of Modern Art.

Figure 4.4   Good Grips potato peeler – alternative form (©OXO Inc.)

Figure 4.5   Good Grips rolling pin and sieve (©OXO Inc.)

Sam Farber sold the company to General Housewares Corporation in 1992; a wise move, as his management style was very 'hands-on' and, to achieve its full potential, the company needed a more collective leadership. Under the direction of current President, Alex Lee, the company has grown consistently, doubling its turnover year-on-year and building up a range of over 850 products; this extends well beyond the original focus on kitchen utensils to embrace implements relating to gardening, cleaning and home organisation.

One of the most interesting aspects of the company is its business model. OXO is a modern, streamlined, design-led organisation that succeeds by focusing on what its core team does exceptionally well: constant innovation in developing and marketing new products. Design is not undertaken in-house; instead OXO has established very close working relationships with up to nine design consultancies, including Smart Design in New York and two in Japan. Product development is a collaborative process, with the consultancies working on a royalty basis,

Figures 4.6 and 4.7 Extending the Good Grips range into garden tools and household storage (©OXO Inc.)

perhaps with a small advance – on the original Sam Farber model. There is a strong rapport between all involved, and a clear focus on inclusive design. Indeed, OXO can be described not just as a design-led business, but as an

inclusive or, to use the US term, universal design-led business.

Important though user-focused design is at OXO, its products are never marketed as inclusive or universal designs. Instead, they are promoted on the basis of fitness for purpose: the best, most convenient, comfortable and easy to use kitchen or garden tools available. Just as the original potato peeler has a unique handle with grip-enhancing fins, so other products feature distinctive elements. Here are two further examples: the measuring jug and salad spinner.

Figure 4.8   Good Grips measuring jug (©OXO Inc.)

The measuring jug has a conventional scale on the outside for liquid measures. However, user tests with traditional products revealed that, after pouring liquid into jugs, people would either lift them up to eye level, or bend down to the level of the liquid to read the volume off the scale: a difficult and cumbersome process. These observations inspired the unique feature of the OXO design: an oval scale wrapped around the inside of the jug that allows the quantity to be read off directly as liquid is poured in. That scale does the job well, is clearly visible – a great help to ageing eyes – and conveys the core values of the OXO brand: distinctive ease of use and fitness for purpose.

Figure 4.9   Good Grips salad spinner (©OXO Inc.)

The salad spinner went through a similar development process: testing existing products, identifying key user issues and seeking innovative solutions. Existing products depended on a winding action applied by a spinner handle, or a swinging action to shake off excess water. Neither action was satisfactory, or efficient in drying salad. A review of possible mechanisms with users pointed to the pump action of children's spinning tops. An equivalent pump action was developed that is much easier to operate – requiring a minimum of grip and a very simple hand motion – and delivers excellent results. Indeed, the one problem with the design was that the bowl

Figure 4.10 Salad spinner – transparent version (©OXO Inc.)

continued spinning after pumping stopped. This prompted the addition of a brake button which, although not technically necessary, introduced a greater sense of user control, while conveying the functionality and efficiency of the product.

Figure 4.11 Salad spinner – opaque lid version (©OXO Inc.)

The fact that both measuring jug and salad spinner sell extremely well is testimony to the way core brand values are conveyed by the designs and reinforce the brand throughout the range. People know what they are buying and do not have to be told about the inclusivity of the designs.

Figure 4.12 Salad spinner – stainless steel version, with brake button (©OXO Inc.)

Manufacture and logistics are contracted out to a small number of organisations with which OXO has long-standing relations. By partnering with OEM companies OXO has the flexibility to increase capacity to meet demands for its products. By adopting such an innovative business model, OXO has enjoyed a compounded annual growth rate of over 30 per cent since 1991. A relatively small team has achieved this – currently staff total just over 50 people – generating production, sales and turnover more typical of a company ten times its size. This highlights the power of an inclusive design strategy.

Industry Barriers and Drivers of Inclusive Design

OXO Good Grips provides a compelling example of business success. However, the fact that it is more the exception than the rule raises the question: what are the real drivers and obstacles for business to adopt the principles of inclusive design? What marks OXO out is that, from the outset, the company led through design, with a lean structure and genuinely inclusive goals. It was also trading into a sector – kitchen utensils – where quality and performance are powerful factors and cost does not dominate. As a consequence, the company started out on a winning track and did not need to rethink its business model, reshape its consumer offer, retrain staff, or build a new knowledge base in order to adopt inclusive design. For most organisations a combination of such factors presents considerable obstacles and challenges.

Strong leadership and motivation are required to make the changes required when organisations adopt a comprehensive inclusive approach. However, with the increase in disability discrimination legislation, it makes business sense to adopt an inclusive design strategy, especially when the British Government is keen to see inclusive design taken up by industry. These factors have led to the development of a growing range of information, guidance and practical support available to assist British industry to adopt inclusive design. In addition, within the voluntary sector there is a growing sense that the needs of disabled and older people will be best served by industry adopting an inclusive design approach when developing new products and services, rather than through specialist products and services that tend to stigmatise. Older and disabled people are also becoming more assertive in their demands – in particular that they should not be excluded from the mainstream of society. This has significant implications with regard to access to buildings, services and, importantly, work and workplaces, especially in the context of changing attitudes to retirement, life-long learning, employment and recent legislation such as the Disability Discrimination Act (DDA). All these developments suggest opportunities for progressive organisations in burgeoning markets for inclusive products and services.

At a 'Disability Summit' organised by Scope for British charities and voluntary sector bodies, there was agreement that inclusive design is a key to integrating disabled people into the mainstream of life and work in the UK. This convinced Scope, a UK cerebral palsy charity, to strive to encourage major organisations to develop inclusive products and services. Initially, Scope thought of establishing a physical Centre for Inclusive Technology and Design (CITD), but this soon became a network of interested research, public and voluntary sector organisations with the expertise to support the Scope initiative and transfer the necessary knowledge to industry. The UK Department of Trade and Industry (DTI), and the Design Council (which is funded by the DTI) have been involved, and this development has led to a number of initiatives that seek to support industrial uptake. For example, the Design Council currently provides guidance in a 'knowledge cell' on inclusive design on its website, while an extensive industry toolkit in the form of a dedicated website is under development within UK land-based telecommunications leader, BT, with the ultimate goal of making it available outside the company. An important driver for this was a DTI-funded online survey of business awareness of inclusive design in UK organisations, undertaken through the CITD network.

The survey set out to measure awareness and understanding of the needs of organisations in implementing inclusive design as advocated by the new British Standard – BS 7000-6 *Guide to Managing Inclusive Design* (2005). Further aims were to develop awareness-raising workshops and in-depth support services to promote and facilitate the adoption of inclusive design in business and industry. At the first stage, over 30 organisations of various sizes were surveyed and then the sample was enlarged to 99 organisations.

The questionnaire was divided into six main parts:

- organisation profile
- current organisation position on inclusive design
- drivers for inclusive design
- barriers to inclusive design
- approaches to increase the use of inclusive design.

Major drivers and barriers listed in the questionnaire had been identified through a previous UK survey by the Engineering Design Centre at the University of Cambridge. These were broken down further into factors such as 'entry into a new market' and 'increase customer satisfaction'. A key finding was that higher awareness leads to a more positive response to drivers and less weight ascribed to barriers: this reinforced the need for a convincing business case.

Principal results were:

- 84 per cent of organisations surveyed had heard of inclusive design
- 77 per cent were interested in making their products more inclusive

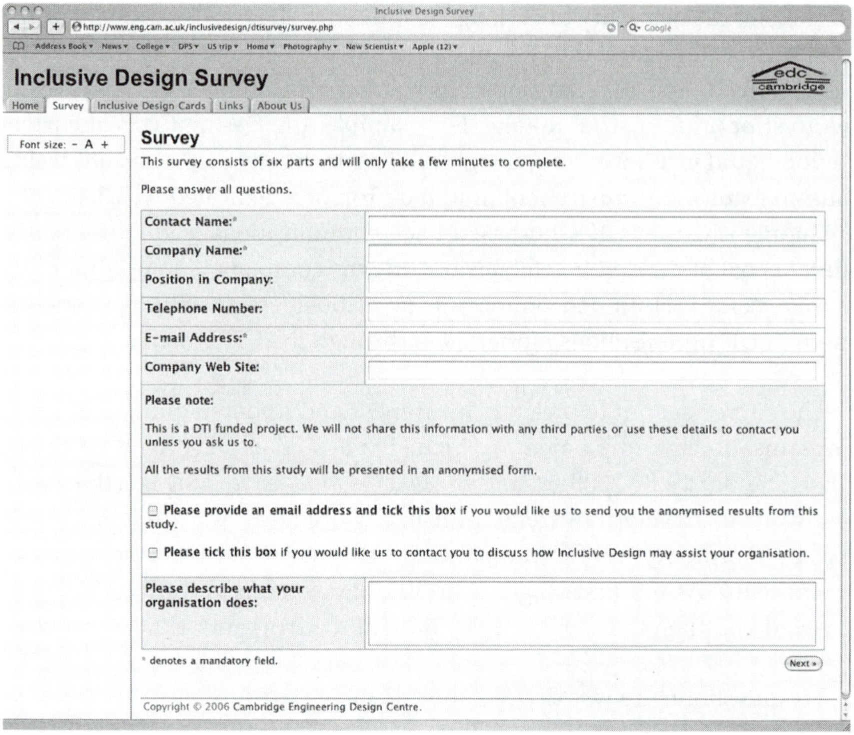

Figure 4.13 Online Inclusive Design Survey undertaken by the Engineering Design Centre, Cambridge

- 61 per cent claimed some level of understanding

- only 13 per cent thought they were already inclusive.

Given the likelihood of organisations over-estimating their level of understanding and achievement, this represented a significant opportunity for knowledge transfer and training to assist UK industry to take the challenge.

The survey was followed by a series of day-workshops with eight leading UK organisations ranging from small to very large. These addressed the need for a strong business case and outlined initial steps towards a practical approach for each company. The workshops were built around:

- an introduction to BS 7000-6, with its five-point business case

- mapping an inclusive design contribution along a generic business cycle and product development process

- distilling the benefits from insights into market positioning

- helping to set priorities so as to maximise commercial value

- inspiring innovative product and service development

- evaluating and validating product and service offerings.

The business rationale and commercial challenges were presented through real examples and key statistics. Then practical group activities focused on understanding inclusivity and evaluating products and services from a range of user perspectives. Participants were introduced to a typical multi-generational family, adopting different personalities and interacting with products and packaging as adults, children, older and disabled people. At the end of each 'day' feedback was sought on the usefulness of the experience, and what else was needed by industry to facilitate the adoption of inclusive design.

Overall, the industry view revealed by the survey, and corroborated during the workshops, was that a good business case complemented by effective marketing tools were essential to encourage the adoption of inclusive design. Moreover, a better understanding of product auditing was crucial for its delivery. Clearly there is a need in business to see a direct connection between inclusive design and profitability – as demonstrated by the OXO example – and better metrics would help. This high-quality industry feedback has shaped the toolkit developed with BT which, along with the Design Council website, will offer the UK business community the support and resources it needs to implement the new British Standard.

British Standard on Managing Inclusive Design

Until recently, manufacturing processes, developments in technology and product innovation were seen as the keys to profitability. However, attention has shifted towards the provision of ever-widening services that frequently achieve higher margins. Factors such as usability and desirability are increasingly important to attract and retain satisfied customers. Organisations that invest in understanding and enhancing the user experience – ideally as part of adopting a professional approach to inclusive design – are more likely to succeed.

BS 7000-6 *Guide to Managing Inclusive Design* was published in February 2005 to help all organisations (private, public and not-for-profit) to evolve such a professional stance. It identifies the 'real world' benefits to be gained as a result of a more inclusive approach, not just during product and service development, but also when managing business generally.

BS 7000-6 is a comprehensive guide to managing inclusive design. It provides the language and framework by which owner-managers, board directors and principal officers down to junior executives – as well as design practitioners – can understand and respond to the needs of diverse users without offending or stigmatising them. The ultimate goal is to meet, as far as possible, the needs of the whole population through mainstream markets.

The standard concentrates on the *management*, not the practice, of inclusive design. This reflects the fact that the outcomes of design projects are influenced far more by those who manage them than by the creative specialists involved. Though formally a guide (as opposed to a specification), the standard is more like a 'code of practice' with state-of-the-art guidance that shows how organisations can effectively lead through design and profit from an inclusive approach to design and design management.

The business case is built around five key drivers and opportunities, and encourages organisations to:

1. Adapt to market changes such as those due to population ageing, new legislation, technological change and the adoption of inclusive design by competitors – to boost turnover, market share and profitability.

2. Understand changing consumer expectations and lifestyles in order to expand the consumer base, extend product lifecycles, and develop brand loyalty.

3. Provide user-centred design through the implementation of ergonomics and human factors principles (and so guard against dissatisfaction due to lack of usability and accessibility) – to minimise the cost of servicing and returns, encourage repeat purchases and build competitive advantage.

4. Maintain workforce loyalty particularly in the context of an ageing population and changing expectations with regard to retirement – to improve efficiency, enhance motivation and ensure that essential skills are retained within the company.

5. Build and sustain corporate reputation through innovation and new product development, leading to user-friendly, high quality design.

Structure and Content

The introduction of the standard sets out the social and organisational context, defines inclusive design and outlines the business case. This is followed by a list of other relevant standards, and a glossary of related terms and definitions.

Two main sections of BS 7000-6 enable executives to codify practice at the organisation and project levels. As such, the standard offers a platform for evolving metrics on performance, and could also form the basis of contracts between parties. Emphasis is placed throughout on close coordination during the development process so all disciplines contribute effectively at every stage. The importance of acute observation and suitable consultation with all stakeholders is highlighted so appropriate approaches are adopted and effective solutions generated.

One appendix sets out the challenge of leading inclusivity in business (including more details on changes in world markets and business practices). Another outlines over two dozen tools and techniques that facilitate the management of inclusive design, grouped under different development phases.

The final section provides a short bibliography and list of useful web links, one leading to the Design Council website where readers can access a significantly wider range of references (Design Council, 2006).

Guidance at the Organisation Level

The first core section covers the management of inclusive design at the organisation level. At the heart of this section is a model process structured under four phases which:

- explore the potential and demands of inclusive design, as well as the commitment to be made when re-orientating an organisation;

- establish a firm foundation for a professional inclusive approach, not least by ensuring that the organisation's inclusive stance is closely aligned with its overall business mission, objectives and strategies, and that this is communicated clearly through a carefully thought-through change programme;

- introduce the appropriate infrastructure to manage inclusive design, draw together the necessary expertise, formulate and implement a master programme of initiatives, then evaluate its impact; and

- build on the experience, refine approaches and consolidate benefits.

Issues addressed at this level include:

- clarification and assignment of responsibilities for inclusive design

- auditing an organisation's operations and facilities

- initiating a change programme to re-orientate organisations

- ensuring products, services, processes and facilities are treated holistically

- different product development and marketing strategies to consider

- impact of product / service launches on subsequent profitability

- evaluation of an organisation's overall performance.

All 18 stages are depicted in a figure that sets out the forward momentum of the process. Several stages could be undertaken concurrently and iteration is likely between all stages. A summary checklist is provided to aid implementation (see Figure 4.14).

Guidance at the Project Level

The second core section covers the management of inclusive design at the project level. Inclusive design projects are tracked from 'cradle to grave' through 11 primary stages, each set out in fair detail (see Figure 4.15 which indicates the forward momentum of projects; several stages might be undertaken concurrently and iteration is likely between all stages). Again, these are complemented by a summary checklist to facilitate implementation.

Issues covered include:

- original triggers, definition of opportunities and planning of projects

- generation of solution concepts, design development and detail design

- launch and sustenance of products and services in the market

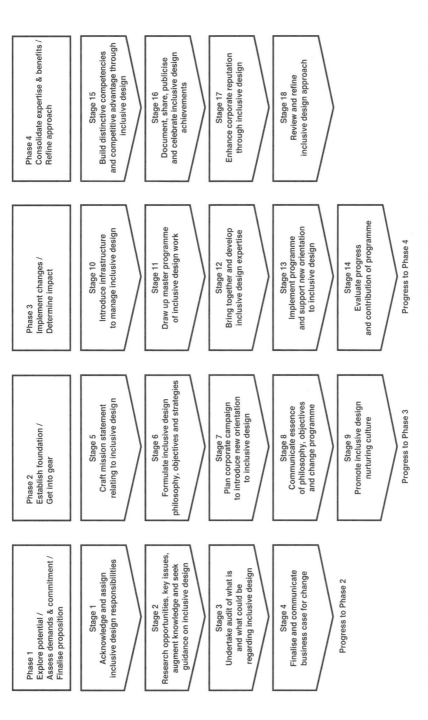

Figure 4.14 BS 7000-6 – process for adopting a professional approach to inclusive design at the organisation level (©British Standards Institution)

- augmentation, improvement and the creation of integrated systems of products in appropriate circumstances

- withdrawal of products and services from market

- 'lifetime' reviews of project, product and service experiences.

Research To Date

Inclusive design research and practice to date have focused primarily on the development of products that are physically accessible. Considerable effort has gone into preparing resources to assist business leaders and designers to understand the benefits of inclusive design and to create more inclusive products. Successes include the:

- provision of websites by the Design Council, the Royal Society for the Encouragement of Arts, Manufactures and Commerce (RSA) and others to promote inclusive design;

- establishment of two international conference series with a focus on business (INCLUDE) and academic (CWUAAT) audiences;

- expansion of the Design Business Association (DBA) Inclusive Design Challenge and Royal College of Art research associate scheme;

- development and provision of Department for Business Enterprise and Regulatory Reform (formerly the Department of Trade and Industry (DTI)) funded training;

- publication of the British Standard BS 7000-6;

- creation of the International Association for Inclusive Design (IAUD), a Japanese network of researchers and product providers from over 130 organisations.

Much of this work has been undertaken by voluntary and public sector organisations including the Design Council, the Royal National Institute for the Blind, the Royal National Institute for Deaf People, and the Centre for Policy on Ageing. Substantial contributions have also been made by key research centres in the subject area, principally driven by the design and ergonomics research communities.

The continuing relevance of the standard will depend on the quality of supporting research, and the data, information, guidance and tools generated. An immediate challenge, spurred on by changing expectations and aspirations

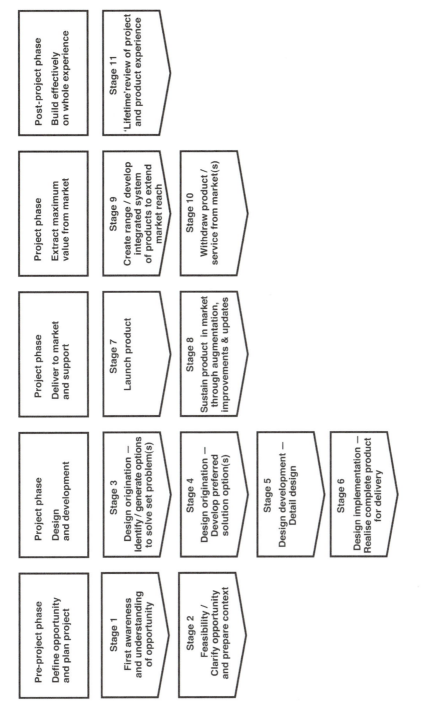

Figure 4.15 BS 7000-6 – primary stages in 'cradle-to-grave' inclusive design process (©British Standards Institution)

among previously marginalised groups, and importantly in the context of rapidly ageing societies, is to shift the focus from core accessibility to social acceptability and desirability that match consumer aspirations, on the OXO Good Grips model. Nielsen talks about practical and social acceptability in his book on usability (Nielsen, 1993), but while he provides much insight into the former, less is known about the latter.

Attempts have been made to categorise the needs of ageing populations by mapping a research agenda (Smith, 1990) and developing an ergonomic description of older people (Fisk and Rogers, 1997). Scientific studies on ageing – for example, the Baltimore Longitudinal Study (Fozard et al., 1993; Fozard, 1997) – have gathered extensive data, focusing on human performance in controlled laboratory situations.

Desirability

A product that is well designed from a functional perspective can be unattractive, unwanted or socially unacceptable. Extensive research by psychologists has identified three basic psychological needs that should be met for people to have a high sense of *well-being*: autonomy (or self determination), competence and relatedness (Ryan and Deci, 2001). However, relatively little is known about the way products satisfy these specific needs, and so enhance the user's sense of well being.

Both observational and experimental research provide firm evidence that subjective well-being is causally related to physical and mental health and productivity (Huppert, 2005). Designs that foster well-being produce benefits in terms of health and productivity which are likely to lead to a virtuous spiral of increasing well-being and improved functionality.

User requirements of products have frequently been compared with Maslow's hierarchy of needs, suggesting that once issues of utility, safety and comfort have been satisfied, emphasis may shift towards the decorative, emotional and symbolic attributes of a product. For the able-bodied population, depending on motivation and context, a product's perceived attributes may have greater importance than its tangible properties. This is because the appearance of a product has a crucial influence on the responses triggered among users and, ultimately, its market success. Judgements are made on the elegance, functionality and social significance of a product; these frequently centre on the satisfaction of consumer wants, aspirations and desires, rather than needs (Crilly, Moultrie and Clarkson, 2004). Moreover, 'consumers don't just buy a product: they buy value in the form of entertainment, experience and identity' (Topalian and Stoddard, 1997; Esslinger and Sweet, 1999).

For an ageing population, this prompts the central question: how does the sense of what is desirable vary across the population, for example by users' age, capability and social background? Answering this question through design has the potential to ensure that inclusive products are highly desirable in addition to being appropriately accessible.

Therefore, a greater understanding is needed of the role of social acceptability in inclusive design and how this might affect all aspects of the product – from initial concepts to detailed design, from advertising and launch to in-service support, then final disposal.

A better understanding is also needed of physical acceptability, and how information and data describing users and products can assist in developing more effective products and services.

Finally, there is a need to understand where and how these issues come together, often with regard to the cognitive capabilities and experience of the users. Social acceptability may depend as much on users' prior experience of a particular technology or product family, as on their functional needs, preferences in styling and so on.

The answers to these challenges are likely to be closely associated with understanding factors that influence user well-being. Researchers are beginning to address these issues, re-directing inclusive design from arguments relating to design exclusion towards those around effective design. This provides a clearer context for a more balanced approach to improve product and service utility and acceptability, as well as how they resonate with consumers and providers alike, without lessening the importance of countering design exclusion.

Challenges in Design Management Research

In contrast to all the research into inclusive design and practice, research into the *management* of inclusive design is virtually virgin territory. As the team that drafted the new British Standard discovered, one should avoid the misconception that managing design is a straightforward extension of design practice. Given the crucial influence of those who manage design activities on their outcomes, this gap weakens all attempts to promote a wider, successful adoption of inclusive design.

Probably the most important difference between design and design management research is that the latter targets those who lead and manage organisations, set their values and direction, and implement business policy (see, for example, Topalian, 1990): this will also encompass the introduction and sustenance of a comprehensive approach to inclusive design. Apart from being the most prolific commissioners of design, business executives constitute the most powerful body of 'designers' in the world. For it is they who:

- select the problems to be addressed

- approve how those problems will be tackled as well as the 'design' of projects set up to solve them

- assign resources to such projects

- sanction the concepts to be developed and how these are presented to markets

- determine how solutions will be supported in the field after launch.

Research in the 1970s also revealed that the most critical problems encountered during design projects are client-centred. Indeed, business executives exert the greatest influence on project outcomes, not the design specialists involved (Topalian, 1980).

BS 7000-6 and BS 7000–2 *Guide to managing the design of manufactured products* (1997) provide guidance on the key issues that define the scope of design management as a rigorous discipline in business (see also Topalian, 2002). Figures 4.14 and 4.15 indicate some that would benefit from research; each stage could form the basis of fruitful investigation. So, for example at the organisational level, research could be undertaken into:

- the formulation of mission statements, objectives and strategies relating to inclusive design;

- ways to plan campaigns to introduce a new orientation towards inclusive design;

- evaluating progress and the contribution of master programmes relating to inclusive design;

- documenting, sharing, publicising and celebrating achievements through inclusive design;

- building distinctive competencies and competitive advantage through inclusive design.

At the project level, research could be undertaken into:

- effective ways of launching new products and services that promote inclusive design values;

- developing ranges of integrated products and services based on inclusive principles;

- 'lifetime' reviews of project and customer experiences with products and services.

The Way Forward

Ideally, all initiatives to introduce inclusive design into organisations should be driven with vision and personal commitment by top executives. Increasing legislation and diverse regulations encountered in markets around the world demand their attention and front-line involvement.

For the vast majority of organisations, inclusive design represents a transformational philosophy in design *and* business practices. It heralds significant shifts in thinking, attitude and approach from top to bottom across organisations and, ultimately, requires close coordination between *all* disciplines in business. The extent of change is indicated by the views of a senior executive who felt strongly that beautiful period office buildings in his city were being ruined by the addition of unsightly access ramps for disabled people. He saw nothing wrong with previous practice: for example, when people turned up in wheelchairs, they would be man-handled up the entrance steps by two burly members of staff. There was no hint of any understanding of the dignity of disabled people or their desire for greater autonomy. Moreover, the UK has more than enough competent designers to create elegant and effective solutions to challenges presented by all styles of building and their locations. Unfortunately, there are all too few enlightened business executives who can harness that talent to achieve outcomes beyond expectation (Topalian, 1980).

A professional approach to inclusive design cannot be switched on and off at the convenience of executives. Effective planning is essential to ensure that they and their staff are aware of what to expect. This, in turn, helps to:

- map out an effective transition programme

- foresee and avoid difficulties

- facilitate 'buy in' among staff and reinforce commitment over time

- raise confidence and resilience

- resist piecemeal implementation that avoids tough challenges

- stick with the implementation programme despite setbacks

- build effectively on experience.

Insensitive implementation is likely to have a serious detrimental impact on the reputations of organisations that adopt a superficial approach. This is highlighted by the example of an organisation that formulated substantial guidance on inclusive design which was publicised in internal and external communications. Initially, those in charge resisted the resulting documentation deviating from the organisation's 'housestyle' even though this would have made it inaccessible to those with poor eyesight: apparently senior executives did not grasp the contradiction of issuing their guidelines in that format though this demonstrated a lack of true understanding of inclusiveness.

The new British Standard is a response to an agenda set by changing consumer demands and expectations. It is promoted by government bodies – such as the Design Council and Department of Trade and Industry – which seek to advance UK competitiveness in rapidly changing business environments. The standard sees business executives and design professionals as potential champions of inclusive design in industry and business. It seeks to encourage the adoption of a more professional approach to inclusive design by arming them with a richer language and a comprehensive management framework to guide them through implementation at both organisation and project levels.

An inclusive business and design strategy delivers a greater understanding of consumer needs and aspirations, and a better alignment of an organisation's consumer offer with them. It also enables a closer association between staff, investors, corporate values and mission, and an enhanced ability to identify and exploit opportunities through innovation.

An increasing number of products and services designed according to inclusive principles are being launched: the Vodafone 'Simply' handset (see Chapter 6), and the Toyota Well Cab are examples.

Supported by the new British Standard, uptake by business is now critically important to the development of inclusive design. No doubt, market results will become the key measure of success.

Figure 4.16 Toyota 'Well Cab' accessible car interior (©Toyota)

Figure 4.17 Toyota 'Well Cab' demonstrates accessibility for all (©Toyota)

To conclude, an area of bright potential in the past few years has been in the public sector. Central and local government are significant purchasers of design, so they could influence the professionalism by which design is managed as well as the quality of outcomes generated. Councils such as Lewisham, Tower Hamlets, Sheffield and Manchester in the United Kingdom have been formulating and refining diversity and equalities policies in response to the Disability Discrimination Act and other recent legislation. Substantial budgets have been allocated to upgrading their facilities to ensure all citizens have equal opportunities and reasonable access to services offered. These achievements could form solid foundations on which to build effective approaches to inclusive design. Indeed, inclusive design provides the ideal means of completing the implementation of diversity and equalities policies. As the Lewisham Council Community Strategy document states: 'Designing in diversity... designing out discrimination...'.

References

BS 7000-1 (1999), *Guide to Managing Innovation* (London: British Standards Institution).

BS 7000-2 (1997), *Guide to Managing the Design of Manufactured Products* (London: British Standards Institution).

BS 7000-3 (1994), *Guide to Managing Service Design* (London: British Standards Institution).

BS 7000-6 (2005), *Guide to Managing Inclusive Design* (London: British Standards Institution).

Permission to reproduce extracts of BS 7000–6: 2005 is granted by BSI. British Standards can be obtained from BSI Customer Services, 389 Chiswick High Road, London W4 4AL. Telephone +44 (0)20 8996 9001; Email cservices@bsi-global.com.

Crilly, N., Moultrie, J. and Clarkson, P.J. (2004), 'Seeing Things: Consumer Response to the Visual Domain in Product Design', *Design Studies*, 25(6), pp. 547–577. [DOI: 10.1016/j.destud.2004.03.001]

DDA (1995), *Disability Discrimination Act* (London: Department for Education and Employment).

Design Council (2006), 'Knowledge Cell on Inclusive Design'. Available at: www.designcouncil.org.uk/inclusivedesign.

DTI (2005), *Department of Trade and Industry Survey on Inclusive Design* (London: Department of Trade and Industry).

Fisk, D. and Rogers, W. (1997), *Human Factors and the Older Adult* (London: Academic Press).

Fozard, J.L. (1997), 'Ageing and Technology: A Developmental View' In *Designing for an Aging Population: Ten Years of Human Factors and Ergonomics Research*, Rogers, W.A. (ed.) (Santa Monica, CA: Human Factors and Ergonomics Society).

Fozard, J.L., Metter, E.J., Brant, U., Pearson, J.D. and Baker, G.T. (1993), 'Goals for the Next Generation of Longitudinal Studies' In *Ageing, Health and Competence: The Next Generation of Longitudinal Research*, Schroots, J.J.F. (ed.) (Amsterdam: Elsevier).

Huppert, F.A. (2005), 'Positive Emotions and Cognition: Developmental, Neuroscience and Health Perspectives in Hearts and Minds: Affective Influences on Social Cognition and Behavior'. Proceedings of Sydney Symposium of Social Psychology, Sydney, Australia.

Keates, S. and Clarkson, P.J. (2003), *Countering Design Exclusion, An Introduction to Inclusive Design* (London: Springer-Verlag).

Nielsen, J. (1993), *Usability Engineering* (London: Academic Press).

Norman, D. (2002), *The Design of Everyday Things* (New York, NY: Basic Books).

Ryan, R.M. and Deci, E.L. (2001), 'On Happiness and Human Potentials: A Review of Research on Hedonic and Eudaimonic Well-Being', *Annual Reviews of Psychology*, 52, pp. 141–166. [DOI: 10.1146/annurev.psych.52.1.141]

Smith, D. (1990), 'Human Factors and Ageing: An Overview of Research Needs and Applications Opportunities', *Human Factors*, 32, pp. 509–526.

Sweet, F. (ed.) (1999), *Frog: Forms Follows Emotion* (London: Thames & Hudson).

Topalian, A. (1980), *The Management of Design Projects* (London: Associated Business Press).

Topalian, A. (1990), 'Design Leadership in Business: The Role of Non-Executive Directors and Corporate Design Consultants', *Journal of General Management*, 16(2), pp. 39–62.

Topalian, A. (2002), 'Promoting Design Leadership through Skills Development Programs', *Design Management Journal*, 13(3), pp. 10–18.

Topalian, A. and Stoddard, J. (1997), 'New R&D Management: How Cluster Nets, Experience Cycles and Visualisation Make More Desirable Futures Come to Life'. Proceedings of Managing R&D in the 21st century; Manchester Business School, Manchester.

Market Advantage: Practitioners' Viewpoints

Hua Dong, Graham Pullin, Ingelise Nielsen, Maria Benktzon, Olle Bobjer and Barry Tanner

Introduction

Can inclusive design achieve market advantage? This chapter aims to answer this question through a conversation with some practitioners working on inclusive design projects.

Earlier publications such as the *DAN Teaching Pack* (Hewer et al., 1995), *Design for the Future* (Coleman, 1997), and *Include 2003* proceedings (Stabler and van der Heuval, 2003), introduced some case studies of inclusive design, for example the London underground ticket machine designed by IDEO, the BAHCO tools by Ergonomidesign and the Selectronic shower by Applied Energy Products Ltd. How do practitioners from these companies view the market advantages of inclusive design? To find out, Hua Dong initiated a conversation with design practitioners from the UK and Sweden. Those involved were: Graham Pullin, formerly Senior Interaction Designer at IDEO; Ingelise Nielsen, Head of Public Relations at IDEO in London; Maria Benktzon and Olle Bobjer, partners of Ergonomidesign, one of Scandinavia's largest and best-known industrial design consultancies; Barry Tanner, New Product Introduction Manager of Applied Energy Products Ltd., a UK-based manufacturer of water, heating and ventilation products.

The conversation was centred on four inclusive design projects, their development processes and market value through practitioners' eyes.

Project Examples

'SIMPLY'

Hua As product development practitioners of inclusive design-aware companies, were you involved in any project that can be considered inclusive design?

Ingelise The London underground ticket machine was a well-known example, but happened some time ago. A more recent inclusive design project was the *Simply* mobile phone that IDEO designed for and with Vodafone.

Graham In some ways I would say that *Simply* is on the fringes of inclusive

design: it is certainly 'inclusive design' rather than 'universal design'. Our brief was to design for people in their 30s, 40s and 50s who were already using (already able to use) a mobile phone, but not finding it ideally suited to them. Minor age-related impairment was part of the picture, but so was exclusion on more cultural grounds.

For example, we found people in this group unlikely to explore and experiment with the interface on their phone, whether through disinterest or for fear of messing something up. This left many of them not knowing how to use quite basic features on their current phone, or even that these were available. Locking the keypad, switching the phone to silent ring and picking up voicemails were common examples.

This was compounded by a deep sense of social etiquette and many people not wanting their phones to misbehave in public by ringing in the cinema, or even on the bus, or dialling someone by mistake. The net result was that a lot of users kept their phones switched off most of the time, which is not good for a phone service provider.

Figure 5.1   Vodafone
***Simply* mobile phone:**
phone lock slider (©Lee
Funnell)

Our solution was to make more explicit those features that had previously been hidden: the keypad lock, instead of an obscure hidden key combination, becomes a physical slider on the side of the phone (there is a padlock symbol on it and the whole screen changes when it is locked); the ringer setting, instead of being hidden in a menu called 'profiles', is again given a direct physical control; voicemail, instead of being accessed by a long press on the number '1' key, is treated like a domestic answering machine (a beacon flashes on the top of the phone when you have a message, and you press this to access any incoming messages, whether voicemail, text or missed calls). There is even a dedicated button at the top of the phone to take you right back to the beginning if you do get lost in a menu.

This approach is not without its compromises: there are inevitably more buttons on the phone, which might make it look no simpler, at least at first sight. And on a mobile phone, with every component fighting for space, ultimately button size is a trade-off between using the phone and carrying the phone. *Simply* is not perfect, but we would like to think we have struck a sensitive balance: a suitable balance for this different market.

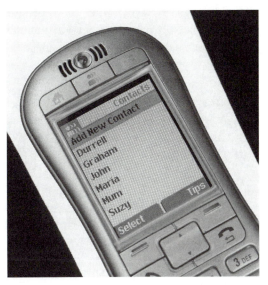

Figure 5.2   Vodafone *Simply* mobile phone: the use of straightforward language on the display (©Lee Funnell)

Ingelise   Three core design principles were established through the research, and all three principles can be thought of as 'inclusive design', whether cultural, cognitive or sensory. They are: Suitable Aesthetic; Explicit Navigation, and Accessible Controls.

BAHCO

Maria   The BAHCO tools are good ergonomic design for professional craftsmen, but I would not say they are good examples of inclusive design: there is only one size of each tool, usually designed for an 'average' man. I would say that the more recent series of Lindstrom Rx electronic cutters and pliers are better examples of inclusive design (Figure 5.3): they have adjustable handle width and spring force, designed to include women users. Also, we have recently designed a range of hammers for a Swedish company Hultafors; they are available in small, medium and large handle sizes to fit an extended range of users' hands: both men and women can use the hammers with ease (see a series of prototypes in Figure 5.4).

Barry Although we have not manufactured other products that are more inclusive than the Selectronic Shower, in the past 2 years, we have made great progress on that project. It has gone beyond inclusive design process to inclusive performance…

Figure 5.3   Lindstrom Rx pliers

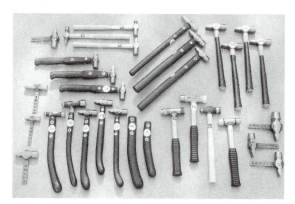

Figure 5.4   Hammers for Hultafors – prototypes

Hua Whatdoyoumean by inclusive performance?

Barry The Selectronic Shower has been approved by the British Electro-technical Approvals Board (BEAB), and it became the first product to meet the new industry standard for thermostatic electric showers being awarded the BEAB CARE mark – this means that it has passed a rigorous testing schedule and complies with the additional safety requirements of the care industry. As an additional safety feature, all Selectronic showers are treated with Microban, an anti-bacterial additive which prevents the growth of fungi and bacteria for the life of the shower. In this sense, it has been through *an inclusive design process* to *an inclusive design product* to *an inclusive performance*!

Design Process

Hua How would you describe the design process?

Figure 5.5   The BEAB CARE certificate for the Selectronic shower

Maria Another inclusive design project with which I was involved is an injection pen for NPS Pharmaceuticals in Salt Lake City, where we changed the stereotype of how an injection pen is usually handled by including critical users in the design process. NPS Pharmaceuticals commissioned Ergonomidesign to design an injection pen that was comfortable and easy for patients to use – including people with reduced dexterity. The goal was to make the injection system as intuitive as possible so that patients, particularly older women, would feel comfortable that they had activated it properly. It should be easy to learn and once the patients got the instruction it should be easy to remember how to use it.

Hua So it was an inclusive design brief, and what was your response?

Maria The injection pen was for treating osteoporosis (porosity and brittleness of the bones due to loss of calcium from the bone matrix). As we knew that people with arthritis might have problems with push buttons, we attempted to change the current design with top triggers and developed six concept models for evaluation. In the evaluation 12 women users were involved, all diagnosed with osteoporosis; half of them had normal hand/arm function and the other half had reduced function.

As a result of that test, we found that the traditional injection pen concept with a top trigger was not possible for some users to activate. We therefore developed a pen with a side activator that also served as a grip and was comfortable for the user's hand. It was designed so you can activate it with either one or four fingers.

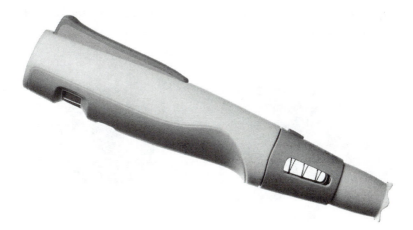

Figure 5.6   The NPS injection pen

Hua   Could you tell me about the new design concept in more detail?

Maria   The injection pen has a colour coding system, which is part of the intuitive design. By following the colours and turning the dosing flip to green, the patients know that they have loaded the dose properly and it is ready to be administered. The pen also has a dose counter that counts down from '14' to '1' so that patients do not have to calculate how many doses are left.

We also incorporated a needle guard that shields the needle from sight. The needle guard is shaped like a daisy so it looks friendlier. As more women are likely to use the pen it has a slightly more feminine touch, and we tried to make it both attractive and less medical-looking.

Hua   You mentioned that some of your users had normal hand/arm function, some not. What is the rationale of selecting such a mix of users?

Maria   It is important to include both critical and non-critical users in the design process to find out if there are any conflicting demands. The non-critical user can often use a much wider range of solutions, compared with the critical user for whom the number of options is more limited.

We also found that experienced users, for example an older woman who was a nurse, might prefer the traditional top trigger solution, as they were used to it, whereas inexperienced users had no preconceptions and were more flexible; the critical users with dexterity problems and little force could use only one or two of the proposed options.

To include as many users as possible we therefore chose the current trigger solution with a side actuator.

Figure 5.7   The daisy-shaped needle guard

Olle   Similar to the NPS injection pen project, the Lindstrom Rx tool range also started with an inclusive design brief. Over the years, a variety of tool designs had been purchased and used in production at a major producer of electronic hardware, Nortel Networks. Most of them were similarly designed with a few exceptions of cosmetic character. BAHCO, a hand tool producer and owner of the trade name Lindstrom, took the initiative to identify and evaluate ergonomic cutters and pliers for use on the shop floor. The ambition of Nortel Networks was to suggest worldwide recommendations on the purchase and use of tools best suited to the user, the production and the quality demands.

Hua   It seems that an inclusive design brief is important for an inclusive design project. I was wondering whether the Selectronic shower project also started from an inclusive design brief.

Barry   Actually, our brief was to produce a high specification shower with operational features suitable for the National Health Service (NHS) and Care Sector market, which complied with current NHS safety guidelines relating to safe showering temperatures.

Figure 5.8   Cutters and pliers are intensively used by operators in the manufacture of printed circuit boards

Hua   So it was not a truly inclusive design brief; rather, it is more focused on the Care Sector?

Barry   Yes but we achieved an inclusive design by working in partnership with the Royal National Institute of the Blind (RNIB). At an early stage, we approached the RNIB with an initial design model of the shower. The RNIB ergonomists helped validate our design, drawing upon their knowledge and experience of product design for older and visually impaired people.

Hua   That was expert assessment. Did you also involve end-users in the development process?

Barry   End-users were involved at a later stage. We found the RNIB ergonomists' early assessment and their initial broad suggestions extremely useful. Based on their suggestions, we improved the ergonomic features of the model and included visual and auditory cues such as colour contrast, print size, font style, flow status light, audible beeps, and tactile feedback. The next stage of the project involved showing the improved prototype to user groups and discussing it with them. With the help of the RNIB, six focus groups were organised in residential homes and local associations for visually impaired people. Among the 50 participants, 17 were carers and home managers. The majority of the users were over 60 years of age.

Hua How was the user assessment carried out and what did you find out?

Barry Small groups of participants were invited to approach the mock-up prototype with fixed buttons, together with an existing shower to provide an impression of button pressure and audible feedback. The RNIB ergonomists observed the process and conducted discussions using a structured questionnaire; they then presented the findings to us. The most important finding was that both *styling* and *usability* were important considerations for older users – this reinforced the case for inclusive design. Other findings from the end user assessment included (the need for) improved colour contrast and use of more distinct tactile buttons as well as reducing perceived complexity. However, I would say that we had got the design 85 per cent right with the expertise of the RNIB ergonomists before it went out to user testing, so the users' role was essentially to validate and improve the design concept.

Figure 5.9   The simple control of the Selectronic shower

Hua As you mentioned, the users tested the mock-up prototype rather than a functional model: did you carry out further tests with real products afterwards?

Barry The phase of development that followed involved longer-term user trials with fully functional Selectronic showers. In addition, RNIB ergonomists also helped us in making the user instructions inclusive, and training our sales people and installers. So the whole process was inclusive.

Hua The Selectronic shower project was not started with an inclusive design brief, but it still achieved inclusivity. What about the mobile phone project?

Graham We are not able to divulge too much about our design process on the Vodafone project, but I can tell you that it began with observations of users in several European countries and resulted in dozens of insights that have been incorporated into the design.

Ingelise This mobile phone is a tool for communication derived directly from user feedback. Vodafone later did extensive market research, which confirmed the design direction.

Market Advantage

Hua How would you describe the market advantage of these inclusive design projects?

Barry We and the RNIB agree that the benefits of the Selectronic Shower project for all parties concerned far outweighed the cost and time of the inclusive design process. For us, the process was cost-effective and the final product became inclusive. For the end users, the shower removes the barriers and improves independence and privacy. For the NHS and Care Sector, it potentially reduces staff workload, complies with the BEAB care performance standard and attracts new customers.

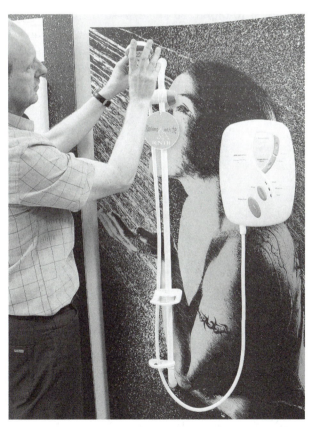

Figure 5.10 The Selectronic shower is endorsed by the RNIB

We launched the Selectronic shower in early 2003. In the first year, its sales increased over a hundred per cent, so we doubled its volume. The second year, sales continuously grew at a very good level. Although we sell the Selectronic range primarily to the Care Market at the moment, it has a potential to reach a much larger market.

The problem is that the Selectronic thermostatic range is more expensive to manufacture. This is because it needs to meet extra requirements for power control, temperature control and has an integral motorised flow control valve – these make it more expensive. However, if the sales volume is increased significantly, we will be able to reduce the unit price.

Maria   The NPS pen was launched in 2006 by Nycomed in Denmark. Previously, there was no injection device on the market that is really easy to administer if you have dexterity problems or very little strength: so it will definitely be a competitive advantage in the long run.

Olle   Following a 10-month on-site exposure and research study in three countries: the US, Canada, the UK, we found one set of Lindstrom Rx cutters and pliers (see Figure 5.11) was significantly more appreciated than the other sets, so this particular set of tools was introduced to the world market.

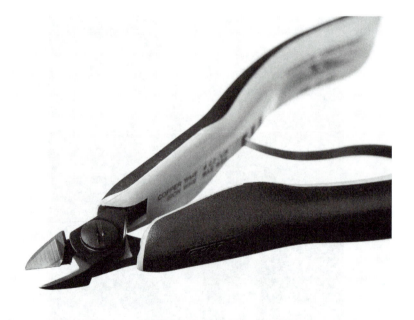

Figure 5.11 A pair of Lindstrom Rx pliers

The design factor mostly appreciated in the Rx cutter was the ease with which the operator could pick up the tool from the table. Operators use the tools not only for cutting, but also for reaching and grasping the shanks to lift them from the desk and place them in the proper position in the palm. This sequence may be a risk factor for epicondylitis (inflammation in the elbow due to overuse), as operators may have to extend their wrist and open their hands very wide in order to get a firm grip over the tool, which is often placed on a workbench by the operator.

Operators with small hands had obvious problems in placing some of the other tools in their hands. To avoid opening their hands very wide, methods were seen by which they picked up the tool in one shank and moved the tool over in their hand in order to get it properly placed. The Rx cutters were equipped with a return spring designed so that the shank width could be set by the operator to reduce it. Moreover, the return spring has a specific force displacement characteristic, which gives the shanks a firmer resistance when fully open to ease the task of picking up the tool. The material and texture on the surface of the shanks in palm contact has been selected to provide optimum friction and least discomfort as a result of palmar friction studies (Bobjer, 2004).

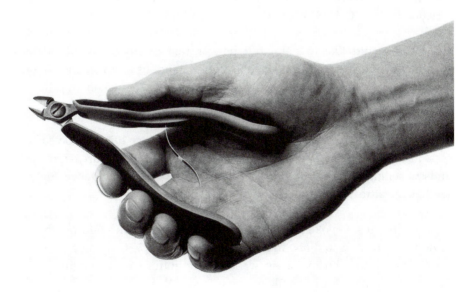

Figure 5.12 Rx pliers in operation

The recommendation from Peter McBride, the ergonomics specialist at Nortel Networks, was that all operators who need to use either wire cutters or pliers should be supplied with the Rx range.

Although the cost of these tools is higher than traditional tools, it can be justified as follows:

- The traditional range of cutters causes considerable pain and discomfort, while the Rx range is comfortable to use.

- Nortel Networks health care providers reported fewer calls concerning upper limb complaints/discomfort since the Rx tools were introduced as the company's regular cutter.

- The samples of Rx tools are in good condition and fully functional after 20 months.

- The spring in the Rx is a separate component, which can be replaced by the operator.

Over a 28-month period of testing, McBride has drawn the following conclusions: although the Rx cutters are more expensive than most of the existing cutters, they last much longer: of the 26 pairs of Rx cutters issued, 22 pairs were still in good condition after 28 months of use, compared with existing cutters which have to be replaced at least 4 times/year. The total cost reduction equates to US$100 per operator per year.

What I would like to point out here is that creating a good working environment and preventing injury to muscles, tendons and joints is not only about having ergonomically designed tools, but also about knowing how to use them at the workstation.

Ingelise   Vodafone *Simply* was recently launched, so it is just too early to assess its market success. There are certainly some promising early signs, with handsets selling out for a while in Britain. And anecdotal evidence suggests that they are attracting a diverse range of customers.

Graham   Yes, I spoke to a Vodafone store assistant who told me that the previous day he had sold one to a woman in her early 30s buying a phone for herself, several to a businessman wanting straightforward company phones and one to a man giving a mobile phone to his mother.

One point I want to make is that the phone itself is only part of the picture. Market success also depends on the way a product or a service is described and presented. The iconic GoodGrips kitchen tools may be a notable exception of an inclusively designed product that 'sold itself'. But *Simply* was aimed at a market segment who had not really engaged with a telecoms industry which they perceived as being focused on younger people. And the issue of inclusion can be a sensitive one: people do not necessarily want to be seen with a phone that looks as though it has been made easier to use.

What was satisfying in this respect about the *Simply* project was that the advertising group, Wieden + Kennedy in Amsterdam, went right back to the initial user observations for their inspiration. Many of their tag-lines were derived from things that the users had said themselves. 'A large, easy-to-read colour screen, because squinting will give you wrinkles' epitomises the spirit of a project at the 'fringe' of inclusive design: age-related impairment is acknowledged, but with a degree of self-deprecating humour. And a lightness of touch, as we hope it was in the design itself.

Hua There are a number of means to achieve inclusive design, and we discussed involving users, both critical and non-critical users, observing users in different cultural contexts, and combining expert consultation and user evaluation. The market advantage of inclusive design is reflected by improved performance, value for money, an increased user range, and 'a lightness of touch' which adds subtle enjoyment to our lives. I hope our discussion will inspire more inclusive designs in the future.

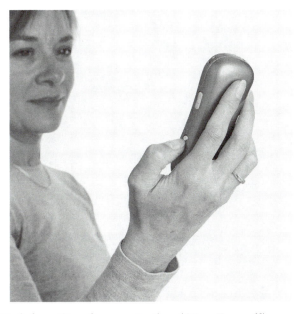

Figure 5.13 Vodafone *Simply*: user testing (©Lee Funnell)

References

Bobjer, O. (2004), 'Friction and Discomfort in the Design and Use of Hand Tools-Exposure to Textures at Different Loads and Velocities with Reference to Contamination'. Doctoral thesis (Department of Design and Technology, Loughborough University).

Coleman, R. (1999), 'Design for the Future', *Design für die Zukunft*, printed by the Helen Hamlyn Centre (London: Royal College of Art).

Hewer, S., Kingsland, K., D'hondt, E., Rietsema, J., Westrik, H., Brouwer, J., Chan, S., Gudiksen, M., Tähkokallio, P. and Coleman, R. (1995), 'DAN Teaching Pack', *European Design for Ageing Network: Incorporating Age-Related Issues into Design Courses* (London: RSA, Waterloo Printing Company).

Pullin, G. and Bontoft, M. (2003), 'Connecting business, inclusion and design' In *Inclusive Design: Design for the Whole Population*, Clarkson, P.J., Coleman, R., Keates, S. and Lebbon, C. (eds.) (London: Springer-Verlag).

Stabler, K. and van den Heuvel, S. (2003), 'The Selectronic Shower: An Inclusive Design Case Study', Proceedings of *International Conference on Inclusive Design*, Royal College of Art, London.

Designer Education: Case Studies from Graduate Partnerships with Industry

Julia Cassim and Hua Dong

Introduction

The post-war period has seen radical changes in the social fabric of the UK with multiple factors hastening the move towards a more inclusive society – gender activism, anti-discrimination legislation and new ways of viewing the social contract have encouraged a wider interpretation of the meaning of civil society in which people of a diversity of lifestyles, abilities, ethnic backgrounds and contesting viewpoints can co-exist however uneasy that mix may sometimes be. In business terms, each viewpoint and population segment can be seen as representative of a potential market or at least an alternative scenario for a product or service. When legislation is enacted to enforce inclusion, the previously deniable can no longer be ignored. As a result, manufacturers and service providers have slowly come around to the idea that perhaps the old stereotypes regarding their core market may have to be adjusted if they are to survive in this brave, greying, multi-cultural and litigious new world.

For designers too it presents a challenge to the one-track *status quo* as described by designer Bill Moggridge (Moggridge 2001):

> *'We find it much easier to design products and services for ourselves than for other people. Entrepreneurs, marketing people, designers and engineers are often selfish in that way.'*

Demographics may show a world that is inexorably ageing but the age map of the design profession is overwhelmingly populated by the young. The Design Council's 2005 report on the design sector in the UK shows 62 per cent of designers aged under 40, with 30 per cent of these in their twenties. A further 61 per cent of the total are men with only six per cent from minority ethnic groups (Design Council, 2005). While this does not preclude empathy on the part of designers with other age, ethnic or social groups, it is not a recipe to ensure inclusive thinking. The associated discipline of marketing is similarly Youth-centric and while the business case for courting older consumers becomes ever more glaringly obvious, only five per cent of overall marketing in the UK is targeted their way.

In view of this, how can the design profession embrace the diversity of the marketplace in a way that actively encourages innovation and inclusivity? How can they expand their vision of the core audience for their work and engage with them in a way that is mutually beneficial? Importantly how can they transmit this reality to those who commission their work? It is a challenge not only for designers but equally for those who train them.

This chapter will look at case studies from the Helen Hamlyn Research Associates Programme, an educational initiative which has been responsible for a series of inclusive design projects undertaken by new graduates of the Royal College of Art (RCA) with external partners in a wide variety of contexts. By offering a compelling good practice alternative, the programme has set a different agenda for the design profession and in the process debunked some surprisingly entrenched ideas. Working with users who are often ignored has helped young designers understand good design as a collaborative process that relies more on substantive user involvement rather than a single Eureka moment.

Five distinctly different case studies have been chosen to reflect the applicability of the inclusive design process to different contexts, external partners and design disciplines. They demonstrate how young designers have used, adapted and at times originated a variety of user research methods alone or in combination to understand the needs and aspirations of their core users and their research partner and thereby drive the design development process.

The Evolution of the Helen Hamlyn Research Associates Programme

When the Helen Hamlyn Centre (HHC) was set up at the RCA in January 1999, it faced three major challenges. The first was to create a meaningful and lasting form of interaction with the RCA design studios and embed inclusive thinking within the educational process. Secondly, it had to find ways to widen the definition of inclusive design and clarify its relevance to the full range of design disciplines being taught at the RCA and practiced in the professional design community outside. Thirdly, it had to develop mechanisms to deliver these aims along with an evidence base of live design projects.

Theoretical Exercises Versus the 'Power of the Prototype'

Two existing initiatives in the US offered insights into how this could be structured within an educational context – one at the Rhode Island School of Design, the other at the Chicago Institute of Design, Illinois Institute of Technology.

At Rhode Island, design students had developed a prototype for a 'Universal Kitchen'. Nothing unusual in design education terms except that this was not a theoretical academic exercise but a live design project that would be subjected to critical evaluation by manufacturers and would succeed or fail on criteria demanded by the market and not design education alone. The experience was an immersive one in the realities of professional practice for the students involved. This new educational model underlined 'the power of the prototype' in contrast to programmes where compelling theoretical design concepts were generated, but which could nonetheless be dismissed by industry on the grounds of impracticality.

At the Chicago Institute of Design in Illinois, MA students were teamed with industrial partners on a range of collaborative projects but within a framework where there was a uniformity of presentation and consistency of approach across the group despite the diversity of the projects. Another important element lay in how external partners were approached for financial support. Traditional models of corporate funding for academia follow a pattern where large amounts are asked for a single design research project, which is viewed as commissioned research and not necessarily collaborative work. Chicago had found that in comparison, if small amounts were requested, the refusal rate dropped dramatically while the acceptance rate soared – for example if 20 potential partners were approached, it was likely that at least half would consider working collaboratively.

The adoption of such an approach by the HHC allowed for the creation of a design research programme, where there was a diversity of projects and partners and the possibility to work across design disciplines. The HHC's added element of co-funding the project with the research partner ensured parity between them and meant that it could not be viewed as a piece of design commissioned on the cheap by a 'sponsor' who could then dictate the parameters of the project. Instead it was a true collaboration based on a transfer of knowledge between the three parties – the RCA studios, the Research Associate and the research partner.

The new yearlong programme was launched in October 1999 and called the Helen Hamlyn Research Associates Programme. A wide range of external partners was secured and this in turn assured a diversity of research issues and user scenarios, a characteristic that continues to this day.

Embedding and Consolidating the Programme Structure

The programme is timed to run from October to June so that the symposium and exhibition are the first things that RCA students see at the start of the new academic year. The year is divided into four distinct research phases – explore, focus, develop and deliver. Its overall aim reflects that of the HHC, which is to address specific user needs related to socially inclusive design. Each year around a dozen RCA new graduates are selected from the graduating year, many having taken part in the Design For Our Future Selves Awards, an annual competition organised by the HHC for Second Year MA students at the RCA. Research Associates are employed full time for the duration of the projects, some of which are extended to a second year. All the design disciplines taught at the RCA are represented – architecture, interiors, furniture, communication, interaction design, product design, vehicle design, industrial design engineering, ceramics and glass and so on. Again this has ensured a diversity of projects, which vary in subject, scale and duration.

The Role of the Research Partner

Project briefs are developed in a three-way conversation between the research partner, the HHC and the host RCA department. They have centred on design for ageing populations, changing patterns of work, mobility for all, independent living and innovation in healthcare. Sometimes the starting point is an MA student project that interests the research partner as in Case Study 2; but more commonly, it is an idea or an issue that they want to investigate or an existing area of research they wish to augment or approach from a different viewpoint.

The range of external partners to date has been wide and included such multinational giants as Unilever, GlaxoSmithKline, Ford, Orange, Hewlett-Packard, Dyson and Levi-Strauss, retailers like Waitrose, MFI and B&Q and creative industry firms such as Reid Architecture, IDEO and Fitch. The participating charities have been similarly diverse with the Peabody Trust, the Guide Dogs for the Blind Association, the British Heart Association and lesser-known names such as Whizz-Kidz, a charity centred on the mobility issues of disabled children.

For the research partners, the programme provides a mechanism whereby they can work closely with RCA design graduates, gain access to innovative thinking on products or services associated with social change, and be part of the RCA's creative research network. For the Research Associates, the scheme serves as an important bridge to full professional practice. Many go on to work with the research partner, developing the project to the point of manufacture as in the case of Matthew White's work with B&Q, the do-it-yourself retail giant. His groundbreaking designs for their own brand power tools have passed the million unit manufacture point with one launched in a new design iteration. The success of this venture has seen a continuing relationship between the HHC and B&Q.

Diverse Contexts, Diverse Partners

The following case studies are representative of this diversity of contexts and partners. Two involve communication design (Case Studies 2 and 5), two product design (Case Studies 1 and 4), and one that was initially thought to involve vehicle design alone resulted in the design of associated service delivery as well (Case Study 3). The rationale for each was varied in character. The research partner for Case Study 4 for example is a large, influential Japanese utilities provider that sets industry standards, maintains an extensive database of consumer information, and has a resident ergonomist and an R&D division. The company has been unable to marshall these characteristics internally to promote inclusivity or innovation in the design of their core consumer products or externally with manufacturers that work with them. In contrast, Case Study 2 was initially a self-generated project based on the designer's personal experience of dyslexia. It became an award-winning beacon project that has gone on to be used in different commercial and educational contexts.

Case Study One: Home Industry – New Tools for Manual Pieceworkers

RESEARCH ASSOCIATE

Yuko Tsurumaru, RCA Design Products

RESEARCH PARTNER

Reid Architecture and the Design Council, in association with the National Group on Homeworking (NGH): a body made up of different voluntary organisations. Reid Architecture's interest in the project centred on the use of low-tech solutions within the tight confines of small working spaces.

THE BRIEF

To research and develop low-cost products capable of improving the lives of pieceworkers working by hand at home using industrial processes.

THE CONTEXT

Pieceworkers working in the home are among the most socially vulnerable and economically exploited groups of workers in the UK. A high proportion of the 800,000 homeworkers in this category are female or from ethnic minorities, since this form of work offers the advantages of combining two roles – the care of children and other dependants, with necessary income generation. The disadvantages can, however, outweigh the benefits. The 175 homeworkers interviewed for the 'Home Truths' report in 1994 by the Leeds-based national group on homeworking

Figure 6.1   Pieceworker assembling small electronic components using the trays

(NGH) cited 'low pay', 'isolation' and 'the mess' (caused by such jobs as sewing, machining, packing and component assembly) as the main disadvantages of this kind of work. The work is often repetitive, dirty, hazardous and carried out in inadequate space and facilities. Given their low rates of pay, homeworkers cannot afford to purchase the appropriate equipment and furniture that would improve their working environment and employers are unwilling to foot the bill.

METHODOLOGY

Tsurumaru worked with the NGH to identify and visit a qualitative sample of pieceworkers across the UK. Six were observed and documented across a span

Figure 6.2 Beech rocking stool designed for textile workers

of age, family composition, geographical location and work functions: in South Wales a couple assembling small-scale electronic components on their kitchen table; in Gosport, a group of women trimming and finishing rubber products with razors; in West Yorkshire, textile workers sticking embroidery kits together at the kitchen sink.

Photographs and drawings were complemented by interviews and questionnaires and the observed processes were compared with factory methods of assembly. Product concepts derived from an analysis of the findings were developed, prototyped and trialled with the homeworkers as part of an iterative, user-centred development process. The problem areas generated a series of design proposals that were further tested with four older users, all with reduced dexterity and mobility. This user group gave feedback at different stages of the design process to ensure that issues facing older workers were factored into the development process.

RESULTS

A series of low-cost vacuum-formed plastic trays with dimpled bases that nestle in a soft foam base were created for small-scale electronic component assembly. The design of the trays was developed from observations of Japanese watchmakers at work. The dimples assist the selection of tiny components and the tray spouts enable them to be poured from one stage of the process to the next. The trays can be removed easily from the kitchen table and stacked without disrupting the flow of work.

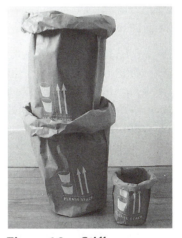

Figure 6.3 Stiff paper bags designed for women trimming rubber products.

For the women trimming rubber products, a set of stiff paper bags was designed in bright colours to blend in with the domestic interior. They replace the dirty, limp and unstable bags they used which scattered trimmings over the floor and were unsightly.

For the textile workers who stood to work at the sink, a simple, low-cost work stool with rockers was designed in solid beech to allow them to perch on it.

Case Study Two: Read – Developing a Typeface for People with Dyslexia

RESEARCH ASSOCIATE

Natascha Frensch, RCA Communication Art & Design

RESEARCH PARTNER

Audi Design Foundation

The project was initiated by Natasha Frensch, a dyslexic Dutch typographer as her final year MA project at the RCA and was subsequently awarded a grant by the Audi Design Foundation under their Young Designer of the Year Award: 'This is the first time we have supported a project by a young graphic designer, but the emphasis on fitness for purpose expressed in the typeface is very much in keeping with the ideals of our awards.'

THE BRIEF

To develop a new sans serif typeface designed specifically to help people with dyslexia improve reading and writing.

THE CONTEXT

Britain has two million severely dyslexic individuals including some 375,000 schoolchildren. Similar patterns are seen in Europe and North America. Dyslexia can occur despite normal intellectual ability and is independent of socio-economic or language background. Innovative responses have emerged in computer software, talking books and other assistive products, but relatively little design research has been carried out in the area of typographic design. Difficulties arise because each dyslexic individual is affected in different ways, with the condition ranging from mild to severe. Many remain undiagnosed well into adulthood. Dyslexics develop lateral strategies to deal with individual difficulties but reading and written communication pose problems with a resulting loss of self-confidence. The incidence in the creative industries is significantly higher than elsewhere. Nearly a quarter of students at the RCA, for example, have some level of dyslexia.

METHODOLOGY

Over a 3-year period, Frensch tested her new typeface against conventional ones with young children who were learning to read and write, older school children and adults aged between 18 and 70, constantly amending and improving her design and incorporating their suggestions. Positive test results encouraged her to persevere with the project and consult leading European type designers for advice on how to integrate unique letterforms into a consistent sans serif typeface.

RESULTS

In designing her new typeface called 'Read', Frensch experimented with hand-drawn letterforms that are independent in character and can be easily distinguished from each other, yet form a cohesive alphabet. The conventional process in type design is to create an alphabet derived from iterations of a few characters. In order to prevent confusion between the b and the d, p and q, f and t, m and n, and so on, Frensch treated each character, number and punctuation mark individually and designed them with a personalised visual look. In this way confusion with the previous or following characters in a word, sentence, paragraph or page was prevented. The inner shapes of the characters were kept large to prevent bleeding and the ascenders and descenders from lower case letters were kept long to encourage legibility. Attention was paid to the spacing of the letters to ensure there were no awkward pairings.

Three typefaces with a complete range of weights were created: Read Regular, Read Smallcaps and Read Space, a specially spaced version for younger children. Frensch wrote, designed and published a special limited edition book in English and Dutch that describes the rationale for the new typeface and details its development. A website (www.readregular.

Figure 6.4   Read Regular: a new typeface design

com) has also been produced to promote the project to an educational audience.

Case Study Three: Optare Alero CSV – A Service Delivery Vehicle for Excluded Rural Communities

RESEARCH ASSOCIATE

Owen Evans, RCA Vehicle Design.

RESEARCH PARTNER

Optare, one of Britain's largest bus and coach makers, is now part of North American Bus Industries. It has established a strong reputation for low-floor, accessible vehicles which are attractive to bus passengers and sells to all of the UK's privately owned operating groups. The company has a strong reputation for its after-sales service.

THE BRIEF

To adapt the new accessible Optare Alero, a 16-seater low-floor vehicle into an all-purpose service delivery vehicle to address the problems of rural and inner city social exclusion and service provision.

Figure 6.5   The new vehicle Alero CSV (Community Service Vehicle)

THE CONTEXT

Despite a raft of social inclusion policies by local and national government, many of the UK's most deprived rural and urban communities remain geographically isolated in terms of transport and services. At least three-quarters of Britain's 17,000 small rural villages have no daily bus service, village shop or school age child care facilities, and many inner-city estates and districts are similarly deprived. Forty percent of the UK population now lives in the 88 most deprived local authority areas, against a backdrop of vanishing local economic outlets. Between 1995 and 2000, Britain lost 20 per cent of its vital community institutions, such as corner shops, grocers, high street banks, post offices and pubs – 30,000 outlets in total.

METHODOLOGY

An analysis of the Alero's capabilities in relation to leisure, corporate, health and local authority markets was carried out and compared with existing mobile services and future community needs. Gradually, a picture emerged of the need for a vehicle with display, desk and storage facilities within a reconfigurable interior that would be capable of providing the widest range of mobile services. Health education, youth outreach work, retail services, IT training, library and literacy services, citizens advice, and police and fire service liaison were among the services identified as community priorities. A series of interior layouts was tested and validated by a group of older and mobility-impaired people, using a full-size mock-up in the Vehicle Design Studio at the RCA. Key

Figure 6.6   The interior design of Alero CSV

findings were then fed back into the design process to shape the development of the vehicle package and virtual modelling techniques were used to demonstrate the capabilities of the new Optare Alero CSV.

RESULTS

The new vehicle called the Alero CSV (Community Service Vehicle) has a number of elements designed to give it maximum versatility. Roof-mounted awnings create the ability to 'host' events in a welcoming, open space in front of the vehicle. A dedicated trailer is included as an option to increase workspace or storage capacity, based on a standard Alero body shell. Roof-mounted air conditioning can be added for extended working periods in hot weather.

Inside the vehicle, an electric generator has been packaged at the rear to provide power for onboard systems. Above this is a storage space that is accessible from the vehicle interior. Two removable tables provide workspace in the rear section, which can also serve as a private meeting room with the addition of a dividing wall. In the centre section, fixing rails provide the means to secure a number of movable elements – small and large desks, seating, storage units, bookshelves, entertainment and catering equipment.

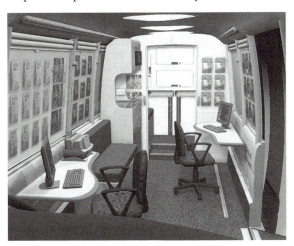

Figure 6.7   Alero CSV provides workspace in the rear section and facilitates a number of leisure activities

Case Study Four: Inclusive 'Konro' – Improving Kitchen Stoves in Japan

RESEARCH ASSOCIATE

Chris McGinley, RCA Industrial Design Engineering

RESEARCH PARTNER

Osaka Gas is the major natural gas supplier to 6.5 million households in the Kansai region in Japan and holds a 24 per cent share in domestic gas sales volume. It employs 16,000 people, has 120 affiliated companies and has a major influence on gas-powered white goods produced by leading Japanese manufacturers, helping determine the industry specifications that govern their design, installation and use.

THE BRIEF

To research and develop a new inclusive footprint for the standard gas stove or 'konro' found in Japanese kitchens that would include the needs of Japan's rapidly ageing population. The project took place over a period of 2 years with the first year devoted to the redesign of the grill alone and the second to the overall redesign of the konro.

THE CONTEXT

The Japanese market is quick to generate new models for most standard consumer products but this has not been the case for such standard kitchen appliances as the 'konro' gas stove which typically consists of three hobs and a small internal fish grill. Over the years, konro have developed technologically with the introduction of sensors, illuminated controls, advanced programmable features and glass top surfaces. They have not progressed sufficiently however to match the

Figure 6.8   'Konro' in use

needs of Japan's growing army of older people, many with reduced dexterity, visual acuity and cognition. The liberalisation of the electricity market, too, has resulted in severe price competition and an increase in the popularity of all-electric houses. Forty percent of new-build houses in the Kansai region are now of this type. With electricity widely perceived as safer and cleaner than gas, induction heating 'konro' have captured a significant share of the traditional market for the gas 'konro'. In addition the change of diet and lifestyle has seen a move towards a fusion of East and West in the design of kitchens and the style of equipment. Osaka Gas selected their most up-to-date 'konro', the S-Class, as a footprint for the design, and the grill was selected as the focal point for the first year of this study. The project aimed to move away from the incremental 'add-ons' commonly found in the 'konro' market, and instead produce a full redesign developed coherently with an inclusive approach from its inception that would be safe, easy to use and simple to maintain.

METHODOLOGY

Showrooms were visited, manufacturers contacted and a product audit of cooking appliances carried out in the UK and Japan with best practice examples highlighted. Visits were made to Japan to meet the product development team at Osaka Gas and ethnographic and ergonomic footage provided by them was studied. Seven housewives of differing ages and social backgrounds were observed and filmed cooking a meal in their own kitchen environments in Japan. Problem areas were identified, including the handling of components, the complexity of the controls, safe and effective cleaning and 'difficult to use' grills. A graphic model was devised in collaboration with Osaka Gas to communicate the goals of the inclusive 'konro.' The key requirements to achieve these goals and reach an agreement on the most relevant factors for the company's design development at this stage were decided, in order to achieve an inclusive marketable outcome.

Sixty improvements were proposed to the design issues raised, and developed into seven concepts, which offered alternatives to existing designs. A focus group of five expatriate Japanese housewives in London evaluated a working example of the S-Class 'konro' and the proposed concepts for the grill, which had been constructed as simple test rigs. The primary barriers to inclusivity were identified as access, visibility, safety and ease of handling. In the second year, the overall design for the 'konro' incorporating the new grill was produced and evaluated through user forums in Japan. It was then fully prototyped as a visual model and displayed at the 2nd IAUD International Conference of Universal Design in Kyoto in October 2006.

RESULTS

McGinley focused on five areas in his redesign of the grill. In the existing 'konro', the door acts as a barrier to access and viewing and dips abruptly when it reaches its final open position. Using a 4-bar linkage, he redesigned the door to dip at the initial stage of opening to allow optimum visual and physical access as the grill was removed from its cavity. The handle dimensions were increased and the shape contoured for better grip. The grill rack was simplified and made symmetrical with cross-wires flush-welded inside the main frame. This allows the tray to be placed in either direction, eliminating the need to locate pins and holes

Figure 6.9   Redesign of the grill

for accurate placement. Its simplified form and reduced surface area makes cleaning easier. A light has been introduced into the grill to improve visibility and comes on only when the grill is ignited. In the second year the project focused on development of an overall concept attuned to the present and future competitive realities of the Japanese market. It contains fourteen design features and improvements as shown in Figure 6.10.

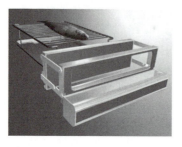

Figure 6.10 Final concept features and key (from McGinley's 2006 report)

Case Study Five: Save Your Sight – A Campaign to Improve Eye Health

RESEARCH ASSOCIATE

Gero Grundmann, RCA Communication Art & Design

RESEARCH PARTNER

The Guide Dogs for the Blind Association is the world's largest breeder and trainer of working dogs. Its mission is to provide guide dogs, mobility and other rehabilitation services that meet the needs of blind and partially-sighted people, to campaign for their rights and to educate the public about eye care.

THE BRIEF

To develop a cross-media cost-effective visual communication campaign aimed at encouraging people over 45 to pay more attention to their eye health.

THE CONTEXT

As we get older, our eyesight deteriorates but there is little awareness of eye health issues and a low eye test uptake in the UK. Lack of knowledge about glaucoma, for example, has resulted in treatment failure and blindness. Bad diet and the incidence of diabetes and diabetic retinopathy are on the increase as is the eyestrain caused by extensive and prolonged computer use. Regular eye check-ups will ensure that such conditions can be detected for early treatment, but there is little information available on eye protection and service provision.

Figure 6.11 'Number Plate' concept

The project had clear short and long-term objectives – to communicate the importance of eye health and measures to protect it; to develop lateral, creative ways to get the message across; to create a sustainable campaign structure to raise awareness and educate the public; and to establish Guide Dogs as a major player in research, education and awareness campaigning. Underlying this was the need to influence future government eye health policy.

METHODOLOGY

Following desk research on the pathology and effects of visual impairment, Grundmann visited eye health charities, specialist hospitals and rehabilitation service providers. He interviewed medical experts, visually-impaired people and rehabilitation workers and visited Finland and Germany for overseas service comparisons in the early phases of research. He then evaluated award-winning healthcare campaigns and carried out a detailed analysis of awareness-raising campaigns of different types conducted by other charities. Successful examples were examined along with those which had been roundly criticised by disabled people. This helped establish a set of parameters for the shape, content and emphasis of the campaign, effective formats that could be used and where best to site the campaign. He concluded that targeting people at the point of denial was crucial.

RESULTS

Grundmann developed a range of creative ideas designed to promote the message about eye health in the context of people's everyday lives – on the street, in the gym, at school, while driving or shopping. The campaign was spearheaded by a high-impact communication idea entitled 'Number Plate', delivered in text-messaging language which encourages drivers to take an eye test before they lose their licence and are forced off the road. This can be expressed either in poster form or as a real number plate and was implemented in 2005. A further concept expands the remit of fitness coaches to include healthier eyes with healthier bodies. 'Eye Coach' is a laminated information guide for fitness trainers for use during their work in gyms and health spas, which is available both as a complete manual and as a quick reference card.

For schools, a 'Little Optician' activity pack introduces eye health to pupils, who can then engage their parents in the issue. The pack includes playful materials to test for visual acuity, field of vision, blind spots, colour blindness and so on.

The three main aspects of the campaign are aimed at drivers, fitness centres and schools and are supported by additional communication materials. These include: recipe cards bearing the message 'feast your eyes' to encourage healthy eating to combat eye disease by increasing lutein levels; eye health information

Figure 6.12 Eye coach information guide

incorporated into packaging for protective eyewear such as sports goggles; and mirrors which reveal campaign messages when they steam up.

All facets of the programme have been evaluated by Guide Dogs for the Blind Association, with key community and business partners identified to roll out the main campaign messages. 'A whole new range of creative opportunities have been developed to enable us to move forward', said Paul Day of the Guide Dogs communication team.

Conclusion

As has been demonstrated, the contexts and the targeted users involved in these five case studies were diverse, while there was a common platform of observation, interaction and prototype testing that helped the designers engage with and understand important issues of design exclusion. This methodology has delivered innovative solutions that can improve people's quality of life in various ways, moving beyond more traditional approaches to 'design for the elderly and disabled' where the focus has been on enhancing physical access to products, environments and services for older or disabled people. As a consequence, the resulting designs are more representative of projects undertaken in professional design practice and have opened the way for inclusive design thinking to penetrate areas in which there were previously few benchmark examples of good practice. Working with users has also helped the young designers involved to understand that good design is based on a collaborative process and not the product a single Eureka moment working in isolation.

References

Design Council (2005), *The Business of Design: Design Industry Research 2005* (London: Design Council).

Frensch, N. (2003), *Read Regular: For More Effective Reading and Writing* (London: Natascha Frensch).

Gheerawo, R. (2003), 'How Can Designers Work with Users and Create Benefits for Business?' Proceedings of *International Conference on Inclusive Design*, Royal College of Art, London.

Moggridge, B. (2001), 'The word according to Bill' In *Magazine, Magazine for the Design Council*, 6, pp. 12–13 (London: Design Council)

Myerson, J. and Gheerawo, R. (2004), 'Inclusive Design in Practice – Working with Industry' Proceedings of *Designing for the 21st Century*, Rio de Janeiro, Brazil.

Empowering Designers and Users: Case Studies from the DBA Inclusive Design Challenge

Julia Cassim and Hua Dong

In preceding chapters, the social, business and legislative drivers underpinning the rationale for the involvement of older and disabled people in the design process have been identified. It is clear that the inclusive design solutions resulting from such collaborations enhance and enable the lives of consumers of all ages and abilities and actively capture new or overlooked markets even for products where saturation point would appear to have been reached long ago. The 'S-Phone' mobile phone launched in November 2004 on the highly competitive Japanese market is one such example. The phone was designed with large single-function buttons, its volume set high, the battery designed so that if its owner forgets to charge for long periods, it will still receive calls and importantly it comes with no thick instruction manual to decipher. The result was a windfall for the Tu-Ka network, which gained 15,500 new users in the first month after the S-Phone went on sale, and attracted significant media interest (Lewis 2005).

New User-Designer relationships through DBA Inclusive Design Challenges

An area less explored in inclusive design literature is partnerships between designers and older and disabled people, where the emphasis has shifted from ergonomic testing alone with the user as passive subject to a more substantive and equal interaction between designer and user. This new style of design partnership raises questions as to how best to integrate user interaction into the design process. Which users should be selected for which project and in what combination? When and at what point should they be involved and in what capacity if they are no longer merely to be used for ergonomic testing or the validation of design features?

The focus of this chapter will be the rationale for the involvement of severely disabled users within the design process and the impact that such partnerships can have on both users and designers, and on the final design outcomes. The six case studies are all taken from the DBA Inclusive Design Challenge, an annual design competition organised since 2000 by the Helen Hamlyn Centre in collaboration with the Design Business Association (DBA), the major trade association for the design profession in the UK. Design teams from DBA member firms work with younger users with severe sensory and physical disabilities over a period of 5 months, the aim being to develop innovative product and service prototypes for the mainstream market. The teams present these at an awards ceremony at the Royal College of Art to an audience drawn from industry and the design, voluntary, public and academic sectors.

To date, seven DBA Inclusive Design Challenges have been organised, including two extreme versions, the 24-hour Challenges held as part of the Include 2005 and 2007 conferences at the Royal College of Art and sponsored by the disability charity Scope (two subsequent 48-hour versions based on the same model were held at the 2nd IAUD International Conference for Universal Design in Kyoto in 2006 and at the Singapore Fringe Festival in January 2007). To ensure that the core element of inclusivity was preserved despite the abbreviated time period, the 24-hour Challenge was framed around the idea of a day in the life of a single individual and a prescriptive brief centred on transport issues given to ensure a tighter focus in comparison with the open-ended possibilities explored in the main Challenge. The users for the five teams were selected to illustrate different aspects of the same theme and ensure a diversity of design responses – one was of restricted growth, one partially sighted, one was a blind guide dog user, one had severe arthritis while the fifth had cerebral palsy which affected her communication and mobility. Each team was put in contact with their user to allow advance documentation of the context of their lives but were not informed of the theme of the Challenge. In this way no preparatory design work could be done and the Challenge's 'rapid response' concept was not compromised. The teams were led by a single firm but included freelance designers, those working for other firms and experts of their own choice. This differs from the main Design Challenge where the prototypes are the work of one firm alone.

The six case studies will be used to demonstrate how such 'extreme' or 'critical' users can empower designers and *vice versa*. They have also been selected to illustrate how designers from disciplines other than the traditional 'inclusive' areas of product and environmental design have been inspired by the process, how their information requirements differ and how all have interacted with users at different stages throughout the ideation and design process.

Context of the DBA Inclusive Design Challenge

The concept of a design challenge was a mechanism originally conceived during the *DesignAge* programme at the RCA. Under the leadership of Roger Coleman, three small-scale challenges were organised which demonstrated the importance of user involvement in the design process. By the time the programme expanded to become the Helen Hamlyn Research Centre in 1999, the academic, creative, business and demographic case for direct user involvement in the design process had been unequivocally made.

In the following year, two reports were published by the Audit Commission (Audit Commission, 2000) and the Department of Trade and Industry (DTI, 1998). The first dealt with the inadequate provision by the NHS of disability aids and equipment, their low design standards and their effect on disabled people and their carers and on government coffers. The DTI study outlined the impact of the poor ergonomic design of everyday consumer products and generic packaging types on older and disabled people and its relation overall to accidents in the home. Absent from either report was any discussion of the psychological impact of 'special needs' design on disabled or older consumers – the emphasis was on function, efficacy and the financial cost of failure. Absent too was any differentiation between the lifestyles, aspirations or consumer patterns of older people with the multiple minor disabilities of age and younger people with more severe congenital or acquired disabilities. There was no discussion either of such users' potential role as advisers to the design process, one which went beyond their usual limited passive status as ergonomic test subjects who could highlight the functional failure of products to one where they became active facilitators of the ideation process.

The reformulated challenge organised by the author and called the 'DBA Inclusive Design Challenge', sought to address some of these issues by shifting the focus from older users with the multiple minor disabilities of age to younger users with more severe physical and sensory disabilities. It was felt that by presenting designers with the alternative scenarios of their disabled contemporaries who represented the extreme end of the user spectrum, two things might be achieved. First that the designers would be enabled to identify generationally with consumers for whom style was as important as it was for themselves but whose needs required the radical rethinking of product or service concepts – a 'back-to-basics' approach which stimulated innovative first-principle thinking and obviated cosmetic solutions. Further, that the designers would be encouraged to move beyond ergonomics and strive for mainstream design that balanced function with aesthetics and eliminated the 'special needs' stigma about which younger users in particular complained. It was felt too that the lateral scenarios offered by these users, many of whom had devised ingenious ways of overcoming the difficulties they experienced routinely with the designed world, would prove a powerful stimulus to creative thinking. By being shown how such users tackled everyday tasks from a different lateral perspective, the designers would be confronted with 'out-of-the-box' thinking in its purest form.

With the shift of emphasis from older to younger users, it was necessary to recruit users who would be willing to work with the designers on a voluntary basis to develop their ideas. User recruitment for the DBA Inclusive Design Challenge and details of the Challenge 2000–2004 are documented in *Innovate* (Cassim, 2001, 2002, 2003, 2004) and *Challenge* (Cassim, 2005, 2006). The case studies in this chapter are selected from the DBA Inclusive Design Challenges held in 2003 and 2004 and the 24-hour Inclusive Design Challenge held as part of the Include 2005 conference at the Royal College of Art. Further details on all these projects are available on the Helen Hamlyn Centre website (www.hhc.rca.ac.uk).

Six Case Studies from the Inclusive Design Challenges

CASE STUDY 1: CLEVERNAME™ – PEARSON MATTHEWS

The company

New product development in the medical and healthcare field.

Initial proposal

To redesign something simple, ubiquitous and tangible – the sticking plaster.

Users

Users with visual impairments (partial sight and blind), severe arthritis, limited mobility, no arms and multiple sclerosis, paramedics.

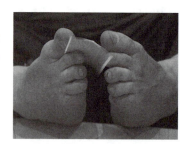

Key issues

- Opening the primary and secondary packaging with one hand

Figure 7.1   Critical user testing of conventional plaster (©Pearson Matthews)

- Selecting a plaster of an appropriate size

- Slippery sterile wrappings

- Wastage due to faulty application

- Circulation cut off by plaster wrapped too tightly, stemming the blood flow

- Painless and efficient removal of the plaster to ensure that the wound does not bleed again

- Identification of the leading edge of the plaster to allow for easy removal

- Application of a plaster on a third party, wearing rubber gloves

- Plasters can stick to and tear rubber gloves of primary care workers leading to the risk of infection.

Design solution

The secondary packaging posed the greatest difficulty for all users. The team was able to reformat the packing and presentation of the plaster to make it easier to apply and remove with one hand. By eliminating the secondary wrapping and redesigning the way it is folded and packed, Clevername™ can be directly accessed from the pack via a single protruding flap and positioned directly on the wound. Both flaps can then be stuck down and the operation is complete. The leading end of the plaster is clearly indicated and curved to offer a single point at each edge, making it easier to peel off. The upper part of the pack provides a large graphic area for

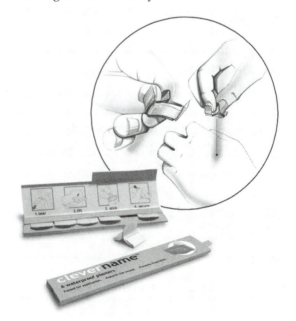

Figure 7.2 Clevername™ – an innovative design of plaster (©Pearson Matthews)

first aid instructions and the design is scalable – it can be a pocket-sized pack for individual use or a larger one for hospitals and schools.

The design team have used the same manufacturing techniques as the conventional plaster and thereby not increased its cost. However, significant functional benefit has been added by improving the design and changing the nature of user interaction with the plaster.

Designer comments

> 'The sort of technologies and devices that we work on are for specific needs. So we have a lot of experience of dealing with people with diabetes, who have glaucoma or poor manual dexterity and the devices that we design take those needs into consideration anyway. I think that by entering the Design Challenge, it certainly opened my eyes to what a broad brush it encompasses in everything we can do.'

> *Stuart May, lead designer, Pearson Matthews team*

CASE STUDY 2: STIK – CORPORATE EDGE

The company

Product and service branding and communications specialists with interiors and architecture division.

Initial proposal

A way to help the many dyslexics in the creative industries take briefs, capture ideas and arrive at design solutions that can be communicated to their clients.'

Users

Dyslexic graphic designers, a creative director, new business manager and dyslexia experts.

Key issues

Six problem areas were identified at the briefing, ideation and presentation stages:

- Fixing things to memory

- Interpreting content

- Focusing on detail

- Capturing ideas

- Establishing a logical progression of ideas

- Explaining how ideas are reached in the first place.

Design solution

The solution centres on these strategies:

- Links are created through storytelling to make language more visual

- Shapes and colour coding act as memory prompts

- Repeated sequences and consistent patterns are used

- Distinctive icons assist memory by association

- Objects bring intangible actions and ideas to life.

Corporate Edge have implemented the strategies internally and now run their projects differently with dyslexic and non-dyslexic designers alike. They envisage an online STIK community updated with new downloadable elements as they evolve and a message board for idea-sharing.

Designer comments

> 'I don't think anyone realises how much dyslexia there is in the creative industries ... in the past, we've recognised that it's difficult for some creatives to remember what's been said or remember even what they've read and for ideas to escape. We've noticed this over the years, and probably made allowances for it both in briefing and then helping people construct presentations, but this particular challenge gave us a focus to

Figure 7.3   Stik – a set of design communication tools (©Corporate Edge)

*start looking at particular issues. We are using the tool as we speak and
actually finding it a real benefit.'*

Stuart Dickinson, Creative Director, Corporate Edge

CASE STUDY 3: FACTORY WARES – FACTORY DESIGN

The company

New product development and design of consumer goods, contract products,
transportation, packaging, environment and futures.

Initial proposal

To design a saucepan that would meet the needs of a wide range of users.

**Figure 7.4   Critical user
forms for the Factorywares
project**

Users

Two elderly users, with arthritis, mobility and
dexterity problems, visual impairments.

Key issues

- Weight, handling, balance and
  drainage

- Need for a multipurpose pan with
  built-in colander

- Radius at bottom too tight making
  cleaning difficult.

Design Solution

The major design element of the re-designed pan is an ergonomic two-part
handle with a fuller cross-section to assist grip, which is angled downwards for
intuitive use. An oval comfort platform at the end shifts the weight of the pan to
the arm away from a single point at the wrist, ensuring greater balance, safety
and less pain. The main structural shroud of the handle is of lightweight, heat-
resistant material overlaid with tactile foam-filled polyurethane to enhance
grip. A secondary hooped handle on the opposite side enables two-handed
use. The universal pan size accommodates different cooking methods. The
saucepan has a traditional round shape but conical sides for easy pouring and
a large radius to assist cleaning. An integrated colander allows for drainage
without the need to lift the pan. The body is of aluminium for lightness, has a
non-stick interior and copper bottom to enhance cooking.

Figure 7.5 Factorywares – a more inclusive saucepan design (©Factory Design)

Designer comments

> *'When we first started, we had an open mind. We didn't go in with any preconceptions: we purposefully kicked off the project, taking on board the feedback from the user groups. We were looking at two-handed operation initially and realised that, to be truly inclusive, we had to make it as effective with one hand and then identify secondary use with two hands.'*
>
> Gavin Thomson, Designer, Factory Design

CASE STUDY 4: 'ELLO' – SEYMOURPOWELL

The company

Product innovation for consumer goods' manufacturers worldwide. Currently, 45 people based on two sites – a studio/product workshop, 'Futures' division and separate automotive workshop.

Initial proposal

An inclusive mobile phone designed to address the needs of the widest possible audience, irrespective of age or ability.

Users

Mobile phone users and non-users with arthritis or visual and mobility impairments.

Key issues

- Inability to access even simple functions

- 'Technopobia'

- Operation is not intuitive

- Buttons are too small, hampering quick and accurate operation

- Interface too complex.

Design solution

A compact folding device, with easy-to-open 'book edges' for one-handed use. The keypad rises when opened for increased tactile feedback, with the prominent five-key convex and the other keys concave to assist navigation. Clear contrasting graphics and memory keys give audio and visual feedback when the operation is successful. There is a one-button direct link to voice mail, which pops up to indicate a new message. The phone vibrates and the '3' key lights up when the caller is unknown, while the memory key flashes if they are known. The larger speaker gives better sound quality and the elimination of a screen increases battery life, which is indicated proportionally by the gauge on the front. The cradle recharger eliminates the need to remember to plug in for that purpose.

Figure 7.6   Ello – an inclusive mobile phone design (©SeymourPowell)

Designer comments

> 'We tried to create a package that would enable people to do the simple
> things well and easily and we tried to make the interface more intuitive,
> more accessible.'
>
> James Samperi, design researcher, SeymourPowell

> 'All the functions and aspects of the phone we wanted to incorporate
> would be things people would understand automatically, and not
> include systems that would require explanation or learning.'
>
> Paul Backett, designer, SeymourPowell

CASE STUDY 5: WHERE'S MY BUS? – LACOCK GULLAM

The company

Specialist in furniture, products, environments, signs and public information
with a special interest in transport and urban environments.

Initial proposal

To make bus travel and the bus-stop environment more accessible for those
with visual and other impairments for whom it is their only travel option.

Users

Regular travellers with vision and mobility difficulties.

Key issues

- Visually impaired people can neither see the bus nor hail it
- Knowing the type of bus is crucial to wheelchair users
- Safety and accessibility of the waiting environment
- Simplicity and reliability of information systems.

Design solution

The environment and features of the bus shelter have been reconfigured and
improvements made to the provision of real-time information via existing
technologies. When the passenger touches their card to a smart card reader in
the shelter, an audio sign is triggered to announce the expected time of arrival
of the bus. The driver is simultaneously made aware of the presence and the
nature of the disability of the passenger, allowing the positioning of the bus

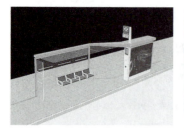

Figure 7.7 Improved bus shelter design (©Lacock Gullam)

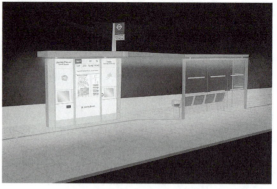

Figure 7.8 The bus shelter provides real time information via existing technologies (©Lacock Gullam)

at the optimum spot. As the bus arrives, a message is triggered in the shelter announcing its number and direction while announcements on board are made at each approaching stop. When a visually impaired passenger alights, the device automatically triggers the shelter announcement, confirming its location. Other passengers with specifically configured smart cards can take advantage of this service.

Designer comments

> *'It's easy to look at single issues from projects and quite often a single issue will get picked up in a brief… but once you start thinking about how people use things, you start broadening out to see how everybody might be included. I think it's going to affect how we play back to clients who may not be aware of the whole issue.'*

> *Sam Gullam, designer, Lacock Gullam*

CASE STUDY 6: BABELFISH – APPLIED INFORMATION GROUP (AIG)

The company

AIG specialise in corporate identities, way-finding schemes and digital services. It worked with Tangerine, Plot Consultancy and Botezco to develop this idea.

Initial proposal

A 24-hour Inclusive Design Challenge project, it responded to the given theme of resolving a clearly defined public transport issue that currently limits or excludes a disabled or older person from using it.

User

Matt Brown, a visually-impaired composer and guide dog user.

Key issues

Way finding in busy and complicated stations can be a real challenge if you are visually impaired or have mobility or cognitive difficulties.

Design solution

Babelfish is a portable navigation device worn as a necklace that gives sonic clues and feedback in large transport hubs. It forms part of a wider service accessed via the Internet and mobile phones.

In its audio form, Babelfish provides a 3D soundscape of the station, using sound to signpost key locations – platforms, exits, amenities, even staff. For a blind person, miniature speakers in a necklace device relay locations to help navigation and allow informed requests to be made of the public.

Babelfish works by using Radio Frequency Identification (RFID) tags, commonly found in the Oyster smart cards used on London Transport but reverses the equation. Usually, RFID tags are mobile and their readers stationary. The AIG team made the tags stationary and the readers mobile. They envisage embedding RFID tags at the key locations around a transport terminal – ticket barriers, cash dispensers, information booths and so on.

The reader would be sited in the traveller's mobile phone. This way, users have control of the technology through their Babelfish-enabled phone which will deliver information in an audio or visual format and enable them to plan the navigation of a journey in advance. Babelfish acts as a virtual escort with real-time location information and guidance delivered to the mobile phone screen or via the necklace device.

Figure 7.9 Babelfish – a wearable navigation device; winner of the 24-Hour DBA Design Challenge 2005

Figure 7.10 The Babelfish project team

Designer comments

> *'Design research is very important and even more so when the information is proactively used and concepts manifest into real life product designs. The fact that the creative industry is so closed to inclusivity is a sad thing, the fact that these forums exist proves that things are changing and hopefully for the best.'*

Tim Fendley, Director AIG

Empowering Designers

For all DBA Inclusive Design Challenge projects, 2-hour project specific user forums are organised at the start of each project involving mixed groups of 'critical' users with severe sensory, mobility or dexterity disabilities to ensure that the major ergonomic issues are covered. In some groups, a 'wild card' user is invited – someone whose usage of products, interfaces or services differs considerably from the norm, even the disabled norm. For example, Tom Yelland, of the Mouth and Foot Painting artists worked with the Pearson Matthew team on the Clevername™ sticking plaster that won the 2004 DBA Inclusive Design Challenge Award. Yelland has no arms, manipulates everything with his feet and although highly dexterous, had never been able to apply a sticking plaster on his own. Such users embody design questions that force the designers to think laterally and from first principles and ensure radical problem solving.

Interviews are conducted with the design teams after each DBA Inclusive Design Challenge. The most cited of all the benefits experienced by the designers was the unanticipated sharp learning curve that results from the user forum experience and the level of stimulus received. 'It is an inspiring process' is a universal opinion and one that helps demystify, illuminate and importantly empathise. 'We were so moved by the critical users! Our director could not help crying after the user session! We have to develop better solutions for them!'

On an objective level, the critical user forum provides a clear picture of the hierarchy of needs and the relative importance of functional, cognitive, emotional and aesthetic issues. These may emerge in user sessions with other groups but in the case of severely disabled users the point is unequivocal and the hierarchy clear. 'Talking to critical users is very important. It offers a fast understanding of the users … . and some headline issues.' This in turn helps designers to consolidate conflicting data, eliminate solutions that are impractical and focus on design directions that make sense in inclusive terms.

The critical and detailed stance of such users to existing products and services is also cited as valuable. 'Disabled people are expert users as they always look beyond product features to detect potential problems. They select their products thoroughly.' Many of the features in the final designs by the teams can be traced directly to suggestions made by the user forum participants – the inbuilt colander for the Factory Wares saucepan (Case Study 3) is one such example.

For the design firms, the teamwork fostered as a result of the project is seen as important to designers and their managers, particularly in larger companies. This feature has been a major incentive to participation. Beyond the creative stimulus received, designers cite the satisfaction of working on a project that they control in its entirety and which is uncompromised. 'It reminded me of why I became a designer in the first place.'

Attitudinal Barriers in the Design Profession

Any desire to empower designers through immersion in the inclusive design process requires prevailing perceptions and attitudes in the profession to be examined, since these are indicative of the state of mind of the design teams prior to entering the DBA Inclusive Design Challenge. At the conclusion of each Challenge, the participating teams are debriefed on the experience. This section details the issues cited by them as barriers to greater awareness or enthusiasm for inclusive design and is followed by the designers' reaction to the experience of participation.

The greatest reservation expressed is the creative restraint that designers fear may arise from having to take account of extreme user needs. Stereotypical images of age and disability based on the medical model and a lack of contact with them contribute to this view as do visions of the poorly designed special equipment upon which disabled people depend, through no fault of their own, but which have given rise to the idea that aesthetics are low on their agenda.

The lack of information aimed at designers in appropriate formats is also cited, as is confusion caused by the mass of information produced since the enactment of the Disability Discrimination Act (DDA), where prescriptive guidelines predominate; as one designer termed it 'creative death by guidelines'. These have led to the appearance of what are seen as limiting new design orthodoxies based on the guidelines such as the idea that black on yellow offers the best contrast available or that certain fonts are *de rigeur* for readers with poor vision.

The enactment of the DDA has prompted a shift from the perception of inclusive design as being relevant only to product and environmental design. An understanding of its applicability to interaction design, communications and graphic design has increased enormously with commissions for public sector projects where an inclusive solution is part of the brief. This in turn has encouraged visual communication firms to enter the DBA Inclusive Design Challenge with the six shortlisted entries for the 2005 Challenge split evenly between communications and product design.

There is, however, a widely-held perception that implementing inclusive design methodologies within the highly pressured constraints and deadlines of commercial design projects is difficult to achieve. This is especially the case where the project is complex, involves other partners who may not share the inclusive agenda or where the client is resistant. Furthermore, there is a perception that inclusive design is *ipso facto* expensive or of relevance to a niche market alone.

Empowering Disabled Users

In September 2005, extreme users who had regularly participated in user forums for the DBA Inclusive Design Challenge were asked to comment on their experience. The major benefits they felt they had derived were:

- Playing an active role in ideas generation had enabled them to articulate design issues, given them the vocabulary to do so and importantly built confidence – 'As a disabled person, it has made me feel more valued for my opinions plus as an amateur designer/gadget maker it gives me a real inspirational buzz'.

- All cited the development of their ability to formally analyse and evaluate products. Two respondents were chosen to carry out detailed product evaluation of special needs cutlery for a major Japanese manufacturer and twelve users have been involved in user forums involving packaging evaluation and new concept generation commissioned by two multinational companies.

- 'I am so much more aware that I look at a product critically when purchasing, thus making a better choice and saving money on products that may not really be suitable.' Another wrote 'I have become very critical of poorly thought-out or researched designs.'

- This growth in confidence has in one case led the participant, an electrical engineer, to design and manufacture an accessible home shelving system that has won an innovation award. Others have cited their increased ability to articulate design ideas and alternatives, and gain understanding of the limitations of the commercial design process. Since they are most affected by the failure of design, a negative viewpoint can be transformed into an active critical awareness of alternatives and possible solutions that has enabled them to become collaborators in the design process rather than mere spectators or critics.

- The fact that the user groups are composed of people with different disabilities from their own has enabled participants to see their issues from a wider perspective and gain understanding of where the specific requirements of each can be reconciled within the greater mainstream design agenda.

- Socialisation and information sharing are cited as major incentives to attend. One respondent commented that the 'cross-section of expertise, experience and need' was valuable. Another said: 'Listening to comments from other users at the meeting alerts me to potential problems and sometimes guides me to a solution.'

User Forum Methods and Documentation

The design teams are free to run user forum sessions as they wish. They are encouraged to record and document them in different media for reference purposes during the design development process and as footage for their final presentation. Clear differences have emerged between projects that centre on the design of products and those involving communications.

For product designers, direct observation of how users interact with products has proved invaluable to advance design ideas. Users or designers will bring examples of products, packaging or interfaces that are analysed through manipulation and discussion. The design team will sketch alternatives, which are evaluated and refined in an ongoing process that the design team is encouraged to record on video. The direct data this 'quick and dirty' process yield allow design concepts to be initiated and progressed significantly during the course of the user forum. Alloy Total Product Design's *Kettlesense*, Factory Design's *Factory Wares* saucepan, Rodd Industrial Design's *Housemate* vacuum cleaner and Sieberthead's *Handle with Care* mug are examples (Cassim, 2002, 2004).

In contrast, design teams involved in communications, service-related or intangible projects such as Corporate Edge's STIK communication toolkit in 2004, and Kinneir Dufort's supermarket system redesign Shopsense (Cassim, 2003) have tended to use more diffuse methods with brainstorming a central feature. Experienced teams such as these will have a clear understanding of the role of each member and will build the discussion around structured questions that are expanded and developed into narratives. These are captured on white boards or post-it notes, classified and then summarised as the discussion progresses. Inexperienced teams may bring lists of questions but are easily diverted into discursive and irrelevant discussion that requires intervention to restore focus to the forum and ensure that they leave with sufficient information to drive their initial concepts forward (Dong et al., 2004).

Information Requirements and Preferences

The information requirements for multi-disciplinary teams involved in complex projects such as Imagination's *Inspiration Park*, BDG McColl's *Mobospace* mobile office design and Fitch-London's 'i-connect' transport communications system, will differ according to the specialism of each member. For *Inspiration Park*, the team consisted of an architect, a graphic designer, a writer, a creative director and a project manager. The architect required specific guidelines on accessibility such as appropriate surfaces for wheelchairs or the kind of navigational features that were suitable for long cane users. The graphic designer was interested in how navigational information could be transmitted by non-visual or non-textual means such as via multi-sensory features embedded into the landscape to inform and delight. The creative director needed information that would drive the overall concept, while the writer was looking for scenarios on which to frame the narrative for the final presentation. Hence the information was delivered in a variety of ways. Besides contacts with individual experts and a list of websites, the resource pack sent to the Imagination design team before their user forum contained guidelines on the accessibility of outdoor environments for the architect; a copy of an exhibition catalogue for *Dialogue in the Dark* with diverse essays and poems from visually impaired contributors (South Bank Centre, 1995) for the writer and creative director; information on public art projects which engaged and informed a wide range of audiences was compiled for the architect and the graphic designer but was used by all.

Although one participant with a cognitive disability and one wheelchair user were included in the *Inspiration Park* user forum, it centred on young visually impaired people – a composer, a singer and an artist – who were expert users of new communications technology. The choice of visual impairment as the major disability was deliberate. The design team was experienced in public projects involving the built environment and were familiar with access issues and strategies as they relate to wheelchair users. It was also possible for them to simulate mobility impairment by using a wheelchair. In contrast, sensory or cognitive disabilities are difficult to simulate or imagine and the team was unaware of the different navigational modes and requirements of visually impaired people. The focus on visual impairment with input from one user with a cognitive disability to underscore issues of information delivery by non-textual means was a mechanism to help the design team to look at the environment from a different perspective. The choice of visually impaired people from creative professions helped trigger not just empathy on the part of the design team, but considerable interest in how sensory impairment impacts on creativity and the innovative strategies developed by the participants to overcome and compensate for such impairments or actively use them as a creative tool.

Thus, although the user forum and subsequent meetings with individual users at a later stage of the project were the major inspirational force behind the final design, information delivery had taken place by a variety of means at all stages of the project.

Overall, the design teams have expressed a preference for web-based information. This is perceived as current, relevant and open-ended. Such information allows design teams to explore a subject laterally and is analogous to the brainstorming sessions to which many are accustomed in which different points of view or discussion topics serendipitously drive concept development.

Conclusion

To date, 36 teams of up to ten designers apiece have been involved in the seven DBA Inclusive Design Challenges, each working in their free time and with budgets assigned for the purpose by the design firm. An informal survey of the participating firms revealed that the costs of participation in terms of staff time and resources alone ranged from fifteen to thirty thousand pounds. Four companies have entered twice, one indication of the importance assigned to the Challenge and its perceived benefits.

The DBA Inclusive Design Challenge has proved effective in alerting the professional design community to inclusive design principles and how they can be integrated into their normal time-pressured working practice and has allowed a new model for user-designer interaction to be developed and refined. A creative rationale has been given to designers for active engagement with a group of consumers who were traditionally seen as beyond the pale in terms of style and whose value to the ideation process has been ignored. This applies not only to goods and services in the special needs market but also to how these consumers' involvement in the design process can improve the design of products and services intended for traditionally defined mainstream consumers.

References

Audit Commission (2000), *Fully Equipped: The Provision of Equipment to Older or Disabled People by the NHS and Social Services in England and Wales* (London: Audit Commission).

Cassim, J. (2001), *Innovate 1* (London: Helen Hamlyn Centre, Royal College of Art).

Cassim, J. (2002), *Innovate 3* (London: Helen Hamlyn Centre, Royal College of Art).

Cassim, J. (2003), *Innovate 4* (London: Helen Hamlyn Centre, Royal College of Art).

Cassim, J. (2004), *Innovate 5 and 6* (London: Helen Hamlyn Centre, Royal College of Art).

Cassim, J. (2005), *Challenge* (London: Helen Hamlyn Centre, Royal College of Art).

Cassim, J. (2006), *Challenge* (London: Helen Hamlyn Centre, Royal College of Art).

Cassim, J. (2006), 'Beyond Ergonomics to Desirability – The Challenge Workshop Model for Inclusive Design Knowledge Transfer to Designers and Industry', Proceedings of *International Conference on Universal Design*, Kyoto, Japan.

Cassim, J. (2005), 'Designers Are Users Too – Attitudinal and Information Barriers to Inclusive Design within the Design Community', Proceedings of *International Conference on Inclusive Design*, Royal College of Art, London.

Cassim, J. and Dong, H. (2003) 'Critical Users in Design Innovation' In *Inclusive Design: Design for the Whole Population*, Clarkson, P.J., Coleman, R., Keates, S. and Lebbon, C. (eds.) (London: Springer-Verlag), pp. 532–553.

Dong, H., Keates, S., Clarkson, P.J. and Cassim, J. (2004), 'Discounted User Research for Inclusive Design', Proceedings of *Home and Electronic Assistive Technology*, King's Manor, University of York.

DTI (1998), *The Home Accident Surveillance System Report* (London: Department of Trade and Industry).

Lewis, L. (2005) 'Old Technophobes Find It's Easy to Talk on the Foolproof Mobile', *The Times* (London) Available at *Times Online*: http://www.timesonline.co.uk/article/0,,3-1487395,00.html.

Involving Older People in Design

CHAPTER

8

Alan Newell and Andrew Monk

Introduction

As described in earlier chapters, there has been a significant amount of progress on design for older people. The new challenge is to ensure that 'new' generations of older people are fully included in the technological advances of the 21st century as they emerge and are integrated in new environments, products and services. In designing inclusive IT systems, the challenge is not simply to design a technical artefact or product, but also to consider a service as comprising a whole socio-technical system involving organisations, people and technology. This chapter presents two case studies addressing the design of IT services for older people, and illustrates the research, design, testing and evaluation processes involved in ensuring an inclusive 'fit' between new services and older users.

In the first case study we consider the challenge of designing an Internet portal for older people – this not only involves the design of the portal, but should also include the challenges older people have in struggling with the installation of hardware and concepts that have no parallel in their experience of domestic appliances. The design problem is to provide an integrated system that is easy for an older and computer naive person to set up and use. Taking lessons from a collaborative design process for this Internet portal, we developed the UTOPIA (Usable Technology for Older People: Inclusive and Appropriate) Trilogy in which data collected from older people were incorporated into efficient dramatic scripts for a video designed to change the mind sets of designers.

The second case study describes the design of a shopping/befriending service. Net Neighbours was inspired by some ethnography that noted how, for many frail older people, shopping is a) difficult, and b) enjoyed as an opportunity for human contact. The service, which is run by Age Concern York, links up older people with volunteers who telephone for a chat once a week and at the same time order shopping using existing online shopping services. The design problem here was to make the human part of the service dependable and usable for the different user groups involved.

Case Study One: Developing an Email System for a Marginalised Group

Successful inclusive design requires designers both to achieve an empathy with their potential users, and to have access to sufficient relevant human factors knowledge about their intended end-users' needs, wants and abilities as well as their often less than positive attitudes to new technologies.

This is particularly noticeable among information and communication technology designers, where much current software seems to have been designed by young male computer scientists who have a limited, or even nonexistent, understanding of the physical and sensory characteristics of older people. It is necessary to develop a different attitude of mind among designers, which in turn requires novel ways of presenting information to designers for whom older people are an unfamiliar user group, a requirement that was underlined by the experience of designing an Internet portal for older users.

This gulf in attitudes appeared when the Scottish UTOPIA Project contributed to the development of a 'Proof of Concept' Internet portal which would be 'attractive to older users (over 60 years of age) who were uninitiated and unconfident in the use of computers and for whom the internet was an

Figure 8.1   An unfamiliar group of users of information technology

alien territory'. Dundee University researchers acted as expert advisers to the company designers who were developing the software, and the experience of this project underlined a major barrier to software design for older people. The company designers were excellent designers, who understood the traditional 'user centered design' methodologies, were aware of the appropriate guidelines, and were given detailed briefings from experts in the field of design for older people and indeed had a meeting with some older people to discuss their ideas. It was not until the designers actually saw older people trying to cope with the prototypes they had produced that they discovered the depth of ignorance of older people of the 'internet' or even 'email'. Comments from the developers included:

> *'The first overwhelming observation is that some of our users start right back at the very basics. That is absolutely NO prior knowledge whatsoever!'*

> *'In the first 5 minutes they were literally just beginning to make sense of what the screen might be about.'*

> *'We have a ready-made framework for interpreting what's on a screen. Our users don't have this. They have to construct it as they go.'*

> *'We take for granted all kinds of metaphors and conventions in user interface design. The lesson for me was that absolutely NOTHING can be assumed.'*

Figure 8.2 Designer working with older people to address issues of the usability of current information technology

Although the developers were well aware of the issues from a theoretical standpoint, the older users' lack of understanding of many 'basic' points came as a great surprise to the designers. It seemed that they needed to 'see with their own eyes' the problems users encountered, before they fully recognised them. Interaction with older users itself, however, often presents particular communication challenges for designers. Older users are rarely aware of the jargon which is second nature to software designers, they tend to be very positive about ideas and prototypes which are presented to them, and, if they cannot cope with technology, they tend to blame themselves, and their own incompetence, rather than poor design. Their confidence in their ability to use technology can also be very fragile, and it is important from an ethical perspective not to put older people in a position where any confidence they have is under threat. In addition cost constraints on design projects may prevent designers from accessing 'real' users.

In many cases, designers are forced to rely on their own experience or intuition to guide their assumptions about user characteristics, which may well have little relationship to the true situation.

It was clear from our case study that it can be very helpful for designers to interact with older people throughout the design process, but this can be expensive and needs careful orchestrating and training of the designers in interaction techniques. Older people are often not good at transmitting the message and designers not always sensitive to these messages. There is, however, a profession which is dedicated to communicating messages to a wide range of audiences with high impact: theatre. We thus looked to theatre to provide high impact method of communicating messages about the challenges that technology provides to older and disabled people.

The Use of Theatrical Techniques

Theatrical methods and actors have been used in the context of product design along with unscripted live drama to capture and understand design requirements for older adults.

In the UTOPIA project, our specific aim was to encourage dialogue within design communities, and between designers and users, as a way of changing the mind sets of designers. To do this we needed a theatrical genre specifically designed to encourage audience participation. The Dundee based Foxtrot Theatre in Education Company had developed a version of 'Forum Theatre' and used these techniques extensively within professional training of

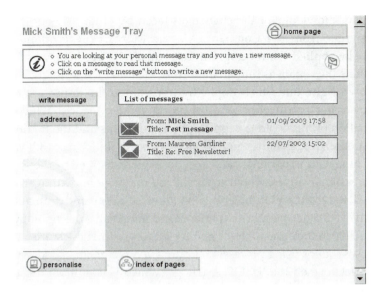

Figure 8.3 Part of the email system developed for the older people

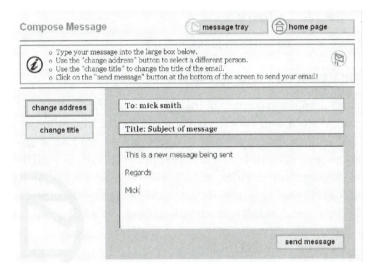

Figure 8.4 Part of the email system developed for the older people

communication skills. This seemed to be a very promising approach, but, as we wished to distribute the results of our work widely, we decided to concentrate on producing videos rather than live performances. In collaboration with Dundee University, this company had also successfully used professionally produced videos to facilitate discussions within focus groups of older people on the technical and ethical issues of a video camera based monitor and fall detection system for older people. The UTOPIA researchers had a great deal of background knowledge of the challenges faced by older users of technology. A script-writer from the Company, Maggie Morgan (Leverhulme Artist in Residence in Applied Computing, Dundee University, 2005/06), was thus asked to instantiate these data as human interest stories – which would be interesting in their own right, but which implicitly transmitted the important messages. The script-writer produced a series of narrative based stories which were an amalgamation of many older people's real experiences and the findings of our own, and other researchers', human factors and usability research with older people. These data, experiences and anecdotes were distilled by the scriptwriter into a series of narratives, which encapsulated many issues within an engaging and cohesive storyline including human interest, humour and dramatic tension. They conveyed older people's experiences of information technology and the situations which they encounter when trying to use it. These stories were then produced as videos using professional actors, a director, and a video team. The video stories formed the 'UTOPIA Trilogy' which was authored to DVD and CD-ROM for distribution and viewing.

The UTOPIA Trilogy

The final videos as illustrated in Figure 8.5 were:

PETER AND JANE BUY A WEB CAM

This concerns an older woman who has limited experience of email, and who has just purchased a web cam so that she can send pictures to her daughter. Her original enthusiasm, supported by the claim on the box of the web cam being 'easy to install', is eroded by repeated difficulties, even with the aid of an expensive 'help line', of installing the software and her lack of understanding of terminology ('what is a USB port?') and is finally destroyed when she eventually discovers that her computer does not have a USB port.

SANDY'S MOBILE ADVENTURE

This deals with the physical and cognitive difficulties older people have when faced with a mobile telephone and the methods they have to employ to be able to use it.

EMAIL EXPERIENCE

Focuses on an older man who tries to use his wife's email system and, due to the complexity of the system, completely fails. His attendance at a computer class underlines the gulf between his knowledge and the knowledge assumed

PETER AND JANE BUY A WEBCAM

Having been given her son's old computer, Jane has set about learning the basics and now feels confident using it for email and word processing. Having come across an article in a paper, she has decided to take the plunge and buy a webcam so that she can talk to her daughter and grandchildren in Australia.

SANDY'S MOBILE ADVENTURE

Sandy has been given his daughter's old mobile phone. He never uses it but carries it around with him to keep her happy. Today he finally finds a use for it when he locks himself out of his house...

A few months later...

After his problems with the phone, Sandy's daughter gave him a quick lesson and a cheat sheet of simple instructions. Sandy still doesn't use the phone, but carries it with him in the car fully charged....just in case.

A year and a half later...

Since saving him a long walk home, Sandy has changed his attitude towards mobile phones and now uses his frequently. Over a glass of wine his daughter brings this change up...

EMAIL EXPERIENCE

Peter is quietly jealous of his wife's confidence with using a computer, but is too proud to admit it. One day he finds that she's left it on when she's gone shopping. He decides that this is the chance to give email a go in privacy...

After the debacle of trying email on his own, Peter has bitten the bullet and signed up to computer classes at the local university. He's feeling his petulant self as ever...

Frustrated with his experiences so far, Peter decides to give email one last try. The computer class is demonstrating a new cut down email application which has been designed for simplicity, clarity and ease of use...

Figure 8.5   UTOPIA Trilogy

by designers ('what is a scroll bar?', 'why does it work in the opposite way to which it ought?', 'why double click sometimes but not others?'). This culminates with his being shown a much simpler email system, and brings out how it is possible to design systems which are not frightening or overwhelming to older people.

The Impact of the UTOPIA Trilogy

The script writer, being an experienced theatre and video director, with a particular knowledge of the use of Forum Theatre to encourage discussion on sensitive issues, had a major impact on the success of the project. The use of professional actors ensured that a good performance could be mounted in a short time, which would achieve the 'suspension of disbelief' required from the audience. A further advantage of using intelligent professional actors, especially on original material, was that they added significantly to the depth of the piece.

A variety of audiences including academics, practitioners, software engineers and relevant groups of undergraduates and trainees, have been shown the Utopia Trilogy and have provided positive feedback about its impact on their views of designing for older people. Evaluation questionnaires, 'focus groups' and other discussions have established that experts in usability for older people, and older people themselves believe that the videos accurately portray the experiences that many older people have with modern technology.

Informal discussions with older users have also indicated very positive reactions to the videos with the exception that older users complained that they did not illustrate the challenges presented to a completely naive user. They did, however, accept that some of the subtleties of the ways in which poor design impacts on the user may have needed to be lost in order to produce an engaging story.

The Use of Theatre in the Design Process

The case studies at Dundee have shown that video based Forum Theatre works well to promote discussions with older people and designers on issues related to new technology. The techniques have provided an important input to the design stages by facilitating the exploration of the ethical and acceptability requirements of such systems. We have shown that theatre can play a significant role in requirements gathering particularly with marginalised groups who are not familiar with computer systems.

The Utopia trilogy expanded on the concept of using narrative based videos to that of raising the awareness of designers of the challenges faced by older users of new technology. The results from questionnaires and focus group indicated that viewing and discussing these videos changed the perceptions of both students and mature designers of IT systems and products. Older users have confirmed that the videos accurately portray a range of challenges that they have found with new technology.

We have shown that the use of theatre (which includes humour and conflict) can be a very powerful method of communicating messages between designers and users of technology. Video was used as a cost-effective way of interacting with large numbers, but it is more restricted than using live performances, and may not have the same impact. Live Forum Theatre has been shown in other areas to be very effective in stimulating discussion, and thus we will also be investigating the use of this and other theatrical techniques, both in conjunction with videos and live performances, for promoting the 'inclusive design' message within the design community.

Our results show that the techniques work well both in certain stages of requirements gathering and in raising awareness. While it is not clear how other, perhaps more detailed, forms of human factors information may be meaningfully portrayed in this way, the general insights which have been conveyed by the Utopia Trilogy represent an important step forward. We are now investigating ways in which we can more closely link such theatrical presentations to scientific and demographic data about older users, so that the messages in such presentations can be grounded in scientific data as well as anecdotes, while still retaining the impact given by the genre.

Case Study Two: Net Neighbours

Case study two was similarly inspired by observations of older people and the difficulties they have living independently. This time we are talking about quite frail people who are not interested in using a computer system. In this case study the computer supports a volunteer who helps the older person in a combined befriending and shopping service.

The Starting Point

A full description of how Net Neighbours came to be is provided in Blythe and Monk (2005). This is a short summary of that paper. The authors were at the time engaged in an ethnographic study of the dependability of telecare services for older people. In the course of home visits and interviews with caring professionals it became clear quite how important shopping is. Many of the frail older people we came in contact with could not get out and had had to make complex arrangements to get their shopping. It was also clear that shopping was seen as a major opportunity for social contact (see Figure 8.6).

'It is a social thing, it means they're not stuck in their four walls and they can actually go out and see somebody.'

Driver of Dial a Bus.

'Meeting people, talking to the shopkeeper, talking to people in the queue ... Even now when I go for me bloody paper sometimes can be quarter of an hour's chat, you know, any shop I go in that doings.'

Jack, 72.

Figure 8.6   Comments made by driver of the 'Dial a Bus service' and an older person with mobility problems that illustrate the importance of shopping as an opportunity for social contact

Online shopping services provide an obvious way that house-bound people could get their groceries and indeed there have been a number of attempts to make such services easier to use by means of special adaptations to PCs. Doing your own shopping from home, however, would not replace the other function of shopping as an opportunity for human contact.

It struck Mark Blythe that there are numerous office workers who have access to high quality computer systems and who might volunteer to use them to help an older person to do their shopping, by telephone. By assigning each volunteer to an older person they would, over time, form a social relationship and fulfil the second social function of shopping mentioned above. We approached Age Concern York who were immediately interested. They had a hospital aftercare service whose clients would be ideally served by such a service. It was obvious to everyone, however, that the service would have to be designed with care. These are very vulnerable people and Age Concern York has principles and requirements governing all of their services for older people. Accordingly, the researchers adapted some user-centred design methods to the purpose.

Human-Computer Interaction (HCI) is a discipline involving computer scientists, psychologists, social scientists and designers. Over the years, HCI researchers have built an armoury of methods for user-centred design, some of which are sufficiently mature to be enshrined in international standards (for example ISO 13407). Readers interested in finding out more about these methods should consult an HCI textbook such as Preece, Rogers and Sharp (2002). Most of these methods have been developed to help design effective and usable ICT based products and services for use at work. The challenge here was to adapt them to the problem of inclusive design, that is, to design a shopping and befriending service that was effective, enjoyable and usable.

A Recipe for Designing a Net Neighbours Service

The Net Neighbours service was designed in five steps. These are outlined below as a recipe that might be used to design a new Net Neighbours Service somewhere else.

STEP 1 – MAKE A FIRST CUT AT IDENTIFYING WHO WILL BE AFFECTED BY THE INTRODUCTION OF THE SERVICE AND WHAT THEIR CONCERNS ARE

Ingredients

The owners of the net neighbours service
A flip chart and pens

Method

1. Arrange a meeting (it took us two meetings of about 2 hours each).

2. List on the flip chart what the service will do for its clients.

3. List all the people and agencies that could be affected by its introduction (the 'stakeholders').

4. List all the concerns each stakeholder will have.

This is the usual first step in user-centred design. Too many systems fail because they have too narrow a view of who the users are. They are built and do exactly what they were intended to do, but they interfere with the work of some critical individual the designers had not thought of and so they are never used.

Our meetings involved two Age Concern York (ACY) staff members and two HCI researchers. Figure 8.7 lists the major stakeholders identified: the client, the volunteer, the charity and the retailer. In addition we identified informal carers

Stakeholders	Their concerns
Charity	Access, risk to client and volunteer; accounting; staffing costs; training; flexibility, avoiding making client dependent on service.
Client	Cost; security; feedback; isolation; fear of change; flexible payment methods.
Volunteer	Ease of use (retail sites); accuracy of order; method and time of reimbursement.
Informal carers and relatives	Cost; security; fear of change; flexible payment methods.
Retailer	Cost; profit; liability; fraud; competition, publicity.
Social services	Allowing people to stay in their own homes.
Medical services	Getting people out of hospital as soon as possible.

Figure 8.7   List of stakeholders and their concerns

and relatives, the York Primary Healthcare Trust (health services) and York social services. Having listed the stakeholders we went on to list their concerns. The ACY staff had a clear understanding of the concerns of the charity and the client (the older person). Those of the others were more a case of informed guesswork, to be clarified in later meetings with the people concerned when this was felt necessary.

The first concern for ACY was access. That is to say, the service should be available to any of their clients who needed it. If for example, the design chosen required clients to write a cheque and some did not have a bank account, that design would be unacceptable. This is also reflected in the concern for flexibility. The other concerns were accounting and staff costs, appropriate training, avoiding making the client more dependent and the risks to client and volunteer identified elsewhere in Figure 8.7.

For the client the principle concerns were: cost and potential isolation. At that time the delivery fee was thought to be an obstacle as many older people do a small weekly shop. In the event this turned out to be unimportant. When we talked to the clients they were all happy to pay the delivery charge which is seen as small compared with the cost of the alternatives.

The principal concerns anticipated for volunteers unfamiliar with online shopping were learning to use the sites and not being out of pocket. For the retailer a number of possible concerns were identified. The advantage of the Net Neighbours scheme however was that it did not change the supermarket's current provision in any way; indeed the supermarkets did not know anything unusual was happening during the pilot study.

STEP 2 – DESIGNING THE TELEPHONE INTERACTION

Ingredients

One volunteer and a few (not too vulnerable) clients.

Method

1. Recruit someone with experience of working with older people to act as a putative volunteer (we drew on the expertise of Jenny Jarred, an ACY staff member who was already running a hospital aftercare service).

2. Get them to recruit a few clients to help you design the service by trial and error.

3. Write down the process used to get shopping lists from the client and refine this description in the light of the problems that occur.

Getting the telephone interaction right, so that it met the concerns of the client, the charity and the volunteer, was very important. We needed to design the interaction to allow a social experience and to get the right goods delivered. Participatory design is a commonly used HCI technique for user-centred design. Users are recruited with the specific aim of jointly designing the service with its technical developers. It is important that they understand that this is what they are doing so that they are not afraid to make suggestions and criticisms. They also have to be carefully selected so that they will not be vulnerable if things go wrong.

The hospital aftercare service involved grocery shopping for a limited period of time after people came out of hospital. It was decided to link the pilot scheme to this so as not to raise expectations about a long-term service among clients in case the scheme proved impractical. Previously, Jenny would visit clients at home, take their orders, drive to the shops, do their shopping and deliver it to their door. During the Net Neighbours pilot study Jenny placed orders on line and paid using her own credit card for clients who agreed to try the new service.

Problem	Change to procedure
Volunteer makes incorrect order	Orders double-checked with client before being confirmed
Mistakes made with orders relating to weight	Metric and imperial conversion table supplied
Mistakes made by supermarkets	Electronic receipts stored as record
Client usernames and email addresses forgotten	Client details stored
New clients confused about how the scheme works	Booklet designed telling them what to expect

Figure 8.8   Examples of problems encountered and the changes made

Figure 8.8 lists some of the problems identified and then rectified in this way. One was that, at least at the start, clients will be upset if their expectations are not met. These expectations may be unreasonable and so it is important to explain what will happen. Extra care has to be taken to ensure that the order is accurate, more so than in a large order for a family, for example. Older people may have regular diets and if four bananas arrive instead of six it will upset their week's meal plan. Both these points are made in the quote from an email from Jenny Jarred to one of the researchers.

Mrs Anderson [all names have been changed] is still in hospital with no immediate discharge date. I have spoken with Mr Anderson who was less than happy with his last delivery. Although within the time slot of 12–2 it didn't arrived until 13.55 and he was getting worried. I think as the first delivery arrived 5 minutes into the time slot I believe he was expecting the same again. There were several items wrong with this delivery [...] He didn't check any of it until later that afternoon. [...] He didn't feel he wanted to continue an[y] more [...] after he had spoken with his wife.

Figure 8.9   Quote from an email from Jenny Jarred to one of the researchers

STEP 3 – DESIGN THE FINANCIAL MODEL

Ingredients

People who can represent the needs of the charity, the client and the volunteers.

Method

1.   Arrange a meeting to discuss how the money will be handled.

2.   Write down the procedure to be followed.

3.   List all the things that could go wrong and how to deal with them.

The concerns, already recorded in step 1, require the service to provide prompt payment and avoid the possibility of fraud or errors. The Charity does not want to lose money. It does not want its volunteers or clients to be out of pocket. There is also the problem of containing the accounting needed so that this does not become a major cost of running the service.

After step 2, Jenny Jarred was in a position to represent the needs of the client and the volunteers. Financial staff at ACY were also involved in this process. The diagram depicted in Figure 9.8 (money diagram) was used to reason about all the things that could go wrong through mistakes or malicious actions taken by the various parties involved. Step 1 had also identified the important requirement for flexibility of payment. It was not acceptable to ACY that a client should be excluded because of their inability to pay by cheque or credit card.

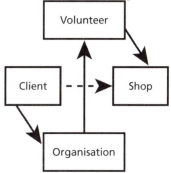

Figure 8.10 The model of how funds might be transferred, used to reason about what could go wrong

The dotted arrow in Figure 8.10 indicates the basic transfer that has to occur, that is, for money from the client to be transferred to the supermarket. Direct payment was not possible because not all clients were expected to have a credit card and anyway, entrusting the volunteer with the client's credit card details was not ethically acceptable.

The solid arrows in Figure 8.10 show the process that came out of this step and is still being used in the service today. The volunteer pays the retailer using their own debit or credit card, and asks the older person to send ACY a cheque for the supermarket bill when the shopping arrives. If the older person does not have a bank account then an Age Concern employee (not the volunteer) visits them to collect the money. The volunteer then claims their expenses back from ACY who transfer funds directly into their bank account.

STEP 4 – DESIGN PAPER OR SOFTWARE SUPPORT FOR THE VOLUNTEER

Ingredients

The putative volunteer from step two and a volunteer who has not, this far, been involved in designing the service.

Method

1. Go through the telephone interaction you have designed in step two and write down prompts that would be useful to the volunteer.

2. Make a printed check list of steps on a form for recording notes and essential details.

3. Test and improve your form with the person who did the testing in step two and then with a volunteer less familiar with the project. Make sure that it does not constrain the order in which they do things too much, or get in the way of chatting to the client.

The York Net Neighbours service started using a printed form to guide the process. We were in the happy position of having programming support available and so we developed this into a secure website to help the volunteers. This records and displays clients' details such as account names and ordering and payment details and also notes on clients' hobbies, interests, children's names and so on to facilitate conversation. The web pages guide the volunteer through each stage of the process, first presenting the clients' phone numbers and details but then showing notes about what they had last discussed (the volunteer would enter, for example, that the client wanted to have a banister painted) stressing the importance of conversation. It incorporates a table for filling in shopping lists (with metric and imperial measures converted automatically) and it links to the various retail sites. Volunteers and account managers at ACY have differing levels of access it. The volunteers for instance, will only be able to access the details of their particular clients. Coordinators at ACY is able to view all details for all clients and all volunteers.

Jenny and Mark co-designed a series of PowerPoint slides mocking up the interface. This, then, was user-centred design from initial discussions to the very first sketch. The notion was that the conversation period would be built into the interface; much as a software wizard directs the user through a complex computing procedure so the interface would offer prompts for the social interaction though in a far less directive way.

A sample page of the website built by Budi Arief, a programmer at the University of Newcastle, is depicted in Figure 8.11, where the volunteer pastes the email sent by the supermarket recording a previous shop into the window, and the website converts it into an easily edited table to act as a prompt for the next order. The 'look and feel' is designed to be recreational, that is, not reminiscent of work-orientated productivity software or E-commerce. For example, each page has a new joke at the bottom of it.

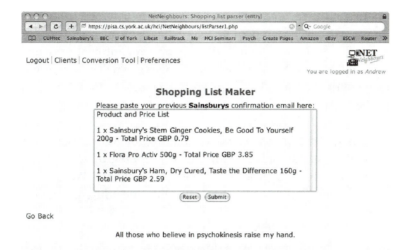

Figure 8.11 A screen from the Net Neighbours York website

STEP 5 – DESIGN THE INTRODUCTION OF THE SERVICE: RECRUITMENT OF VOLUNTEERS AND CLIENTS, TRAINING OF VOLUNTEERS, MANAGING THE SERVICE

Ingredients

Funding, an organiser, volunteers, clients.

Method

1. Obtain the resources needed to run the service.

2. Recruit someone to run it.

3. Devise a way of covering for volunteers who are on holiday or sick.

4. Organise training for the volunteers.

5. Recruit some volunteers.

6. Design a procedure for introducing volunteers to clients.

7. Recruit clients.

8. Review all procedures after they have been used for a while.

9. Record statistics to impress current and future funders.

Funds to run the system for the first year were obtained from York Social Services. The post of administrator was advertised by ACY and given, in the event, to Jenny Jarred. Jenny will organise recruitment and training in conjunction with Active York. In the initial stages she will cover for volunteers who are on holiday or off sick, and pick up the pieces in the event of anything going wrong.

Volunteers go through the standard training for Age Concern volunteers and then familiarise themselves with online shopping by shopping for each other. There has been no problem in recruiting clients! We are talking to potential corporate sponsors for a larger service, including the supermarkets themselves.

At the time of writing we have a dozen volunteers, paired with people who are unable to get out to do their own shopping. The care taken to identify all the concerns of all stakeholders seems to have paid off and we look forward to increasing the size of the operation in the near future.

Conclusion

The two case studies described here illustrate different ways of involving designers with users in order to develop the empathy needed for successful design. In the first this was mediated by researchers. They initially conducted an ethnographic study to understand the users' needs, involving detailed discussions with, and observation of, older people trying to use existing web portals. This was then communicated to the designers using theatrical techniques via a video. In the second case study older people and volunteers worked directly with the designers of the Net Neighbours service in a systematic participatory design framework. What they have in common is a willingness to put a part of the design effort into gaining a detailed understanding of what the users want to do and how the design fits into the wider context of their daily lives.

A central tenet of user-centred design is summed up by the axiom 'know your user'. Usability is only possible, and actually only definable, with regard to a particular user group, doing a particular task in a particular context. Both case studies emphasise the need to know the characteristics of your users, particularly if they come from a group not usually represented within the design community. The email project showed that 'knowing' was not enough, it was also necessary to develop an empathy with users – and the use of theatrical techniques was an effective way of achieving that.

In the Net Neighbours case study there were three distinct user groups, each with different tasks to do and different contexts of use. The design process was successful because it gave all these user groups the power to influence the design. By working together in this way it was possible to identify points in the early design that were not compatible with the needs of a particular user group and resolve the problem without creating new problems for someone else.

The inclusive design of software and services is not a matter of designing for the maximum possible proportion of the general population. It is about defining and understanding your target users, what they want to do and the context in which they do it; and then and only then, making sure that the real needs and wants of this user population are catered for, while enabling wider access by the general population.

References

Blythe, M. and Monk, A.F. (2005), 'Net Neighbours: Adapting HCI Methods to Cross the Digital Divide', *Interacting with Computers*, 17, pp. 35–56. [DOI: 10.1016/j.intcom.2004.10.002]

Boal, A. (1995), *The Rainbow of Desire* (London: Routledge).

Carmichael, A., Newell, A.F., Dickinson, A. and Morgan, M. (2005), 'Using Theatre and Film to Represent User Requirements'. Proceedings of *International Conference on Inclusive Design*, Royal College of Art, London.

Danowski, J.A. and Sacks, W. (1980), 'Computer Communication and the Elderly', *Experimental Aging Research*, 6(2), pp. 125–135. [PubMed: 7389782]

Eisma, R., Dickinson, A., Goodman, J., Mival, O., Syme, A. and Tiwari, L. (2003), 'Mutual Inspiration in the Development of New Technology for Older People'. Proceedings of *International Conference on Inclusive Design*, Royal College of Art, London.

Foxtrot-theatre, www.foxtrot-theatre.org.uk.

Howard, S., Carroll, J., Murphy, J., Peck, J. and Vetere, F. (2002), 'Provoking Innovation: Acting-Out in Contextual Scenarios'. Proceedings of *People and Computers Human Computer Interaction Conference*, London.

Hwang, F., Keates, S., Langdon, P. and Clarkson, P.J. (2003), 'Multiple Haptic Targets for Motion-Impaired Computer Users'. Proceedings of *Computer-Human Interaction*, New York, NY.

Light, A. (2005), 'Tools of Inspiration', *Interfaces*, 64(autumn), pp. 10–11 (Swindon: British HCI Group).

Mckenna, S.J., Marquis-Faulkes, F., Newell, A.F. and Gregor, P. (2003), 'Scenario-Based Drama As a Tool for Investigating User Requirements with Application to Home Monitoring for Elderly People'. Proceedings of *International Conference on Human/Computer Interaction*, Crete, Greece.

Newell, A.F. and Gregor, P. (1997), 'Human computer interfaces for people with disabilities' In *Handbook of Human-Computer Interaction*, Helander, M., Landauer, T.K. and Prabhu, P. (eds.) (Elsevier Science B.V.).

Newell, A.F. and Gregor, P. (2000), 'User Sensitive Inclusive Design – in Search of a New Paradigm'. Proceedings of *ACM Conference on Universal Usability*, Washington, DC.

Newell, A.F., Dickinson, A., Smith, M.J. and Gregor, P. (2006), 'Designing a Portal for Older Users: A Case Study of an Industrial/Academic Collaboration', *ACM Transactions on Computer-Human Interaction*, 13(3), pp. 347–375.

Preece, J., Rogers, Y. and Sharp, H. (2002), *Interaction Design: Beyond Human-Computer Interaction* (New York, NY: John Wiley and Sons).

Salvador, T. and Howells, K. (1998), 'Focus Troupe: Using Drama to Create Common Context for New Product Concept End-user Evaluations'. Proceedings of *Computer-Human Interaction*, New York, NY.

Sato, S. and Salvador, T. (1999), 'Playacting and Focus Troupes: Theatre Techniques for Creating Quick, Intensive, Immersive and Engaging Focus Group Sessions', *Interactions*, Sept-Oct, pp. 35-41.

Designer-Orientated User Research Methods

CHAPTER

9

Hua Dong, Colette Nicolle,
Robert Brown and John Clarkson

Introduction

Central to inclusive design is understanding users (as people, not as 'consumer', 'customer' or 'end-user'). 'Few designers today have the luxury of creating their own vision with no input from others' (Laurel, 2003). The user-orientated approach, highly valued these days as a panacea for a successful design, still produces user-unfit designs. One reason for this is that user needs often are not seriously researched and addressed (Sin, 2003).

There are many user research methods, for instance:

- traditional ones adapted from social sciences such as 'focus groups', 'interviews', 'observation', 'questionnaires';

- increasingly popular ones applied by design researchers such as 'ethnography': a research method directed at studying the social character of groups and the activities of their members in their natural settings;

- 'Digital Ethno': a modern, digital evolution of traditional ethnographic forms;

- 'persona': a user archetype (based on ethnographic research) that describes a specific behaviour pattern and set of goals related to a specific product's domain;

- 'informance': techniques in which actors and/or researchers study what is known about consumers and role-play potential consumers.

Attempts have been made to collect such methods and specify their strengths and appropriateness in the design process. *The Methods Lab* (Aldersey-Williams, Coleman and Bound, 1999) collected 53 user research methods (Figure 9.1), with the aim of building the definitive resource of user research methods in design. It was written primarily for design students, students of user research sciences, and designers and researchers in their first few years of professional practice.

The range of methods was graphically demonstrated in the Methods Map (the diamond shape in Figure 9.1) which provides a ready-reckoner for designers seeking methods of a particular kind. The map positioned each method at a point along two axes that reflect designers' concerns. The horizontal axis represents the external reference a method requires (Designer-centred vs. User-centred). The vertical axis depicts design projects concerned with purely visual qualities at the top, ranging to those where functional qualities are predominant at the bottom.

The Design Council has compiled a 'method bank' Website (Figure 9.2 shows an early prototype) with around 70 user research methods for industry use (Figure 9.3 shows the hard copy version of the methods), and some of the methods are now available at its website (www.designcouncil.org/en/About-Design/Design-Methods/). The *USERfit* handbook (Poulson, Ashby and Richardson, 1996) describes more than a dozen popular methods of user-centred design for assistive technology, although these methods should also be seen as appropriate for inclusively designed products; the *Design Research: Methods and Perspective* book (Laurel, 2003) reviewed a number of emerging user research methods with a focus on interaction design.

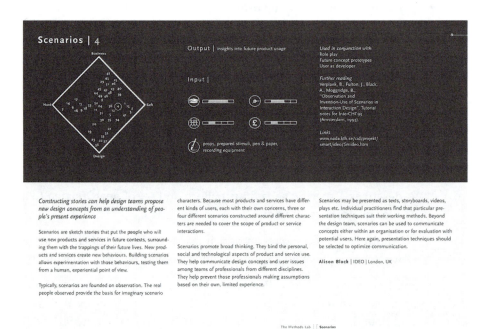

Figure 9.1   Methods Lab page

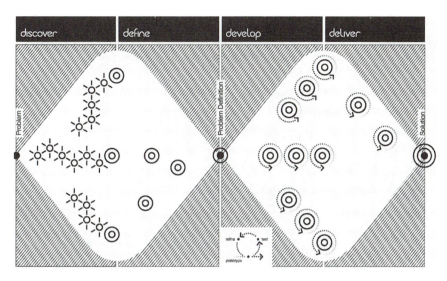

Figure 9.2   Method bank – an early prototype of the website

Figure 9.3   Method bank – hard copy

This chapter is focused on such designer-orientated user research methods, including designer-generated user research techniques and tools. It will first present a classification of the methods, before providing a number of examples.

Classifying Designer-Orientated User Research Methods

Designer-orientated user research methods can be categorised into three basic forms:

- *Forum*: the basic activity is 'to ask'; methods include interviews, focus groups, and those derived from focus groups, and so on;

- *Representation*: the basic activity is 'to observe'; methods include ethnography, simulation, personas, and so on, as well as user data such as anthropometric data and user capability data;

- *Co-design*: the basic activity is 'to participate'; methods include empowerment games, development panel, co-decision, and so on.

It should be noted here that many user research methods are derived from basic ones; depending on the numbers of users recruited or specific tools/ techniques used, they may have various names. For example:

'Focus group' has evolved into an extensive family of related methods (Ireland, 2003), such as:

- 'one-on-one interview'

- 'dyads' (or 'friendship pairs')

- 'triads' (three people)

- 'mini focus groups' (six to eight consumers)

- 'party group' and 'super groups' (50–100 or more people)

- 'online discussion group'.

'Ethnography' can take forms of:

- 'field ethnography'

- 'digital ethnography' (or so-called Digital Ethno)

- 'photo ethnography'

- 'ethnofuturism'

- 'real world ethnographic enactments'.

'User participation' can be categorised in seven major forms (Sanoff, 1992):

- representation (designer represents the user)

- questionnaires

- regionalism (with consideration of specific cultural heritage within a geographically limited area)

- dialogue (user consultation)

- alternative (users are given the choice of several alternatives within a fixed set of boundaries)

- co-decision (direct and active user participation)

- self-decision (the decision is made by the users themselves).

The advantage of classifying these numerous user research methods into three basic types is that it emphasises an essential activity (that is 'ask', 'observe' or 'participate') and gives freedom for designers to create their own means of understanding the user.

A good example of the presentation of designer-orientated and generated user research methods is the IDEO Method Cards (Figure 9.4), which can be used as a knowledge management tool. There are 54 cards; each represents one type of user research method, with illustrations and a short description of 'How' and 'Why' to use the method.

The IDEO Method Cards have the following characteristics:

- *Visual* (use of visual aids such as pictures)

- *Versatile* (different cards can be used for different projects)

- *Inspiring* (not too descriptive, open for interpretation)

- *Playful/fun* (card-sorting can be a fun experience).

These can be regarded as successful characteristics of designer-orientated methods and tools. A design tool 'Flowmaker' (www.flowmaker.org) also bears similar characteristics.

Designer-orientated methods should also take into account time constraints

for design projects. As Plowman (2003) argued, when companies like IBM, IDEO, Apple, Design Continuum, Cheskin, Intel, Xerox, Herman Miller and Microsoft say they conduct ethnographic research, they are not conducting ethnographic research in the same way as academic ethnographers. It is simply not practical for business entities to invest the same amount of time or to engage in the same form or extent of ethnography as is practised by academics. So

Figure 9.4   IDEO cards

another characteristic of a designer-orientated user research method is to be 'practical'.

Examples of Designer-Orientated User Research Methods

This section will illustrate three examples of designer-orientated user research methods: a traditional method, 'task analysis', and two modern methods; 'persona' and 'informance'.

Task Analysis

DEFINITION AND CLASSIFICATION

Task analysis is a process by which detailed information is gathered from users about what they are required to do, in terms of actions and/or cognitive processes, to achieve a task objective. More simply, it is used to gain an understanding of what people do in the tasks and jobs they carry out (Shepherd and Stammers, 2005). It can be used as both an interview method ('to ask') and an observational method ('to observe'), depending on what type of information needs to be collected and what is to be done with it. Using both interview and observation, however, will lead to even richer data, especially when combined with other user research methods.

Task analysis can be used whenever a designer wants to know more about the users and the tasks they are performing. Understanding the users' requirements and abilities better and which product functionalities will meet them will lead to a more inclusive design, whether designing a new product, a new version of an existing one, training manuals or operating procedures.

The information provided by the task analysis can then help to predict human performance, to identify the skills or knowledge needed by the user to perform the task or to use the product, and any safety issues, along with any tools or specific equipment needed by the user.

The IDEO Method Cards (Figure 9.4) include a number of task analysis techniques. Those with a basic activity of 'asking' include: *Narration*, whereby participants would describe what they are thinking, and the *Five Whys*, whereby participants are asked 'Why' questions in response to five consecutive answers. Other methods enabling the researcher 'to learn', by identifying patterns and insights from the information collected, include *Error Analysis*, *Cognitive Task Analysis*, and *Activity Analysis*.

ORIGINS

There are a number of different techniques of task analysis, for example Hierarchical Task Analysis (HTA), first proposed by Annett and Duncan (1967). This form of task analysis examines what people need to do to attain a particular goal, breaking it down into sub-tasks, in a hierarchical form in order of complexity until a suitable stopping place is reached ('stopping rule'), and following a plan on when to do each sub-task. When to stop the analysis is down to the analyst and the purpose to which the data are to be used, so the stopping rule is flexible.

In addition to interviewing and observing the users, further details about the task can be elicited through verbal protocol analysis, or 'thinking aloud' (Robson, 2002), whereby users can be asked to think aloud their thought processes as they actually perform a task. What are they doing? Why? How are they going about it? Can they easily see, hear, feel, and understand what needs to be done? When do they go to the next operation? Is it difficult? Is it boring? Is it enjoyable? Are any special skills or abilities needed? Are any aids or support required to do the task, for example, reading glasses or human help? Knowing the answers to such questions will more effectively ensure a more inclusive design, which will meet the real needs and preferences of its users.

BASICS

While interviewing users, it is important to take notes to record the tasks and behaviours. One such note-taking method is called Personalised Task Representation (PTR) (Gregory, 1979), where rough notes, probably on large sheets of paper, full of scribbles and corrections, can later be represented more clearly to check their accuracy with the users. This is where some creativity can be shown, for example, loops can be included in the notes, indicating yes/no options, and colours can be used to indicate critical issues of time, visual/audio inputs, information availability, and so on. These may highlight areas which could be particularly problematic for users, as illustrated by a 'quick and dirty' PTR (Figure 9.5) to identify an older person's difficulties when going on a bus journey (Dekker, Nicolle and Molenbroek, 2004). Colour coding was used to indicate where timing was important, and where additional information was required by the traveller. The numbers above the diagram referred to a list of possible solutions to each of the issues or difficulties.

The same data can also be further described in the form of HTA, using either a diagrammatic or tabular form. The key here is to be flexible – choose from whatever techniques or 'building blocks' are available, or make up your

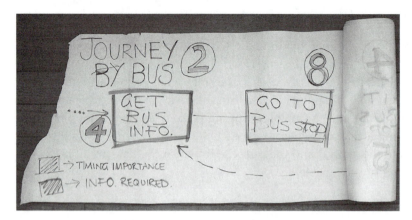

Figure 9.5   Using task analysis to plan a bus trip

own to suit your own experiences or preferences. Capturing a large amount of data can, however, be a time-consuming and tedious process, and a software tool called TaskArchitect is now available to help record, display and analyse the results (Walls, 2006).

EXAMPLES

Brown's work at the Helen Hamlyn Centre designing garden power tools for B&Q illustrates how task analysis can help designers think through usability issues when designing a product. Integrating task analysis with observational research, he broke down the steps required to climb a ladder and trim a hedge with an electric hedge trimmer. Task steps were recorded as users were observed and the users were asked to describe their experience as they went through the steps (an example of 'observation' and 'verbal protocol analysis' being used together). In this case, rather than constructing a definitive model of how hedge trimmers were used, Brown used the process to help him to think through usability issues at all stages. He found these issues fell into the following broad categories: assembly, handling, lifting, applying force (for example to operate the trigger or remove the battery), storage and safety. For example, the weight of the hedge trimmer, largely due to the motor (and battery in the case of the cordless version), made it difficult to handle, especially at arm's length. This discovery led directly to the 'backpack hedge trimmer' concept, where the battery and motor are mounted on the user's back on a backpack. A flexible drive shaft powers the handheld cutting head which becomes a small fraction of the weight of the original product.

People can also find it hard to do the reaching required in cutting hedges – reaching down to the ground, reaching up to the top of hedges and reaching over

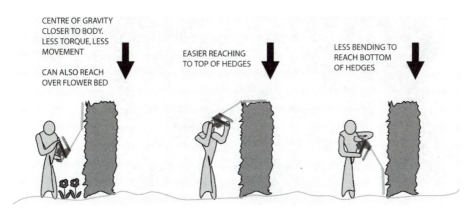

Figure 9.6   Task analysis used in garden tool design

flowerbeds. Robert's research highlighted this issue and inspired a concept for an extended hedge trimmer, where the cutter is mounted on the end of an extension bar at an angle. This makes all reaching operations much easier, reducing the reach, stretch and strength demands made by the product (Figure 9.6). In many cases, this idea means the user can reach the top of a hedge without needing to climb a ladder, and so this (often dangerous) task step is avoided completely.

Brown's project clearly demonstrates how research carried out by designers can directly inspire new ideas. He has since set up Sprout Design, which uses exactly this approach to innovate more inclusive products, on an overall product concept level as well as on a product feature level.

Sprout Design and the Cambridge Engineering Design Centre are developing a software-based tool (Figure 9.7) that uses task analysis to estimate the number of people in the UK who would be excluded from using any particular product. A simple building-block graphical interface guides operators in constructing their own task analysis, using input from real users if available.

Tasks are broken into steps and the difficulty of each task step is then assessed in terms of the cognitive, sensory and motion capability a person would need to carry out that step. People who do not have that level of capability are excluded. Results are shown graphically and the task analysis serves to highlight the steps where the most people will have difficulty. The software identifies specific issues which need to be addressed in the design and therefore works as an innovation driver. Improvements to the design can be assessed in real time, the software instantly showing the impact on exclusion. Knowing what proportion of a company's market their products are excluding can also be a powerful business case for adopting a more inclusive approach to design.

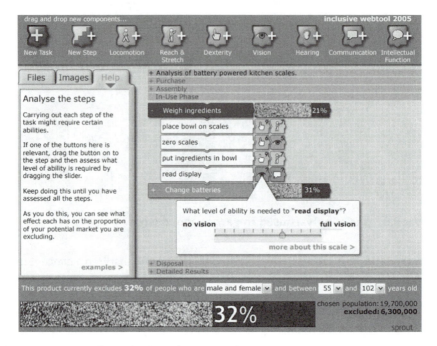

Figure 9.7   A task-analysis software tool

SUMMARY

Task analysis has been used by human factors practitioners for many years, and designers should feel free to use it as they see fit. As a designer-orientated user research method, task analysis has the following characteristics:

- *Visual*: It can be presented in either graphical form, or in page or sheet form.

- *Versatile*: It can be used during the analysis phase or in planning evaluation studies; for both existing systems or a hypothetical product; information elicited from users through, for example, 'interviews' or 'observation'; can use flexible forms of note-taking and representation.

- *Inspiring*: Decomposition of tasks is useful to explore how activities fit into a wider context; in later stages of the development the current solution can be checked against the original task or activity analysis to see how the design deviates from the intended solution, and what consequences this leads to.

- *Playful/fun*: Flexibility enables more light-hearted applications, such as in Figure 9.8, where task analysis is used in the Design Business

Association (DBA) Critical User Forums; can also use colour/loops, and so on, to add meaning and interest.

- *Practical*: The tasks can be broken down to the level of detail felt to be needed for the purpose of the analysis.

Persona

DEFINITION AND CLASSIFICATION

Personas are hypothetical archetypes, representing real people throughout the design process. They are defined with significant rigour and precision, backed up by actual user research data (Cooper, 1999). Personas can be used as both a design tool and a communication tool. It is a typical 'Representation'-type user research method.

ORIGINS

As a user profiling or user modelling tool, personas are often used for developing consumer hardware and software products, but they can also be applied to information-intensive Web design projects and industrial design projects.

BASICS

A persona description includes typical work flow, attitudes, skills, frustrations, goals, and environment. A persona set (in general between two and seven

Figure 9.8   Task analysis used in practice by designers

personas) is the entire collection of distinct behaviour patterns relevant to a product or system. The primary value of personas is in focusing the design on the most typical users to optimise the product for them. Its purpose is 'to get everyone thinking in a unified way from a user's perspective'.

EXAMPLES

There are numerous examples of successful personas developed for various design projects (see www.stcsig.org/usability/topics/personas.html). For a website redesign project the clients told the developer that they had cut development time by as much as half using persona-based design (www.cio. com/archive/111503/play.html).

A programme sponsored by the DTI was undertaken by the Centre for Inclusive Technology and Design (CITD) in early 2005 to understand the level of awareness of Inclusive Design in industry and deliver a high impact training package to eight major companies in the UK. Persona cards were produced by the project team, representing seven members of a fictional family. The characters reflected different ages, lifestyles and levels of capability. They gave the workshop participants empathy and helped them think through the experience the fictional characters would have using each example product.

Each persona raised specific usability issues – for example, Jenny is a single mother with an active eighteen-month-old son and a 4-year-old daughter. Consequently her time is very precious and she has little patience with anything that unnecessarily wastes her time. She is also concerned with the safety of her children. The function of her card was specifically to make workshop participants consider product usability issues for someone with small active children. Other persona cards covered issues such as a broken wrist, arthritis, deafness, visual impairments and reduced intellectual function. The results from these workshops showed that the cards stimulated lively discussion and directly inspired new ideas for how to make the products easier to use.

SUMMARY

Personas are a type of designer-orientated user research method, because they are:

- *Visual*: Each persona has an image which makes it unique, memorable and 'realistic'.

Figure 9.9   An example of persona

- *Versatile*: Personas are defined by goals. In general, they should not be recycled from a previous project for a new project. But relevant interviews and research data can be used for creating new personas. Personas can be used in combination with other user-centred methods, such as task analysis, card sorting, and usability testing.

- *Inspiring*: Personas are not real people; although they can be identified with their technical skills and fictional details, there is always space for individual designers to imagine scenarios associated with each persona.

- *Playful/fun*: Personas are not abstract or generalised user models; by using personas, designers tend to think of individual users such as 'Mary' or 'Craig', rather than the stereotyped over 50s. There exists a dialogue between the designer and the fictional user.

- *Practical*: The number of personas created for a project should be kept relatively small and manageable – usually between two and seven. If needed, both primary personas and secondary personas can be created for design projects.

Informance

DEFINITION AND CLASSIFICATION

Informance is a short word for 'informative performance'. It is a set of techniques in which actors and/or researchers study what is known about consumers and role-play potential consumers. Informance subsumes both ethnography and empathy. It is rooted in performance ethnography (captured an interesting scene on video and have memorised it and can perform it from the perspective of its main character) and design improvisation (speak the character's thoughts aloud as you perform the scene – a step further to the performance ethnography) (Laurel, 2003). Informance is a type of user research method that features both 'Representation' and 'Co-design'.

ORIGINS

The goal of 'informance' goes beyond understanding consumers' culture or even having an 'inside' understanding of consumers. Its goal is to create, through performance, characters that can speak about their world, express informed opinions about product features, answer questions about design possibilities, and even design products.

BASICS

Informance begins with ethnographic study – questioning and observing people in particular consumer segments. Researchers move on to interpreting their data through empathy: seeing situations, uses, and elements as the studied consumers would see them. The next step is informance itself: acts of pretending which transform empathy into action. The idea of informance is to allow typical consumers to say what they cannot say themselves by transforming them into characters in a performance. The power of informance lies in embracing the paradox: using a sound empirical basis as springboard for the skill of the researchers and designers to create characters. Pretending has value in many ways for design researchers. It allows researchers to give a voice to their understanding of consumers. These consumers become 'we' rather than 'they', and as such, join the design team.

EXAMPLES

A good example of the successful use of informance is the ElderSpace project (Dishman, 2003). The research team, comprising three social scientists, one artist, and an industrial designer, set out to produce informance after spending weeks analysing videos and photos from the nursing home. They each adopted a character based upon representative combinations of actual people they had studied (that is personas). Using theatrical techniques and through scripting, memorising, embodying and acting out the lives of those personas in a fully staged set, they learned more by 'doing' and 'being' those characters than they could have by any other means. As a design process, most saw informance as having enormous power in two areas: 1) helping the designer to consider how each individual user is embedded in larger social systems; and 2) forcing technologists to evaluate the whole electronic ecosystem and interaction infrastructure when trying to bring in new technologies. The UTOPIA Trilogy (Chapter 8) is also a type of informance, where actors rather than researchers role-played the users.

SUMMARY

As a designer-orientated user research method, informance is

- *Visual*: It is performed on the stage.

- *Versatile*: Two situations especially call for informance. Design for entirely new categories of products calls for informance because new kinds of products are particularly difficult for most people to imagine. Informance is also particularly useful with potential users who have little in common with the designers. A product may be for a segment that is demographically remote from the designer; for example, 30-year-old designers creating products for people who are 70; or a product may be intended as 'worldwide' and thus culturally remote from any individual designer (Dishman, 2003).

- *Inspiring*: A later stage of informance can integrate the designer's solution into a performance of the original subject in the same situated context but with new interfaces or affordances. This allows the designer to explore the design solution in all sensory and cognitive modalities, thus providing inspirations. The final 'show' can give the design team another chance to revise their concepts, forcing them to move the ideas from paper to tangible prototypes and obtain feedback from the audience.

- *Playful/fun*: Role-playing is fun, especially when the aim was to explore those unknowns.

- *Practical*: Informance can take many forms, for example 'performance for an audience' (Dishman, 2003) and 'design improvisation' (Laurel, 2003). The advantage of 'performance for an audience' is that many people can be brought into the research and design process; the advantage of 'design improvisation' (no audience apart from the team members who are performing for each other) is that it requires less polish and probably fewer props.

Conclusion

This chapter has classified designer-orientated user research methods into three types: Forum ('to ask'), Representation ('to observe'), Co-design ('to participate'), and summarised the characteristics of designer-orientated user research methods, that is *visual, versatile, inspiring, playful/fun* and *practical*. Three examples, that is task analysis, persona and informance, were used to illustrate these characteristics. Many user research methods are derived from basic methods, so designers should not feel overwhelmed by the large numbers of methods with various names. New tools/techniques have created chances for 'new' user research methods, and designers have freedom to create their own user research methods or adapt methods as they see fit.

References

Aldersey-Williams, H., Coleman, R. and Bound, J. (1999), *Methods Lab* (London: Royal College of Art).

Annett, J. and Duncan, K. (1967), 'Task Analysis and Training Design', *Occupational Psychology*, 41, pp. 211–221.

Cooper, A. (1999), *The Inmates are Running the Asylum: Why High-Tech Products Drive Us Crazy and How to Restore the Sanity* (Indianapolis, IN: SAMS).

Dekker, M., Nicolle, C. and Molenbroek, J. (2004), 'GENIE Workshop for Curricula with User Involvement and Inclusive Design', *Gerontechnology*, 3(1), pp. 35–42.

Dishman, E. (2003), 'Designing for the new old' In *Design Research: Methods and Perspectives*, Laurel, B. (ed.) (Massachusetts, MA: MIT Press).

Gregory, R. (1979), 'Personalised Task Representation' *AMTE(E) Report TM79103*, Copyright Controller HMSO (Not commonly available).

Ireland, C. (2003), 'Qualitative design research', In *Design Research: Methods and Perspectives*, Laurel, B. (ed.) (Massachusetts, MA: MIT Press).

Laurel, B. (2003), *Design Research: Methods and Perspectives* (Massachusetts, MA: MIT Press).

Plowman, T. (2003), 'Ethnography' In *Design Research: Methods and Perspectives*, Laurel, B. (ed.) (Massachusetts, MA: MIT Press).

Poulson, D., Ashby, M. and Richardson, S. (eds.) (1996), *USERfit −A Practical Handbook on User-Centred Design for Assistive Technology* (Brussels: ECSC-EC-East Asian Economic Caucus). Available at: www2.stakes.fi/include and www.education.edean.org

Robson, C. (2002), *Real World Research*, 2nd edn (Oxford: Blackwell Publishing).

Sanoff, H. (1992), *Integrating Programming, Evaluation and Participation in Design: A Theory Z Approach* (Aldershot: Avebury).

Shepherd, A. and Stammers, R.B. (2005), 'Task Analysis', In *Evaluation of Human Work*, 3rd edn, Wilson, J.R. and Corlett, N. (eds) (London: Taylor & Francis).

Sin, K.W.M. (2003), 'Users' Creative Response and Designers' Roles', *Design Issues*, 19(2), pp. 64–73.

Walls, M. (2006), 'TaskArchitect (review of software)', *Ergonomics in Design*, 14(1), pp 27-29.

Practicalities of Working with Users

David Yelding and Julia Cassim

Introduction

This chapter looks at recruiting and working with users from a practical perspective. It takes account of what can be achieved within likely budgets, administrative constraints and schedules. In doing this we have borne in mind that time and resources are unlikely to be available to enable the more elaborate studies carried out by academic researchers.

The chapter is based mainly on the experience of Ricability (the Research Institute for Consumer Affairs), an independent research charity set up by *Which*? some 40 years ago which specialises in research for older and disabled people. Unlike other consumer organisations, its ultimate objective is to improve the standard of products and services, mainly by publishing information based on product tests and other research. Although Ricability uses standard research techniques such as focus groups, surveys, interviews and observations, their application is focused on people with a diverse range of impairments. We argue that it is research and design partnerships with these groups that can lead to truly inclusive design – products and services that can be used by a wider range of people and which are easier for everybody to use, able-bodied or otherwise.

Why Work with Users?

Some designers may consider that consulting with users has limited importance while others may regard it as an unwelcome distraction. After all, they know about products because they design and use them. Colleagues or friends can always be asked without the complicated apparatus of a formal consultation. Many consider that working with users with impairments will put boundaries on their creative thought or push them towards conventional products that lack distinction or style.

In practice, wide-ranging consultation is likely to yield a richer set of information and scenarios on which the design can be based. On the most mundane level, talking to potential consumers can reveal the sometimes surprising way in which products are used such as screwdrivers used to open cans of paint. It can also reduce the risk of fundamental errors such as kettle or saucepan handles that are too hot to touch as well as suggesting the more subtle characteristics that may make a product desirable. Providing the right people are consulted, there will be insights into cultural or environmental considerations that may affect the design. In many Asian households, for example, the cooking is done by the grandmother, who may have limited ability to carry heavy objects. Most importantly, perhaps, the input from users provides a stimulus for new ideas and approaches, an example being the computer mouse which was inspired by watching the way children moved objects. Finding out what irks people about products may lead to some lateral solutions – electric drills that do not need a key, wheeled shopping trolleys that double as seats and so on.

Useful Guidance

TAKE A HOLISTIC APPROACH

Inclusive design requires a holistic approach. For example, travel is made up of a chain of events. Before the design of the train, coach or bus is even considered, passengers must be able to book tickets easily, to get to the station, find and use an accessible toilet and so on. Every aspect of the journey needs to be accessible if the journey is to be problem-free. Thus, website design, the training of staff, the availability of help with luggage and all other aspects of service delivery must be considered. Uniting all these considerations is the need to know and understand what consumers want, how they behave and what they can do. Thus, an inclusive approach demands much closer contact with consumers and a coherent understanding of all the elements that make up a single activity.

THINK MAINSTREAM

This chapter necessarily gives emphasis to disability. However the focus of inclusive design is not disability. Rather it aims to eliminate disability caused by design by making sure that as many people as possible can use a product, irrespective of the nature of their impairment. The social model of disability demonstrates that it is poor design that turns an impairment into a disability. Good design can make the impairment irrelevant to use of the product. Designers may think of positioning their product for a particular and sometimes very narrow market but where an inclusive and mainstream design approach is adopted, disability should not rule designers out of any of these markets.

Mainstream and assistive products have traditionally been two separate entities and consequently have largely existed as two separate industries. Designers of mainstream products sometimes simply ignored or were ignorant of the needs of those who did not fit into what was then considered the norm while the market for 'special products' was thought to be too narrow to support innovative design. The result has been stigmatising, poorly-designed and undesirable products that no one would choose freely. Their users were rarely consulted or given much choice in products provided by statutory authorities that were essential to their ability to maintain a degree of independence and therefore quality of life. Inclusive design should mean that the need for assistive products or adaptations is much reduced.

START EARLY

Most R&D projects involve some consumers, but older and disabled people tend to be involved at the periphery of any consultation, if they are involved at all. In some cases, small numbers of older or disabled people are added at the end of the consultative process with the result that their input is attenuated and too late to be useful.

LOOK AT HARD CASES

There is compelling evidence to show that the conventional method of carrying out consumer research needs to be inverted. Development work should concentrate on those who have the most difficulty rather than on the able-bodied majority. Designing for disabled people makes products easier to use for everybody else.

USE COMMON SENSE

When planning consultation, managing the sessions and interpreting the information, common sense is likely to be your best guide. Many research techniques have evolved a jargon all of their own where esoteric-sounding techniques are merely familiar processes newly wrapped. Do not use any technique unless you can explain it in plain English.

Some Misconceptions

WORKING WITH USERS IS NOT A PANACEA

Consultation provides information but is unlikely to answer every question or provide a blueprint. The small-scale consultation described in this chapter should bring any major limitations of a product or service to the fore and suggest realistic improvements. But by its very nature consultation is unlikely to produce definitive cut and dried answers, and may reveal more issues than solutions. One consequence of working with users is a need for more creative thought and leaps of imagination from designers. There is a tendency to consider that inclusive design is only about products. As illustrated by the case study chapters, inclusive design is not just about product design but applies to every design discipline. Written instructions for example, are notorious for being badly organised, badly conceived and given in print too small to decipher. Many simply assume a level of knowledge consumers simply do not have.

Other common design failures revealed by our research include:

- Small print on labels – often pale grey on white

- Instructions in small print with poor colour contrast

- Poorly lit, small read out panels

- Complicated menu systems

- Rotary knobs with smooth sides

- Small controls which require high dexterity to grip

- Controls which require too much force to operate

- Lack of tactile feedback, which mean controls cannot be used by feel

- Multi-function controls on electronic devices that confuse the user

- Tasks which require the use of two hands

Practicalities

For the practicalities of user consultation, we have considered work that is designed to reach evaluative conclusions about how well a product meets the needs of different users, about their attitudes and about their aspirations towards it. In the following section, we describe the various stages involved in recruiting people, eliciting information and interpreting the results. This is not intended to be prescriptive nor can it be complete in a chapter of this length. However, it should serve as a starting point for designers when considering working with users.

Recruiting

HOW TO START?

Some consultations take the form of trawling. Researchers explore as many areas as they can in the hope that something will rise to the surface. This can be useful in areas about which little is known but sometimes it is because research has been carried out without clear consideration of what it is needed for or how it may be acted on. From the outset, be clear about what you need to know, and to what level of detail. This process should suggest the techniques you will use and the criteria for selecting the users you will work with.

WHO TO RECRUIT?

The accuracy of large-scale surveys based on random-selection techniques can be calculated statistically; however, the essentially qualitative techniques described here are likely to yield samples too small to allow this. When using small groups for research, deciding on the profile of users for work of this type is more a matter of common sense and of reducing the risk of those consulted being representative only of themselves. Most researchers aim for as wide a spread as possible within their target group of consumers. Small samples may not be an inhibiting factor because major issues of design – whether good or bad – will be identified relatively easily by small groups, and discussions should provide sufficient stimulus for ideas and further development. However, when selecting small groups, whatever you do is likely to be a compromise: some of the factors you may need to consider are outlined below. Since you will be dealing with small numbers, it will not always be possible to draw generic conclusions from different groups. It is surprising how often general attitudes can colour views about the utility of a project; people for whom function is not the first priority can persuade themselves that a design whose appearance is pleasing is easy to use. Having a diverse sample, even if it is small, can help cancel out these and other biases.

PREVIOUS EXPERIENCE

The criteria for choosing your sample will depend on what you are trying to discover. For example, you may have to decide whether you want to consult existing users of the type of product in which you are interested or those encountering it for the first time. When testing responses to style and aesthetics, the age, social group and background of the subjects will be important.

DEMOGRAPHIC GROUPS

It is usually desirable to include people with differing experiences and attitudes. The demographic groups often considered centre on sex, age, terminal education age, socio-economic group and some type of lifestyle group.

IMPAIRMENT

A radical view is that tests carried out entirely by people with more severe impairments will automatically encompass the needs of able-bodied people and those with less severe impairments. Few organisations are prepared to take this risk. A decision needs to be made on what impairments must be represented and to what level of severity. Diagnoses of medical condition alone are not relevant because they do not tell you what people are able to do.

There are particular problems associated with carrying out assessments which will be useful for people with disabilities. The first and most obvious one is that there is no standard for disability which can be used as a benchmark. The severity of any particular impairment varies considerably, affects people in different ways, and may change from day to day. What individuals are able to do also depends on motivation and to some extent on their determination and ingenuity.

If conclusions are to be drawn about people with particular impairments, it will be necessary to consult a sufficient number of them to understand their diversity. As an example, for comparative tests Ricability aim to recruit a minimum of twelve people with a single characteristic we wish to treat separately. Depending on the product being tested, these separate groups may include people who have impaired strength, dexterity, cognition, vision, hearing and mobility. Increasingly tests take account of the needs of people with combinations of disabilities, including those who are generally frail. It follows that at least 50 people need to be recruited for each test, a number that increases substantially if the number of products to be tested results in each user being only able to assess a proportion of them. Before conclusions can be drawn for any disability group, we carry out an analysis about the variation of results by that group – the more diverse the group, the more careful one must be about drawing conclusions. In the context of design development, samples of this size may be neither possible nor essential and thus a decision will need to be made as to which impairments are relevant and at what level of severity.

ELIMINATING BIAS

Since techniques of random selection used by statisticians are likely to be unavailable, it will be necessary to use more informal methods. Here one should be aware of possible sources of bias. These include:

- avoid people you know, including colleagues. Your relationship to them, and their knowledge of your work may serious distort your findings

- try to get people from a multiplicity of sources and contexts. If you recruit from a single day centre, for example, you may only be talking to a very narrow group

- avoid recruiting people who know each other

- recruit from as many contrasting geographical areas as is practical.

WHERE TO RECRUIT?

Organisations to approach include local disability organisations and groups (listed under 'disability' in the phone book or available from your local council), day centres and social clubs. The local council may run or fund groups who can provide practical help. Other approaches include advertising (local papers, community newsletters, postcards in shops, chat rooms). Where a budget is available, people can be found by population screening, which has the advantage of allowing a great deal of control over who is chosen. This involves cold calling on households in likely areas to identify people who fit your criteria. Large companies may work regularly with a market research company who might offer help – their interviewers are experienced in recruiting samples and have identity cards, which can help alleviate suspicion of doorstep callers. Otherwise, research organisations can be sourced from the Market Research Society. 'Snowballing' is another well used technique – every person you recruit is asked if they know someone who might also be interested. Take care to avoid coteries of people who know each other well.

ALLOWING ENOUGH TIME

As a rough guide, recruiting a reasonably diverse group of 25 people may take 5 days work spread over 4 weeks. Informing people of what you wish them to do when you make the initial approach is important. Be specific about the length of the task, about dates, the accessibility of the venue and the reimbursement of out of-pocket expenses. Stress that their contribution will be confidential and that you are following approved ethical procedures for your institution. And, importantly, recruit some reserves to replace those who are unable to come at the last minute.

Techniques of Eliciting Information

All the techniques described here are methods of eliciting information. What needs to be considered is who you consult, how you do so and how you interpret the information. The main techniques, which can be carried out on a small scale, include: focus groups, depth interviews, quantitative surveys, user panels, user tests, observation and expert panels.

FOCUS GROUPS

These are informal groups of usually 6–8 people. The main advantages of focus groups are speed, the opportunity to bounce opinions between participants, the fact that groups can develop a dynamic that encourages frank and free discussion and general flexibility (unexpected leads can be followed at will). Careful moderation is needed to guide the discussion, to keep it on track and ensure that some members do not dominate, or that group pressure does not inhibit others. Mini-groups (usually 4 people) may be more productive if some experimental work (such as trials of a prototype) are to be carried out, or if it is important to confine the group to people with, for example, similar backgrounds. Only one group may be necessary for your purposes. Where you have more than one, you will need to decide whether to mix participants or 'match' them – for example by holding a separate group for different age groups, for each sex or for people with particular impairments.

Some practicalities

Pay participants. This makes recruitment easier, and can be done in the form of a contribution to travel or other expenses. Be careful that the payment does not cause difficulties for those who are receiving benefits. Typical payments for participation in a group range from around £25, to include travelling costs. Be prepared to make travel arrangements or lay on transport.

If you can afford a professional moderator (around £500 a day if employed directly), do so. Prepare a topic guide – a list of subject areas, around which the interviewer improvises. Start with a list of issues you consider relevant and circulate it among colleagues and talk it through with a small number of users to check. Be prepared to improvise in the group as you may find unanticipated issues arise. Limit the number of observers in the group to two at the most and do not let them intervene, since the moderator needs to keep control of the group. Record the group where possible, but seek the participants' informed consent for this form of documentation. Many focus groups routinely include older consumers but their opinions can sometimes be eclipsed by younger more vociferous participants. Given the propensity of older people to blame themselves rather than poor design, their opinions have not always been widely heeded. Selecting older people who are active, articulate and open-minded is important but the opinionated should be avoided.

Premises need to be fully accessible – not only for wheelchair users but also for those with sensory and other impairments. Ask participants about their requirements. For example, you may need to avoid glare (bright light through windows) for participants with some visual impairments while people with hearing impairments may need induction loops. Toilets should be accessible and disabled parking available. Unless your tests are to be carried out by post (see below) location will be important. Travelling distances need to be as short as possible, particularly if participants have mobility impairments.

DEPTH OF INTERVIEWS

In some circumstances (where in-depth information is needed from each individual or if respondents may have difficulty getting to a group, for example) individual interviews based on a topic guide will be a better option. Interviews are likely to be discursive and exploratory rather than consisting of sets of formal questions. The group interaction is lost but this format allows the individuals' opinions and ideas to be explored in great depth. It takes longer and may be more expensive depending on whether you are paying the interviewer or not. Providing potential respondents can be identified, interviews may be easier to arrange than a focus group.

Some practicalities

The number needed will vary according to the diversity of consumers to be consulted and the diversity of their opinions. A cautious approach would be to interview ten people with different demographic characteristics and then review the results to decide whether further interviews are likely to add significantly to what has been discovered.

QUANTITATIVE SURVEYS

If you need information from a representative sample of people, the most economical option is using a commercial omnibus survey. These are run regularly by market research companies and you will be buying into pre-scheduled surveys by paying for your own questions.

EXPERT PANELS

Groups of experts (designers, ergonomists, occupational therapists, physiotherapists, home economists, and so on) are often used as a quick way of getting an insight into how products are used and the advantages and disadvantages of particular designs. There are risks, since the accuracy of the information depends on the experts and on the nature of their experience. It is possible that old assumptions may be reiterated. Finding experts can be easier than recruiting users and the process of consultation faster and cheaper. An expert panel can be a preliminary stage in designing and organising user trials.

USER TESTS/TRIALS

User tests of products can take different forms. They are valuable because they provide highly realistic and accurate information on products as they are actually used. Wherever the trials take place, users fill in questionnaires, are interviewed or attend a focus group to discuss their experience of the product and attitudes to it. If the test is of instructions or of other written materials, the techniques are similar but are more likely to take place in controlled conditions.

The purpose of the test needs to be explained and each task carried out in the right order and in the right way. You may need one member of staff for each respondent if you are interviewing, if the tasks need lots of explanation or if the respondent has a severe disability. This will be essential if respondents are severely visually impaired or have learning disabilities.

OBSERVATION

Observation is a useful tool used in conjunction with user tests. Some users are accustomed to experiencing difficulty using products that they will nevertheless describe as being easy to use because they present no more difficulty than other products in their experience. Observation may reveal that in fact they have had to adopt quite awkward strategies to use the product. Observation also allows some analysis of generic basic tasks. This is useful where you are trying to rethink the ways in which the product might be configured. It is better not to combine observations with other duties during a user test.

USER PANELS

If user tests are to be carried out regularly, recruiting a panel may be cheaper overall as its costs can be spread over several projects. The other advantages are that the panel can be designed to be large enough to provide a choice of participants for later work, which makes future consultation much easier. With panels it is also possible to collect and accrete detailed background data over time which allows for the more sophisticated interpretation of results.

The disadvantages are the time involved in managing the panel and the theoretical possibility that panel members lose their value as typical consumers by adopting a professional critical stance.

QUESTIONNAIRES

Several techniques involve questionnaires. Designing a questionnaire is an art as well as a science. Keep the language simple and colloquial – try not to use complicated or arcane words. Avoid questions which presuppose developed opinions.

When using multiple choice answers, check that all possibilities are covered – in most cases you will need a category for 'other'. Keep questions balanced so they do not prompt or suggest a particular answer. Start with an easy multiple-choice question to ease the respondent into the questionnaire. Avoid portmanteau questions which are capable of two separate responses (How satisfied were you with the weight and size of this ...?).

Make a common sense check on what you have done – for example do not have a single question about the size of the buttons if there are buttons of different sizes on the product being tested. If you are using rating scales, include a mid neutral point. Try out the questionnaire on real people and ask them to think aloud to you as they complete it; this will rapidly expose any ambiguities or illogicality in the questionnaire. Look carefully at the answers to check that they tell you what you want to know. If you have missed a question, asked one that gets ambiguous answers or if a mistake in the sequence directs people to the wrong question, filling the gaps afterwards will be problematic. Keep the questionnaire short (not as easy as it sounds) and avoid too many open-ended questions – blank pages can be daunting and tend to get minimal answers. Questionnaires should be road-tested by trying them out beforehand; three or four may be enough for a small scale study; more if you are using them to suggest pre-codes for possible answers in a larger scale survey. A dry run to test administrative arrangements and timings is also useful.

Some practicalities

The key lies in the planning. Tasks should be clearly described and in a logical order. Explain the purpose of the test, but take great care not to hint at the answers you are seeking. If possible, make any test samples anonymous to eliminate bias. Have enough samples for people to try without waiting or you may find that fatigue has set in before the test is completed. Allow participants to fill in questionnaires as they go, while the detail is clear. Start off with a dummy question that demonstrates what you want. If you are testing a group of alternatives comparatively, emphasise that it is permissible to go back and change ratings if participants consider they have previously over or underrated a product. If self-completion questionnaires are used, check at convenient stages, and while the respondent is able to clarify any uncertainties, that each question has been answered clearly and sufficiently. Some researchers prefer interviews to self-completion questionnaires because they ensure a more even quality of response and allow for the possibility of intelligent probing for full answers. If there is time, and respondents have the energy, a group discussion to summarise can be helpful. If at all possible, carry out a pilot to test the practicalities of the test. If you are using written materials, they should be appropriate for those attending – large print, tape, screen, for example. If visually impaired people are participating, you will need staff to guide them and perhaps a scribe to record their answers to questionnaires. Ensure that you have sufficient space to allow people to move around in or be interviewed in privacy.

Ethical Considerations

If you are a student or tutor, your college, university or institution should have its own code of ethics governing user research. You should ensure that you have a copy of this, fully understand it and follow the guidance given. It may well include pro forma documents for securing permission and obtaining informed consent. In addition, there are legal requirements that govern what information you may and may not share with others. For example, the Data Protection Act limits what you can do with personal information stored in any electronic medium, and you should also ensure that any personal information, however it is stored, is kept confidential. If you are working with other organisations or institutions it is important to make sure you are aware of their ethical codes and requirements; for example, in healthcare-related design projects you may well have to obtain and conform to medical ethics provisions. Finally, the fact that you may be collaborating with other institutions does not necessarily mean that you can share user data, and you should be careful to respect the rights and confidentiality, not just of users, but of other researchers.

You also have a duty of care for those you are working with and you cannot ask users to carry out any task that puts them at risk. The element of risk can be hard to evaluate since many people exaggerate the extent to which they can carry out common tasks with ease. Talk to them, and stress that they should not carry out any task they have doubts about; make sure such warnings are included on questionnaires, instructions and informed consent documents. If the project involves lifting people, hire qualified staff to help. Users, particularly those who are older or have disabilities, get tired; so keep the testing sessions to a reasonable length (1½–2 hours) and build in tea and rest breaks. If you are carrying out tests with people who are vulnerable, ensure that you include people with relevant knowledge to help in an emergency. You need to take great care that any prototypes or equipment do not contain hidden risks when used by novices.

If you are taking photographs, get written permission to use these photographs in all likely situations – to illustrate speeches, in publications, annual reports, and so on. You will need public liability insurance to cover the users – tell the insurance company what you are doing, and be prepared for a supplementary premium.

Costs vary according to the facilities and time available. Assuming focus group members are recruited from scratch, the moderator is paid and direct costs include fees to respondents, the hire of a venue, refreshments and transport, audio and/or visual recording, the cost may be between £3,000 and £4,500 depending on whether you use a specialist research agency / researcher to do everything or you are using your own facilities. Professional interviewers cost some £150–175 per day, plus travel and other necessary expenses. The cost per interview will depend on how many can be achieved per day and excludes development of the questionnaire and analysis. Analysis costs vary depending on who does it, the software you employ and the level of detail you want. A formal report on group discussions would include the cost of transcriptions, and a report (usually written by the moderator). You may not need the transcriptions, or indeed a written report, if the ideas that emerged from the group are sufficiently clear.

If your respondents are likely to be consulted later on in the project or for subsequent work, maintain contact. Inform them of your conclusions and how the project is developing.

Resources to Help Interpreting Findings

It is helpful to interpret your findings with reference to other work. Anthropometric data on adults, children and the older population have been compiled into useful reference works.

Usability ratings are often a key part of the testing carried out by the consumer organisation *Which?* and its counterparts in other countries which are listed on: www.international-testing.org

Prizes or approval labels could be given for some products. The Owlmark is an approval scheme run by the Centre for Applied Gerontology at the University of Birmingham. Finland and Spain have schemes which allow companies to display a 'design for all commitment' label. All these are worth checking for details of positive product features if you are working in a similar field. An independent approval and labelling scheme for popular mainstream appliances has yet to be established to identify products with accessible features.

The designers of assistive technology products in related fields may have useful information as well as experience of particular groups of potential consumers. For example, over 100 specialist firms design or manufacture equipment that enables disabled people to use standard production cars. Most of them work entirely independently of motor manufacturers yet many may have information that would help car designers make more accessible vehicles.

Ricability assesses products comparatively against *Design for All* principles and publishes comparative reports but funding rarely allows Ricability to continue to carry out the necessary user tests for every update of our reports. We have pioneered a system of checklist assessments based on a pilot survey which showed that this technique would produce consistent results providing four main conditions have been met. These are:

- the assessment document is based on tests in which an adequate number of participants with each of the disabilities to be covered took part

- the original user test covered the range of features and designs available on the products to be assessed

- assessors are properly trained in the implications of each type of impairment

- detailed guidance is provided by the assessment document.

These checklists may provide a prompt for key factors that affect the usability of products and can be found at www.ricability.org.uk/reports/report-design/guidelinesforproductdesign.

References

Aldersey-Williams, H., Coleman, R. and Bound, J. (1999), *Methods Lab* (London: Royal College of Art).

ICO (1998), *The Data Protection Act, 1998* (London: Information Commissioner's Office). Available at: www.opsi.gov.uk/ACTS/ acts1998/19980029.htm.

Market Research Society Code of Practice. Available at: www.mrs.org.uk/code. htm.

Norris, B. and Wilson, J.R. (1995), *ChildData: The Handbook of Child Measurements and Capabilities* (London, Department of Trade and Industry).

Peebles, L. and Norris, B. (1998), *AdultData: The Handbook of Adult Anthropometric and Strength Measurements* (London, Department of Trade and Industry).

Smith, S., Norris, B. and Peebles, L. (2000), *Older AdultData: The Handbook of Measures and Capabilities of the Older Adult* (London, Department of Trade and Industry).

Countering Design Exclusion – Theory and Practice

John Clarkson

Introduction

Product design has the potential to exclude users, a fact that is sadly all too prevalent in an age of increasing technological advancement. The current generation of mobile phones, for example, includes more features than the previous generation and as a result is potentially much more difficult to use. Recent research has also shown that exclusion is also no longer the preserve of those with reduced capability and two out of three Americans report having lost interest in a technology product because it seemed 'too complex to set up or operate' (Philips, 2004). Furthermore, a US-wide survey by Microsoft shows that the majority of working-age adults are likely to benefit from the use of more accessible technology (Microsoft, 2003, 2004).

The principles of inclusive design have the potential to significantly advantage able-bodied as well as less able users, while approaches that reduce exclusion are likely to reduce difficulty and frustration for those users who are not excluded, yet do not find a product easy to use. In this chapter, the principles and mechanisms of exclusion are discussed, along with an approach that may be taken to carry out an exclusion analysis. Relevant data sources describing user capabilities are also identified along with details of their application to exclusion analysis.

Finally, examples of exclusion analyses are presented in order to provide some sense of the levels of exclusion to be encountered with a range of common domestic products.

Design Exclusion

Design exclusion arises when the demands of using a particular product, within a given environment, exceed the capabilities of the user. At worst this leads to

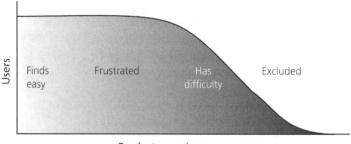

Product experience

Figure 11.1   Level of exclusion

the user being unable to use the product; at best the product may be difficult or frustrating to use. Put simply:

If Demand > Users' Capability then Exclusion

The user's capability is derived from their cognitive, sensory and physical characteristics, which include a mix of simple physical measures (for example anthropometrics and strength), functional measures (for example the ability to climb stairs or to read newsprint) and experiential measures (for example prior use of computers).

The product's demands are derived from its physical and behavioural characteristics, which may be described by its interface features (for example screen, text, buttons, and so on) and design variables/attributes (for example colour, dimensions, shape, force, interaction sequence, and so on).

The interplay between the product's demands and a user's capability, in the context of a particular activity or task, determines the level of exclusion experienced by that user. For example, a product placed on the top shelf in the supermarket may be inaccessible to users due to their height and/or their ability to reach to the shelf – the same product placed lower down is likely to be more accessible. Similarly, a television screen near a window may be perfectly viewable on a dull day, yet difficult to watch on a sunny afternoon – a situation that may be exacerbated if the user's vision is compromised by bright light.

The model also accommodates the view that design exclusion describes a spectrum of user / product interaction challenges, from total or partial exclusion, to difficulty or frustration for those users who are not excluded. It also allows for the fact that demands and capabilities may change with time,

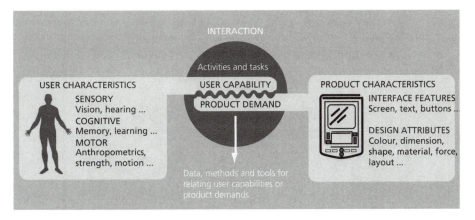

Figure 11.2   A model of user/product interaction

with variation both in the long term (for example due to ageing) and the short term (for example due to changes within a daily cycle).

Exclusion may also be a function of the frequency or duration of the activity or task. An infrequent, difficult task is less likely to lead to the same levels of frustration as a frequent, difficult task. For example, the infrequent, yet difficult, replacement of a battery will not frustrate as much as the regular and difficult activation of the on / off switch. A similar argument may apply to short and long difficult tasks.

However, an infrequent (or short) task that excludes the user may lead to exclusion for the whole product. For example, a user who is unable (in the absence of help) to 'programme' a new cooker may not be able to access features that are temporarily disabled – in particular where use of the oven is typically governed by a 'child safety' interlock. Herein lies the key difference between exclusion, where a single infrequent excluding task can compromise use of the whole product, and difficulty / frustration.

Approaches to Exclusion Analysis

Studies show that by 2020, half the adult population in the UK will be over 50 (Coleman, 1993) and that similar trends are observable elsewhere. Such ageing populations are known to exhibit an increasing divergence in physical capabilities (Clarkson and Keates, 2003), where in general the population becomes less capable with recorded levels of disability ranging from 1 to 20 per cent for different countries (United Nations, 1990). At the same time,

Figure 11.3   Designed to exclude?

the products that we use each day seem to become ever more complex, making increasing demands of their users.

For example, a mobile phone demands that its users can read the legends on its keys. If the size of the keys is reduced, with a corresponding reduction in legend size, to meet a marketing need for a smaller, lighter phone, then the demand made on the users' visual capabilities is increased. When such demands exceed the capabilities of the user, then the user will find it difficult or, at worst, impossible to use the product. Hence, as populations age and user capabilities fall, it becomes increasingly

Figure 11.4   A typical mobile phone

necessary for products to support a wider range of physical capabilities (Cooper, 1999).

In order to identify populations who can (or cannot) use products there is a need to assemble relevant data describing prospective users. Fortunately, there are many sources of such data available, each tailored for different purposes, including, for example, descriptions of:

- physical characteristics – the size (and strength) of the user

- socio-economic studies – the educational / social background of the user

- disability data – what the user cannot do

- capability data – what the user can do

- medical conditions – the health of the user

- longitudinal studies – the variation of health / abilities of the user with time

- market surveys – the likes or dislikes of the user.

Any, or indeed all, such data may be relevant to product design and much of it is certainly related. However, in terms of understanding whether users are physically excluded from using a particular product, the disability / capability and physical data are more important. Indeed, anthropometric data provide the predominant source of physical data used in product design, allowing designers to knowingly accommodate users within extremes of physical size.

Such data are usually assembled from a variety of sources with no single group of users providing all the data. The data can also be age related, as is the case with data available in the UK for children (Norris and Wilson, 1995), adults (Peebles and Norris, 1998) and older adults (Smith, Norris and Peebles, 2000).

Knowing which and how many people cannot use the product and why they cannot do so immediately highlights the aspects of the product that need to be improved. This forms the basis of an exclusion audit. For example, if a product excludes a significant proportion of the population because the users either cannot hear or cannot see the output from the product, then designers know they need to re-design the features involved in providing the output to the users.

The underlying principle of the exclusion audit is that, by identifying the capability demands placed upon the user by the features of the product,

Figure 11.5   People come in all shapes and sizes

it is possible to establish the users who cannot use the product irrespective
of the cause of their functional impairment. Consequently, by re-designing
the product to lessen or avoid the demand, users from a wider range of user
groups can potentially be included. Levels of exclusion can be estimated if the
prevalence of capability (relative to the demands of the task) within the user
population is known.

The Prevalence of Capability Losses

A series of surveys of disability and family resources in Great Britain
(Martin et al., 1988), (Grundy et al., 1999) and (Semmence et al., 1998) aimed
to provide up-to-date information about the number of disabled people in
Britain and their domestic circumstances. The purpose of the surveys was to
provide information to allow the planning of welfare benefits and services
provision.

The results showed that an estimated 8.5 million adults in Great Britain
– 20 per cent of the adult population – had a disability according to the
definition used. Of these 34 per cent had mild levels of impairment, 45 per cent
had moderate impairment and 21 per cent had severe impairment. It was also

found that 48 per cent of the disabled population were aged 65 or older and 29 per cent were aged 75 years or more.

The surveys, undertaken by the Office of Population Censuses and Surveys (OPCS), identified 13 different types of disabilities based on those described in the International classification of impairments, disabilities, and handicaps (WHO, 2001) and gave estimates of the prevalence of each. They showed that musculoskeletal complaints, most notably arthritis, were the most commonly cited causes of disability among adults living in private households. Ear complaints, eye complaints and diseases of the circulatory system were also common. For those living in communal establishments, cognitive complaints, particularly senile dementia, were mentioned most often, followed by musculoskeletal (for example arthritis) and nervous system (for example stroke) conditions.

• Locomotion
• Reaching and stretching
• Dexterity
• Seeing
• Hearing
• Personal care
• Continence
• Communication
• Behaviour
• Intellectual functioning
• Consciousness
• Eating, drinking, digestion
• Disfigurement

Figure 11.6   OPCS categories of impairment

For the purposes of product assessment, seven of the 13 capabilities identified by the surveys are of particular relevance. These may be grouped into three overall capability categories:

- motion – locomotion, reaching and stretching, and dexterity

- sensory – seeing and hearing

- cognitive – communication and intellectual functioning.

A summary of the capability data is presented in Figures 11.7 and 11.8 for the GB populations aged between 16 and 49, and aged 75 and above.

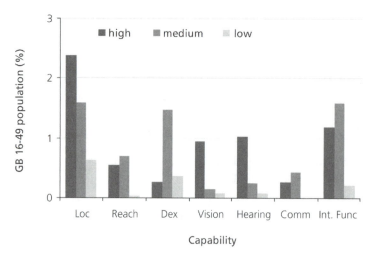

Figure 11.7   **Prevalence of disability for GB population aged between 16 and 49**

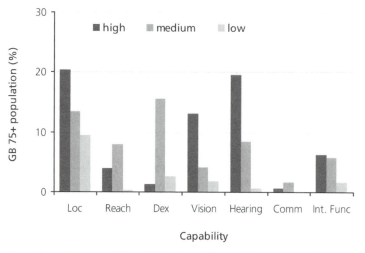

Figure 11.8   **Prevalence of disability for GB population aged 75 and above**

Perhaps the most striking feature is the order of magnitude difference in the scales used for each figure. While the graphs have similar distributions, the percentage of those with a loss of capability in the 75+ age band is 10 times higher than for the 16–49 band.

The analysis of capability data generates useful information for designing for a wider range of user capabilities. However, multiple capability losses present particular challenges for designers and if their importance is to be fully appreciated, comparable capability data are essential. Again, capability data, taken from a single sample, can provide some insights in this area.

Case-Studies of Design Exclusion

The following sections provide exclusion analyses for a number of well known domestic products. They serve to provide an indication of typical levels of exclusion likely to be encountered in the home.

DOMESTIC PRODUCTS

A range of domestic products have been assessed to quantify typical levels of design exclusion. In each case, the demands made by the product were estimated using the seven capability scales; an overall demand was calculated as a weighted sum of the three highest demands and the number of users unable to meet the demands was evaluated, taking account of multiple capability losses. The results are shown in Figure 11.9 superimposed on a pyramid.

The product demands are divided into ten levels, with the top band (1) corresponding to the highest capability demand and the bottom band (10) to the lowest. Different shading is applied to differentiate high user capability (score 1–2); moderate capability (score 3–6); and low capability (score 7–10). The whole user pyramid represents 8.5 million adults with functional impairments. The percentages shown represent exclusion in Great Britain for those over 15 years of age.

THE KETTLE

A typical 1.7 litre stainless steel kettle is shown in Figure 11.10. Assuming that the kettle is positioned to suit the height and mobility of the user, the basic

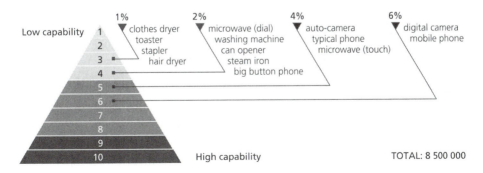

Figure 11.9   Levels of exclusion for a number of common products

Figure 11.10   A typical 1.7 litre stainless steel kettle

actions required are: to pick up the kettle; carry it to the nearby water tap; fill the kettle with water; return it to its base; switch it on; and pour the boiling water into a cup. A level of user exclusion can then be calculated by assessing the levels of each of the functional capabilities required to undertake these actions and estimating the number of users unable to meet these demands (Figure 11.11). In Great Britain 5.3 per cent of those over 15 would not be able to use such a kettle.

One could argue that the predominant purpose of a kettle is to provide hot water for making drinks and, in that context, an ideal kettle might be one that is no more difficult to use than drinking from a cup. The target population for an ideal kettle could therefore be all those users who can safely drink from a cup full of hot drink.

Further analysis shows that those excluded from this task number less than 500,000 for those over 15 in Great Britain (Figure 11.11). In fact, the results suggest that there are over two million people in Great Britain who can drink from a cup, but are unable to use a typical 1.7 litre metal kettle to boil water. An inclusively designed kettle (Figure 11.12) has the potential to include many

Kettle	Total excluded	
	(%)	(people)
Typical	5.3	2 506 000
Inclusive	2.6	1 229 000
Ideal	1.0	486 000

Figure 11.11   Exclusion levels for the kettle

Figure 11.12   An inclusively designed kettle

of those excluded by the heavier metal kettle (Figure 11.10). However, at the time of writing, such a product is not available.

Digital Television

Digital terrestrial television (DTV) equipment and services are significantly different from their current analogue counterparts, often using a separate set-top box with its own, additional, remote control (Figure 11.13). An assessment of current equipment undertaken for the UK Department of Trade and Industry

(DTI, 2003) suggests that two million people in Great Britain (4.4 per cent of those able to access analogue television) could be excluded from viewing the new digital services using digital television set-top boxes.

A further 700,000 people (1.6 per cent of those able to access analogue television) would be excluded from using advanced features such as digital text and interactive services. This problem is compounded by the fact that providers of different parts of the system (television, set-top box, interactive television services and digital teletext) all use different interaction approaches.

Figure 11.13   Difficulties with a remote control

The integration of the set-top box electronics with the television (iDTV) provides the means to solve a part of the first problem, but much effort is required to coordinate the design of the whole system to ensure that the new digital technology remains at least as accessible as analogue television.

A subsequent report, also for the UK Department of Trade and Industry (DTI, 2006), extended the analysis to estimate the number of UK households that would have difficulty adopting the new digital technology and identified four products that might be expected to meet the majority of user needs. The results of the analysis may be summarised as follows (Figure 11.14) for households in the UK:

a)   1.2 million households contain someone with severe sensory, cognitive or motion capability loss;

b)   3.5 million households contain someone with mild sensory, cognitive or motion capability loss;

c)   6.2 million able-bodied households contain someone who has a fear of or unfamiliarity with technology.

Consequently, it is estimated that:

•   2.0 million households contain someone who will be excluded from using current DTV equipment (including all those in group (a) above and 0.8 million from group (b));

- 8.9 million households contain someone who may have difficulty using current DTV equipment (including 2.7 million from group (b) above and all those in group (c)).

Design outlines that might provide assistance (Figure 11.14) for those who face exclusion and difficulty fall into four categories (DTI, 2006):

1. a reduced functionality set-top box for those with mild capability loss or technophobia (UK market size = 2.2 million);

2. an ultra-usable fully-featured set-top box for those with mild capability loss or technophobia (UK market size = 5.1 million);

3. an assistive set-top box (with audio description, audio feedback keys, talking electronic programme guide and distinct well-spaced buttons) for those with severe dexterity and visual capability loss (UK market size = 0.6 million);

4. an adapted set-top box (with options such as signing and voice activation) for those with other severe and multiple capability losses (UK market size = 0.3 million).

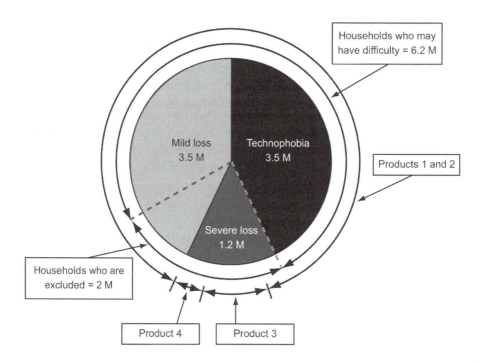

Figure 11.14   Exclusion analysis for digital television set-top boxes

Countering Design Exclusion

Assessing capability demands is only a part of a larger process required to counter design exclusion. There is a need for a range of tools and techniques to help designers and design managers with this task. The inclusive design cube (Figure 11.15) was proposed to assist in the visualisation of the scale of exclusion and the resultant design task (Keates and Clarkson, 2003). The axes represent sensory, cognitive and motion capabilities. Hence, the cube conveys a sense of the overall level of exclusion and some indication as to its source.

The cube also helps to illustrate the fact that for every product family there is an ideal population who may be able to use a well-designed product. This is likely to be smaller that the whole population. The included population, who are actually able to use the product, may also be significantly smaller than the ideal population.

The concept of an exclusion audit (see Chapter 12) has also been developed to combine the exclusion analysis described above with an expert analysis of the product interaction process and trials with actual users. This approach has proven to be particularly successful if the users involved in the trials are 'boundary' users, that is those who are right on the limit of being able to use the product. However, there remains a need to develop the means to train the expert assessors and provide guidance on the selection of suitable users for the trials.

In addition, trials of the exclusion audit have highlighted the shortcomings of the existing user data, and research is underway to develop a new database specifically for use in inclusive design that would integrate the capability and anthropometrics-based views of the user.

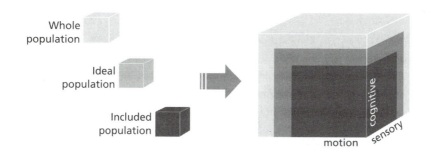

Figure 11.15   The inclusive design cube

Summary

Exclusion by design is commonplace, both at home and in the workplace. It also represents the extreme reaction to poor design which leaves many frustrated or facing difficulty, even if not excluded.

The level of exclusion, or difficulty, may in principle be determined if the prevalence of capability losses within the population is known. This is not an exact science and is critically dependent upon the quality of capability data and its applicability to product audit. However, preliminary findings from a number of analyses suggest that there is scope for improvement with many domestic products.

Research continues to improve the quality and availability of capability data and to develop robust audit tools both for products and services, and for the specification of employment opportunities for an ageing population. This is important because the quality and availability of data in appropriate formats for business leaders, design managers and designers are key drivers in the uptake of inclusive design.

References

ADA (1990), *Americans with Disabilities Act*, US Public Law: pp. 101–336.

Clarkson, P.J. and Keates, S. (2003), 'Inclusive Design – A Balance Between Product Demands and User Capabilities' Proceedings of *ASME Design Engineering Technical Conferences*, Chicago, IL.

Coleman, R. (1993) 'A Demographic Overview of the Ageing of First World Populations', *Applied Ergonomics*, 24(1), pp. 5–8. [PubMed: 15676889] [DOI: 10.1016/0003-6870%2893%2990152-Y]

Cooper, A. (1999), *The Inmates are Running the Asylum: Why High-Tech Products Drive Us Crazy and How to Restore the Sanity* (Indianapolis, IN: SAMS).

DDA (1995), *Disability Discrimination Act* (London: Department for Education and Employment).

DTI (2003), *Digital Television for All – A Report on Usability and Accessible Design* (London: Department of Trade and Industry). Research conducted by Sagentia assisted by Cambridge Engineering Design Centre. Available at: www.digitaltelevision.gov.uk/publications.

DTI (2006), *The Equipment Needs of Consumers Facing Most Difficulty Switching to Digital TV* (London: Department of Trade and Industry). Research Conducted by Sagentia Assisted by Cambridge Engineering Design Centre. Available at: www.digitaltelevision.gov.uk/publications.

Grundy, E., Ahlburg, D., Ali, M., Breeze, E. and Sloggett, A. (1999), *Disability in Great Britain* (London: Department of Social Security, Corporate Document Services).

Keates, S. and Clarkson, P.J. (2003), *Countering Design Exclusion, An Introduction to Inclusive Design* (London: Springer-Verlag).

Martin, J., Meltzer, H. and Elliot, D. (1988), *OPCS Surveys of Disability in Great Britain (Report 1): The Prevalence of Disability Among Adults* (London: Her Majesty's Stationery Office).

Microsoft (2003), *The Wide Range of Abilities and Its Impact on Computer Technology* (Redmond, WA: Microsoft Corporation). Research conducted by Forrester Research, Inc. www.microsoft.com.

Microsoft (2004), *Accessible Technology in Computing – Examining Awareness, Use, and Future Potential* (Redmond, WA: Microsoft Corporation). Research conducted by Forrester Research, Inc. www.microsoft.com.

Norris, B. and Wilson, J.R. (1995), *ChildData: The Handbook of Child Measurements and Capabilities* (London: Department of Trade and Industry).

Peebles, L. and Norris, B. (1998), *AdultData: The Handbook of Adult Anthropometric and Strength Measurements* (London: Department of Trade and Industry).

Philips (2004), *The Philips Index: Calibrating the Convergence of Healthcare, Lifestyle and Technology* (New York, NY: Philips Electronics North America). Study administered by Taylor Nelson Sofres. www.designcouncil.org.uk/Documents/About design/Design techniques/ Inclusive design/Philips Index (US version).pdf.

Semmence, J., Gault, S., Hussain, M., Hall, P., Stanborough, J. and Pickering, E. (1998), *Family Resources Survey – Great Britain 1996–1997* (London: Department of Social Security).

Smith, S., Norris, B. and Peebles, L. (2000), *Older Adult Data: The Handbook of Measurements and Capabilities of the Older Adult.* (London: Department of Trade and Industry).

United Nations (1990), *Disability Statistics Compendium* (New York, NY: United Nations Publications).

WHO (2001), *International Classification of Impairment, Disability and Health* (Geneva: World Health Organization).

WIA (1998), *Workforce Investment Act*. US Public Law, pp. 105–220.

Product Evaluation: Practical Approaches

John Clarkson, Carlos Cardoso and Ian Hosking

Introduction

Product evaluation plays a valuable role in many product introduction processes:

- providing input into product requirements

- demonstrating adherence to specifications

- reducing technical and commercial risks

- ensuring compliance with standards

- enabling feedback on user opinion.

It also has a valuable role to play in evaluating the accessibility, usability and utility of a given product.

Product evaluation may be undertaken by product users, consumer groups, product developers, independent agencies or experts, competition judges and even competitor organisations. All, for a variety of reasons, will be keen to judge the product and voice their opinion as to its performance.

Evaluation may range from the informal request for the opinion of a friend, to the deliberations of a focus group; from a carefully planned and executed user trial, to the formal application of standard tests by an independent test house; each approach meeting the need for a balance between the time and cost required to undertake the evaluation, the utility of the results and the formality with which the results need to be presented.

The ultimate evaluation remains the performance of a product in its intended market. The Cambridge Engineering Design Centre has been developing a number of evaluation approaches that focus on accessibility. These range from making designers more aware of accessibility and usability issues to user trials and exclusion audits. This chapter will describe the rationale for these approaches and describe their application to a number of familiar products.

Evaluation in the Product Development Process

Evaluation plays a key role in the product introduction process, marking the transition between the major stages in the development and delivery of a new product. The initial 'need' is likely to be evaluated before funding is committed to *conceptual design*; the product 'concept' will be evaluated before funding is released for *detailed design*; and so on. This 'stage-gate' approach, as illustrated in Figure 12.1, is widely used in industry.

The nature and extent of evaluation undertaken at each stage might be expected to be determined by the impact of progressing with the wrong design. However, this is not always the case. All too often the majority of the evaluation effort is focused on ensuring that a product meets its specification rather than checking that the specification is right in the first place.

Effective and timely evaluation is a critical factor in determining the ultimate success of a product. Undetected errors can, at best, harm product sales and, at worst, cause harm to users.

Evaluation in the Inclusive Design Process

Evaluation is particularly important in the inclusive design process where design decisions at all stages of the design process have the potential to exclude users. Inappropriate product requirements can exclude users; a poor concept can exclude users; detail design decisions can exclude users; inadequate testing can exclude users; and poor delivery, through packaging and instructions, can exclude users. This is a cumulative process, where users excluded by a poor concept are unlikely to be included by good detailed design.

Figure 12.1   **The stage-gate approach to product development**

It is important that all those associated with the product development process are able to make informed decisions with regard to the demands that the product will make of its users. Difficult decisions inevitably will have to be made, but they will be better made in the presence of good information about the product, its potential users and its use environment. Such information will come in the form of direct contact with users (through the use of interviews, focus groups and trials, and so on) and through indirect contact (through the use of simulators, personas and data, and so on) at appropriate stages of the design process.

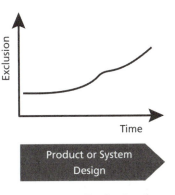

Figure 12.2   Exclusion by design

The following sections discuss a variety of approaches to evaluation in inclusive design, including the use of:

- guidance for inclusive design: mechanisms for exclusion and general approaches to product improvement

- life cycle analysis: analysis of product use from purchase, through use, to disposal

- expert appraisal: expert review of product features to highlight potential usability/accessibility issues

- capability loss simulators: tools to simulate impairment and their role in product design

- exclusion audit: detailed task-based analysis to identify specific reasons for user exclusion or difficulty

- user trials: use of lab-based trials with users to identify potential reasons for exclusion or difficulty

- an integrated approach: using more than one of the above methods to audit products.

Each approach will be described with reference to its role in product evaluation and its likely place in the design process. The sections on expert appraisal (also known as expert panels) and user trials complement those that were introduced in Chapter 10. Discussions will also make reference to case studies of mobile communication devices and household products. Finally, suggestions will be made for more advanced audit approaches, supported by the provision of appropriate methods and data.

Guidance for Inclusive Design

Design evaluation may be undertaken as a discrete activity following a period of design or integrated into the design activity. Designers engaging in the later activity must have a deep understanding of the functional and physical requirements for the product or service they are designing; its environment of use; and the capabilities of the proposed users. Guidance can play a part in raising such awareness, particularly with regard to understanding users and use environments.

As discussed earlier in the book, designers are generally able to design for themselves, understanding their own capabilities and limitations with regard to using the product or service they are designing. However, they are often less able to relate to other, potentially less able, users in the same way. This may be due to naivety, lack of experience or even lack of motivation if the client specifies a product for the younger market. Guidance can help to bridge this gap, enlightening designers with regard to the diversity of human capability and experience, and describing user-centred design activities that may enhance their design process.

GENERAL GUIDANCE

Guidance that describes the motivation for inclusive design can provide designers with an understanding of the key drivers for inclusive design. To recap:

- Knowledge of population demographics and the rate of population ageing can be used to help form a picture of the potential market for a new product or service;

- An understanding of the range of capability within the population and its variation with age provides insights as to the levels of exclusion, difficulty and frustration that may be encountered with new products or services;

- Descriptions of user capabilities and their impact on the take-up of new products or services can encourage innovation to reduce levels of exclusion, difficulty and frustration;

- Knowledge of social and educational trends can have a significant impact on the adoption of new technology.

General guidance will inform the business case for inclusive design, providing decision-makers with the information required to identify potential benefits for their intended market. General guidance will also improve design, providing designers with a framework for user-centred design.

DESIGN PROCESS GUIDANCE

Since inclusive design is an extension of normal design practice, the inclusive design process can usually be based upon an organisation's normal design process. The addition of a number of user-centred evaluation activities can transform most processes and enable the design of more inclusive products or services.

The design process may be inspired by an existing product or be driven by the desire to develop a novel concept. In either case evaluation activities can be added to inform the designer and improve the design. Since all decisions taken during the design process have the potential to exclude users it is important to continually evaluate the emerging product or service, from requirements to concept, from concept to prototype and from prototype to finished product. At each stage of the design process appropriate and cost-effective evaluation approaches must be used. These may take many forms, some of which are detailed below.

USER GUIDANCE

It is important to understand the characteristics and capabilities of the target users of a product or service so that it can be designed to meet their needs and desires. This requires a good understanding of anthropometrics and functional capabilities, and their impact on product and service use.

Anthropometry is the study of body measurements, such as height, weight and hand size, and functional measurements, such as arm reach and strength. The distribution of these measurements in a population tends to follow a typical 'bell-shaped' curve, the size and positioning of which depends on factors

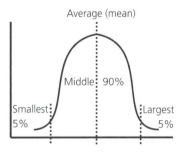

Figure 12.3   Typical anthropometric variation

such as gender, age and country of origin. It is common practice to design for the middle 90 per cent of the variation for a given population. However, this can exclude the smallest 5 per cent and the largest 5 per cent, who are likely to find the product hard or impossible to use.

People's capabilities have a significant impact on their ability to interact with most products, where interaction involves each of three main stages:

- *Perceiving*: sensing the state of the product;

- *Thinking*: determining how to respond;

- *Acting*: carrying out the movements required to respond.

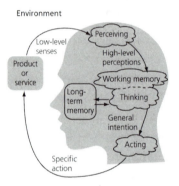

Figure 12.4   The model-human processor

Hence, performing an action as a whole involves each of the three stages and a combination of sensory (for example vision and hearing), cognitive (for example thought, intelligence and communication) and motor (for example dexterity, reach and stretch, and locomotion) capabilities.

In order to understand the possibilities (and limitations) of product interaction it is necessary to understand each capability in terms of: the function it provides; how that may be reduced through age or disability; and potential design responses to such capability loss. It is also important to understand the particular challenges that arise when designing for multiple capability losses.

It can be helpful to understand the prevalence of different capability levels within the target population since this provides insights into potential product performance targets. This is most easily done using a four-point scale:

- *Full ability* – has adequate use of the capability for everyday activities;

- *Moderate ability* – experiences some difficulties with the capability in several everyday situations;

- *Partial ability* – has significant problems with the capability in most everyday situations;

- *Minimal ability* – cannot use that capability for practical everyday purposes.

These descriptions can also be used to relate specific capabilities to population estimates for the UK population (Grundy et al., 1999). In addition it is possible to identify the prevalence of multiple capability losses that can compound the challenge facing many less able users. Multiple losses are often the result of particular medical conditions, but also arise as a result of the ageing process.

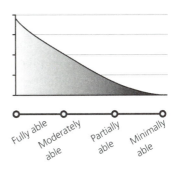

Figure 12.5   An example of levels and prevalence of capability

Evaluation Methods

There are a number of evaluation processes particularly suited for inclusive design, ranging from methods that involve users to those that do not, and from those that can be used early in the design process to those best suited to the later stages of development. The following represent a number of the more useful evaluation approaches.

LIFE CYCLE ANALYSIS

In order to evaluate a design, it is necessary to consider its use throughout its life cycle, from purchase, through use, to disposal. As the British Standards Institute (BSI) points out: 'it is manifestly counter-productive when a well-designed product is installed inappropriately, such as a telephone fixed too high on a wall for people to reach' (BSI, 2005).

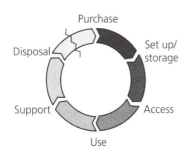

Figure 12.6 A typical product life cycle

Life cycle analysis leads the designer to consider all potential causes of user exclusion during the life cycle of a product or service. Many products 'fail' users due to over complex demands for set up or excessive demands on user capability in use. For example, mobile communication devices generally use small text and complex menu structures even for the most basic of actions. This excludes potential users not only on the basis of excessive visual demands, but also as a result of the assumed experience of menu-driven systems; both factors that particularly impact older users.

Product life cycle analysis can be extended by further dividing each part of the life cycle into a series of simple steps or tasks, utilising approaches such as those described in Chapter 10. The life cycle and task analyses form the basis of much of the observation and analysis that is described in the following sections and should also form an integral part of the design of a new product or service. In particular, they provide a framework within which to identify critical tasks that prohibit further progress if they cannot be accomplished. For example, a set-up task that is essential to allow use of the product is critical and should not be designed so as to exclude users.

EXPERT APPRAISAL

Expert Appraisal is the broad review of a product's features coupled with a detailed task-based interaction analysis to highlight potential usability and accessibility issues. It is usually undertaken by someone who has the professional training or experience to make an informed judgement on the design, for example, usability professionals, engineers, designers, experts in the product or its particular environment, or existing users.

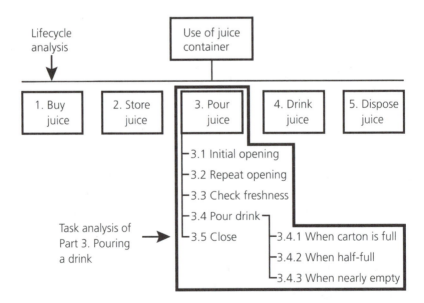

Figure 12.7   An example life cycle and task analysis

Although expert appraisal can be carried out informally, it often involves checking a design against predefined guidelines or recognised principles, and is likely to be accompanied by a life cycle and task analysis.

Expert appraisal is usually used to detect critical problems before a product is released for more thorough, and potentially more expensive, evaluation. However, it can be applied at any stage of the design process. The

Figure 12.8 Expert appraisal in action

quality of the appraisal depends on the availability of appropriate experts and their knowledge of the users and of the circumstances of use of the product. The participation of several specialists is recommended, in order that a variety of perspectives and problems can be identified.

CAPABILITY LOSS SIMULATORS

Simulators can be used to 'reproduce' the effects of different types and levels of physical (motor and sensory) capability losses, allowing the wearer to assess the accessibility and usability of a product. Their use is most appropriate when a three-dimensional model or prototype of the product is available for examination (see also Chapter 13).

Some simulation kits can be obtained commercially, for example, the Royal National Institute for the Blind (RNIB) provides sets of glasses representing different eye conditions. However, simple simulators can also be created from everyday products, for example, kitchen gloves and sports knee and elbow braces can be used to reduce freedom of movement in various parts of the body. Similarly, earmuffs and spectacles smeared with grease can be used

Figure 12.9 Cambridge 'Gloves and glasses' in action

to simulate decreases in hearing and vision capabilities.

Depending on their accuracy, simulators can provide a quick and cheap method of supplementing user trials. They can also be particularly useful in helping designers to better understand and empathise with the situations and needs of a wide range of users.

Simulators have been successfully employed in automotive design where a 'suit' has been used by designers to restrict movement and vision. 'Gloves and glasses' developed by the Cambridge Engineering Design Centre have also been used in the assessment of central heating controls and a range of household products and portable communication devices. However, it is important to remember that any simulation, no matter how good, does not enable the assessor to fully understand the consequences of constantly experiencing a reduction of physical capability. In addition, effective methods of simulating losses in cognitive capabilities are yet to be produced.

EXCLUSION AUDIT

An exclusion audit is used to estimate quantitative measures of design exclusion, indicating how many people can use a product and how many are excluded from its use. It is based on the premise that *activities* lead to *demands* on the user, and that these demands are to be met by the *users' capabilities*. Exclusion then arises if, in a given situation, the users' capabilities are insufficient to meet the demands for the particular activity.

In order to estimate levels of exclusion the demand a product places on its users must be determined. This is best achieved using task analysis to divide up the process of using the product into smaller activities or tasks, where each task places a particular demand on the users' capabilities. Demands may be estimated using available scales, for example, for vision, intellectual function and dexterity, those that have been used to estimate the prevalence of disability in the Great Britain population (Martin et al., 1988).

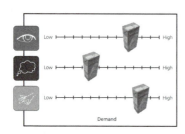

Figure 12.10   A simplified exclusion audit

By mapping product demand to national scales, it is possible to estimate how many people are likely to be excluded from using the product on the basis of each demand. These figures can be broken down to identify specific causes of exclusion, and their relationship to particular capabilities, or amalgamated to obtain an overall figure. The figures for each capability can also be compared to each other to determine which areas give rise to the highest levels of exclusion or show the most potential for improving the product's inclusivity. For example, an exclusion audit may identify that a small decrease in visual demand would include a large number of additional people, while a similar decrease in dexterity demand would only include a few more.

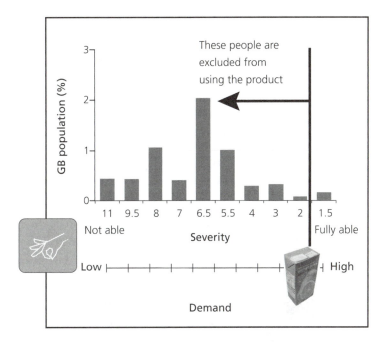

Figure 12.11   Calculating exclusion from product demand

Exclusion audits enable the comparison of existing products and new design prototypes. They can be used early on to compare competitive products and to identify elements to focus on in the redesign of an existing product. They are also valuable in later stages of the design process when a model or prototype is available to handle and examine. At this point, an exclusion audit can help to identify how to improve the product so as to increase its usability.

Figure 12.12   User trials in action, extreme users

USER TRIALS

Involving real end-users in product evaluation can provide invaluable input to all stages of the design process, providing insights into what they can and cannot do, and into their requirements and desires.

Different stages in the design process require different kinds of information and so the type of users it is best to involve also varies from stage to stage. Experience has shown the following classification of users to be helpful:

- *Extreme* users, that is those with pronounced capability loss, are valuable early in the development process to inspire creative thinking by asking questions such as 'how can a blind user use this device?' and through demonstrating coping strategies necessarily adopted for existing products;

- *Boundary* users, that is those with moderate capability loss and on the edge of being able to use a product, can most easily identify points of difficulty and exclusion in existing and proposed products.

- *Able-bodied* users, that is those with limited or no capability loss, represent the users for whom most products have been designed and are able to provide feedback about product usability at all stages of the design process.

Figure 12.13   Able-bodied users

In practice, all three user types can provide valuable insights into understanding user needs and preferences, while a mix of boundary and able-bodied users is particularly well suited to evaluating existing and proposed products.

Trials can take place in the user's home or at the design office. Both bring some advantages and disadvantages. Observations in the home are more likely to expose 'real' behaviour with familiar products, while trials at the office allow for easier setting-up and recording of controlled experiments. In both cases, the ethics of the trial and the comfort of the users are paramount.

An Integrated Approach

All of the evaluation methods described above have their strengths and weaknesses. Some are easy to use, but provide limited results. Others are more expensive, but provide valuable insights. In practice, it is useful to use more than one of the methods to address the issues that arise at different stages of the product development process. For example, an exclusion audit can provide valuable input into the business case for a new product, extreme users can inspire creativity during concept generation, while user trials with boundary users can confirm that design targets have been met.

The following sections illustrate evaluation approaches that can be taken to support product development by reference to two recent design projects.

Mobile Communications

Sagentia, with assistance from the Cambridge Engineering Design Centre, have been working with Vodafone to develop the framework for a more inclusive mobile phone.

The company was aware of the potential of inclusive design to provide technology for the widest range of users, including those with various levels of auditory and visual impairments, and have identified a big opportunity in the gap between mainstream and specialist products. However, they wished to gain a true picture of the diversity of the population and the market potential to help inform and rationalise medium- to long-term product and service development plans.

The first stage in addressing this challenge was to undertake a broad-based accessibility audit of five mobile phones, comprising:

1. detailed life cycle and task analyses of key phone functions from purchasing through set up to use;

2. expert appraisal, by two independent teams, of each product and its use throughout its life cycle;

3. an exclusion audit of each product and its use throughout its life cycle;

4. user trials of each product with older users;

5. consolidation of the assessment results and development of a business case and requirements for an improved product.

The audit provided many interesting results, identifying numerous opportunities for developing a more inclusive product. However, it also reminded the team that users with impairments still want phones that are small, stylish and desirable. Compromise will be necessary, but inclusive design can inform the compromise to improve the end result.

Sagentia continue to assist companies in the development of better phones, where the key lesson learned, in line with the findings of Philips (2004), is that simplicity is the ultimate, and often illusive, sophistication.

Household Products

Sprout Design, with the assistance of the Cambridge Engineering Design Centre, have been working with a major supplier of household products to review and improve a number of products from their range.

The company was aware of inclusive design and keen to engage in a range of activities to improve their understanding of the subject. As a result they:

- attended an inclusive design conference;

- sent key management, design, marketing and production personnel on a 1-day general inclusive design training course;

- read key texts on inclusive design;

- undertook extensive user trials to observe customers using existing products;

Figure 12.14   Product exclusion life cycle begins in the store

- encouraged staff to identify good and bad examples of inclusive design;

- commissioned the Royal College of Art and The Helen Hamlyn Centre to organise a workshop with extreme users and designers;

- developed a number of novel product packaging concepts.

In addition, they identified a number of products for further evaluation and redesign. For each product the team undertook a market survey, limited user trials and used product with 'gloves and glasses' simulators. They also undertook an expert appraisal and exclusion audit for each product and its use throughout its life cycle, identifying limiting tasks and reasons for exclusion. Finally, exclusion targets for a more inclusive product were set and a number of improved design concepts proposed, which were subsequently subjected to a further exclusion audit. In later projects, Sprout Design also advised the company during the re-design of the products.

Typical findings from such evaluations included:

- all products had a strong brand identity that assisted their location in the supermarket, but product variants were not always as easy to distinguish;

- instructions for use were typically compromised by attempts to make packs multi-lingual, resulting in the use of small fonts and figures;

- much of the packaging was impenetrable without the aid of a sharp object and set up procedures tended to be overly complex;

Figure 12.15   Product evaluation with gloves and glasses

- product features designed to assist use were often not visible due to lack of colour contrast;

- product use was compromised by the need for two-handed operation or understanding of overly complex use sequences;

- simple changes to the product or packaging design could potentially yield much lower levels of exclusion or difficulty in using the products.

This dual approach of improving the company's general awareness of inclusive design along with undertaking specific product audits proved successful. They are now better able to specify more inclusive products and work with external designers to deliver them.

Summary

Design evaluation plays an important role in the design of more inclusive products and services, enabling designers and product managers to identify areas for special attention and improvement. There are many evaluation approaches that can be employed at various stages of the design and development process to increase understanding of general accessibility issues as well as to provide qualitative and quantitative assessment of specific task sequences.

Effective use of evaluation must balance the ease of theoretical studies with the potential benefits of a well-planned, but more expensive, user trial. Above all else it is important to realise the particular benefit of evaluation in inclusive design, where a broader, and possibly less familiar, range of user capabilities must be considered. Good design will be dependent upon good and robust evaluation.

References

BS 7000-6 (2005), *Guide to Managing Inclusive Design* (London: British Standards Institution).

Cambridge Engineering Design Centre (2003), 'Inclusive Design Website: Assessment Section'. Available at: www.eng.cam.ac.uk/inclusivedesign.

Card, S.K., Moran, T.P. and Newell, A. (1983), *The Psychology of Human-Computer Interaction* (Hillsdale, NJ: Lawrence Erlbaum Associates).

Grundy, E., Ahlburg, D., Ali, M., Breeze, E. and Sloggett, A. (1999), *Disability in Great Britain* (London: Department of Social Security, Corporate Document Services).

Martin, J., Meltzer, H. and Elliot, D. (1988), *OPCS Surveys of Disability in Great Britain (Report 1): The Prevalence of Disability Among Adults* (London: Her Majesty's Stationery Office).

Philips (2004), *The Philips Index: Calibrating the Convergence of Healthcare, Lifestyle and Technology* (New York, NY: Philips Electronics North America). Study administered by Taylor Nelson Sofres. www.designcouncil.org.uk/ Documents/About design/Design techniques/ Inclusive design/Philips Index (US version).pdf.

The Center for Universal Design, (1997), *Principles of Universal Design*. Available at: www.design.ncsu.edu/cud/about_ud/udprinciples.htm

User Simulation in Product Evaluation

Carlos Cardoso and John Clarkson

Introduction

The involvement of real users during the design process is typically accepted as an essential approach to developing products and services that fulfil the needs and requirements of the wider population. However, despite user involvement being a very useful and inspiring approach, it is not always feasible in everyday design practice. Time, cost, logistical and sometimes ethical approval requirements prevent many design companies from having access to real end-users. Consequently, when assessing the ease of use of their design solutions, designers tend to use their own personal and professional skills to predict how users will interact with products and what type of difficulties they might encounter. This approach is often defined as self-observation. Whereas most designers might be skilful enough to predict a wide range of typical usability problems, an obvious shortcoming of this approach is the designers' assumption that they can be representative of a wider and heterogeneous population.

Trying to guess and commit to memory the different user attributes that may result in unexpected behaviours or difficulties when interacting with certain products is an overwhelming task to accomplish. On the other hand, the use of design support tools, such as literature on ergonomics and software packages, are sometimes avoided because of the format in which they display information or the time it takes to learn how to use them. This suggests that the implementation of more interactive and quick-to-use evaluation tools could potentially support designers in performing more objective judgements during the design process.

This chapter reviews the use of physical (motor and sensory) capability loss simulators as an evaluation tool aimed at helping designers to experience and anticipate more objectively some of the problems that people, exhibiting varying degrees of physical capability loss, may encounter when interacting with a wide range of everyday products, services and environments.

Simulation: Background

Simulation, as discussed here, involves a person (usually able-bodied) wearing physical restrainers to feel the effects of different types of capability loss. For instance, the wearer can use simulators that restrict movement in key parts of the body such as hands, elbows and knees. Also, earplugs and fogged spectacles can be used to simulate auditory and visual capability loss, respectively.

At this stage, it is important to clarify why this chapter talks about simulating *functional capability loss* and not simulating *impairments*. Within the context of inclusive design, a *disorder* is a medical condition such as osteoarthritis, which can affect several different joints in the body (for instance, hands, knees and hips). This disorder may cause an *impairment* that describes how particular body parts are affected due to the effects of the condition, such as osteoarthritis causing bone cartilage to become pitted, rough and brittle resulting in pain and stiffness of the joints. These symptoms of impairment may affect a person's *functional capabilities*, for instance limiting the hand's or arm's freedom of movement and/or strength.

Disability, which is caused by products and surroundings, occurs when the capabilities required to use a product or service surpass those of the user. Simulation involves reducing the wearers' sensory and motor *functional capabilities*. The aim is to alter the wearers' experience of their environment by imposing sensory and/or motor capability losses upon them. Ultimately, the aim is to show how everyday products often 'disregard' (and hence *disable*) a large number of users, due to a lack of consideration of their capacities. For this effect, several simulators have been developed within the field of user-centred design, ranging from simple to more sophisticated devices.

SIMPLE SIMULATORS

One of the first capability loss simulations took place in the early 1980s and involved a group of architects wearing spectacles that reduced their visual capabilities, while carrying out several tasks in everyday environments. Other more recent studies, especially in the field of design education, included simulation workshops where undergraduate students wore simple simulators to learn about the problems disabled people may experience when performing daily activities. The students tried to simulate, for instance, the effects of arthritic fingers by affixing buttons with tape on the knuckles of each finger. Visual capability loss was simulated by wearing blindfolds and fogged spectacles. Also, some experiments have been carried out involving students dressed up with ice hockey equipment, to simulate motor losses, such as difficulties reaching for and manipulating objects.

Other interesting exercises include, for instance, breathing through a straw while climbing stairs to simulate fatigue related problems. Some people also suggest putting dried beans inside the shoes to simulate the effects of gout and, ultimately, affecting the ability to walk and keep balance. Despite being low-fidelity tools, these and other simulation approaches are an economical and effective way of raising awareness about the effects of capability loss variation, which a large number of people may exhibit.

SOPHISTICATED SIMULATORS

More complex simulation apparatus include the Third-Age Suit, developed by Ford Motor Co. and Loughborough University in the UK; and the Age Explorer, developed by Meyer-Hentshel, a consulting firm in Germany (www.dw-world. de/dw/article/0,,782623,00.html).

Both suits are made of coveralls with components (for instance, elbow and knee braces) sewn on, which attempt to simulate average levels of physical capability loss that older adults (over 60 years) may exhibit. These suits restrict movement in hinge points of the body, such as hands, elbows, knees and neck. Additionally, earmuffs and yellow spectacles try to simulate hearing and visual capability losses, respectively.

The Third-Age Suit has helped Ford's designers to understand and anticipate the special driving requirements of their older customers. This contributed to the commercial success of the Ford Focus, which has been described as easy to use, especially in terms of getting in and out of the car and of operating the driving controls. The Age Explorer has been used by Meyer-Hentschel as an in-house audit tool for training young professionals from a variety of companies, such as automotive, white goods and travel.

Despite the usefulness and popularity of these simulation tools, recent studies recognised the limitations of the Third-Age Suit when taking into account the combination of multiple impairments as well as the simulation of different levels of physical capability loss. Consequently, those studies pointed out the need to develop practical simulators, which provided designers with meaningful data, simulated different levels of capability loss and did not restrict design creativity.

LIMITATIONS OF THE SIMULATION TOOLS

It is important to be aware that any simulation, in spite of being a useful way of experiencing temporarily the symptoms of impairment, does not enable designers to fully understand the consequences of being constantly impaired. People who exhibit real capability losses may have lived with that problem for a long time and may have developed alternative strategies for interacting with their surroundings, which designers would probably not predict even if using very accurate simulators. Equally, poor or imprecise simulation could lead designers to assume that the user characteristics and needs have been understood, which might result in inadequate assessment decisions.

Consequently, simulation is suggested here as a supplementary assessment tool and not a replacement for the experience and benefits of working with real users. Resorting to simulation as the only assessment technique to be implemented throughout a typical design process is likely to be insufficient at milestone stages when involving real users is of most importance. Another limitation of this type of tool is the difficulty in simulating cognitive capability losses. It has been suggested (but not recommended) that cognitive loss could be induced temporarily by consuming alcohol and other drugs or by undergoing sleep deprivation. However, safety is an obvious issue and it would be more appropriate, for instance, to ask people to perform several tasks at the same time, such as doing some mathematical count backwards while using the device being assessed. Due to the complexity of incorporating the simulation of cognitive capability loss into existing toolkits, these have been hitherto focusing on mimicking the effects of sensory and motor capability losses.

A Calibrated Simulation Toolkit

One of the main aspects that differentiate the simulation toolkit presented here from other existing solutions is the incorporation of the concept of capability loss as a continuum. The toolkit aims at counteracting the common misconception that capability variation is split between the minimally able and the able-bodied. In fact, since people's capabilities can range from low through medium to high levels, the toolkit is designed so as to enable a graduated simulation of different levels and combinations of physical capability losses. The toolkit focuses, primarily, on the simulation of visual, hearing, locomotion, reaching and stretching, and dexterity loss.

An integral part of the development of this toolkit was to go beyond the issue of raising awareness about the physical capabilities of older and disabled users and provide designers with a tool that was as accurate as feasibly possible. However, designing simulators that enable their wearers to experience what it is like to have their capabilities reduced is only part of the problem.

It is also important that the type and the level of capability loss being simulated are realistic and capable of producing meaningful data. This involves a thorough simulation of the capability losses that real end-users may exhibit, and ideally a direct mapping to the number of people with such characteristics across the wider population. Unless the levels of capability loss being simulated by the toolkit are related to real numbers of people, it will be very difficult to perform an objective and informed assessment of a particular product. For instance, while wearing visual and dexterity restrainers to assess the ease of use of a dishwasher, a designer may feel more physically affected by the capability limitations imposed by the visual simulator. This may lead the designer to consider that the visual attributes of the dishwasher (the labelling, colour of different features, and so on) may be a more urgent problem to address, than for example the shape of the door handle, or the ease of turning of different buttons. However, if in the wider population there happen to be more people exhibiting dexterity rather than visual limitations, such an assessment decision may prove inadequate. Hence the importance of knowing about the number of people behind each level of calibration of the toolkit. Without this information, and solely based on their own physical perception, designers may overlook such problems.

Ultimately, the goal is that, by imposing particular capability losses upon someone wearing the simulators, it is expected that they will experience similar types of disabilities to the ones encountered by real users when interacting with their surroundings. This understanding, along with information on numbers of people affected, would potentially enable designers to identify the most difficult features to use with the device being assessed.

In order to achieve this quantifiable calibration, however, it would be necessary to have access to statistical demographic data on how peoples' capabilities vary across the wider population. Such a complete source of information does not presently exist. In fact, data sources comprising information about people with impairments and disabilities vary widely. Also, they are more likely to focus on single capabilities rather than all the necessary human characteristics that should be considered when assessing user-device interaction. Therefore, until a new and thorough population survey on the relevant human characteristics is carried out, it is not feasible to accurately and realistically calibrate a wearable simulation toolkit.

Nevertheless, as an exploratory study, the toolkit presented here was calibrated against an existing population survey of disability carried out in Great Britain (Martin et al., 1988; Grundy et al., 1999). The simulation toolkit was built with the purpose of replicating each of those levels. For instance, the visual loss simulators comprised different pairs of spectacles that gradually reduced the wearer's ability to see people and objects at different distances, or read varying text sizes. Similarly, the dexterity restrainers reduced the ability of the wearer to manipulate objects of different sizes (kettles, cups, scissors, safety pins). As previously mentioned, the simulators aimed at mimicking capability losses and not impairments or disabilities. However, these population disability scales contain very little information about capability loss and the impairments that may have caused it, which makes it difficult to accurately calibrate the different components of the toolkit. Therefore, a series of assumptions had to be made while designing the calibration of the toolkit, inevitably involving some degree of subjectivity.

Ultimately, the map between the different levels of capability loss simulated and an estimate of the number of people exhibiting such limitations, would help designers to uncover and prioritise problems, increasing the opportunities for (re)designing more usable solutions. However, prioritising problems merely based on the number of users excluded may be too simplistic in many circumstances. It is also important to take into account the frequency of the problems identified, the relative importance of the interface element being used and sequence of actions being carried out, as well as the time and budget available for any design change. That is why it is important to consider the simulation toolkit as a part of a wider assessment structure and not as a stand-alone tool.

DESCRIPTION OF THE TOOLKIT

The toolkit presented here is made of modular components, each one addressing the simulation of physical capability loss in different parts of the body. The advantage of using modular components is that the assessors need only put on the parts of the toolkit that will enable them to affect specific capabilities. Previous simulation tools (such as the Third Age Suit or the Age Explorer) were generally made of coveralls with restrainers sewn on, making it necessary to put on the whole suit even if the objective was only to simulate, for instance, arm movement limitations.

The simulation toolkit presented here is basically divided into the number of capabilities that it tries to impair: vision, hearing, locomotion, reaching and stretching, and dexterity.

VISUAL CAPABILITY LOSS SIMULATORS

The visual simulators comprise nine pairs of spectacles that try to reproduce decreasing levels of visual acuity (the ability to perceive details presented with good colour contrast) through increasing the blurriness on the lenses (Figure 13.1). As the wearer puts on the different spectacles, the ability to recognise people and discriminate detail in the surroundings diminishes. The spectacles also affect the ability to perceive objects with poor colour contrast.

HEARING CAPABILITY LOSS SIMULATORS

Figure 13.1   Visual capability loss simulators

These simulators include a set of earmuffs and ear plugs. These devices affect mainly the ability to perceive different sound levels. They make it difficult to hear clearly people talking, or some feedback sounds, such as bells and ring tones. Unlike the majority of the other components in this toolkit, which were either designed from scratch or adapted from existing gear, the hearing loss simulators were bought off the shelf.

LOCOMOTION CAPABILITY LOSS SIMULATORS

Since locomotion is related to the ability to walk and climb steps, but also to bending and straightening, these physical restrainers decrease both the wearer's ability to easily perform flexion of the legs but also to bend the torso (Figures 13.2 and 13.3). Knee braces with a metallic structure interfere with the ability to walk, climb steps and squat down, for instance to pick something from the floor. A large waistband, with inserted vertical plastic strips, inhibits the action of bending forward and laterally.

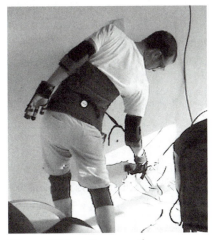

Figure 13.2   Locomotion capability loss simulators

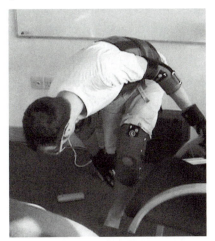

Figure 13.3   Locomotion capability loss simulators

REACHING AND STRETCHING CAPABILITY LOSS SIMULATORS

This part of the toolkit limits arm movement in two main hinge points: the elbow and the shoulder (Figure 13.4). Flexion of the forearm is constrained by

braces with inserted plastic strips placed at the back of the elbow. Shoulder flexion and extension are limited by adjustable straps that are connected to the waistband, which are also part of the locomotion restrainer. Adjustability of the shoulder movement enables the wearer to set the range of motion of both arms to specific angles. According to the level of severity to which these components are calibrated, the wearer will have difficulties, or even be prevented from, reaching at various heights, for instance to pick up an object from a shelf in front of the body, at head level or above.

Figure 13.4   Reaching and stretching capability loss simulators

DEXTERITY CAPABILITY LOSS SIMULATORS

The main impairment effect of the dexterity restrainers is to restrict the flexion of the fingers, for instance when trying to close the hand to pick up, manipulate and hold different objects (Figure 13.5). These simulators are composed of loose finger pockets that are placed at the back of each finger and that can be adjusted according to the size of the wearer's hand. Inside these finger pockets increasing numbers of plastic strips can be inserted to augment the difficulties in closing the hand. This dexterity simulator also includes a wristband that limits movement of the wrist.

Figure 13.5 Dexterity capability loss simulators

TESTING THE TOOLKIT

The development of the simulation toolkit presented here was the result of consecutive refinements carried out throughout the implementation of three major studies. The studies involved observation of several groups of older adult users (exhibiting varying levels and different types of capability loss) and able-bodied young design practitioners. All groups were involved in the assessment of a number of everyday devices (electric kettles, domestic central heating control units, and digital television receivers).

The older adult participants acted as potential end-users and the designers as assessors. Whereas the former group used each device once only, the designers performed self-observation evaluations first, followed by simulation assessment (while wearing the toolkit). The results gathered from the observations of the end-users enabled the identification of a large number of problems of several types that the devices placed upon them. The number and types of problems identified by the designers during self-observation were in turn compared with those revealed by the users. The study then compared how many and what type of problems designers identified after having undertaken the simulation assessments, and compared these results against the previous two assessment stages.

The findings from these studies, and the feedback provided by the designers throughout, influenced the reformulation and further development of the simulation toolkit.

OVERVIEW OF RESULTS

Apart from minor exceptions, the simulation toolkit (Figure 13.6) enabled the

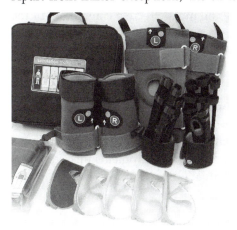

designers to always identify more problems than those found during their self-observation assessments. The problems designers identified while wearing the simulators were also generally consistent with those that the users had previously encountered. The physical restrainers prompted the designers to revisit problems identified during self-observation, being particularly useful at helping designers to uncover several new ones.

Figure 13.6   The simulation toolkit

Ultimately, it was the simultaneous capability loss imposed by the toolkit that increased significantly the level of physical effort required to perform even the most trivial actions. Designers were surprised at the impact that the simulators had upon their capabilities. This was clearly verbalised, for instance, by one of the designers wearing the simulators while trying to bend down to plug a cable to the main socket: 'this is very difficult… how am I supposed to go down? This is exhausting, every single movement becomes a big act when you think about whether you really have to get up and down or not, whereas normally I would not think about it'. Designers had not anticipated how common, everyday actions could become exceedingly difficult to perform when their capabilities were severely reduced.

This was especially the case with the identification of the products' interactive demands in terms of vision and dexterity. Most of the products assessed in these studies involved either the ability to see and read specific product features, or the skills and strength to handle various components. For instance, one designer described the effort required to undo a set of small cable ties, which were holding together some electrical cables of a digital set up box receiver, saying: 'if I had one disabled [hand] or eyesight it would be much easier, but since I have simultaneous disabilities, this makes it even harder to [do] it'. Another designer talks about the difficulties in using a remote control: ' … is like hard to read and [you] can't actually press the right button'; or as another designer also commented 'very difficult to press buttons… [the] remote is very small, so I cannot hold it with one hand properly'. Both the visual and dexterity simulators were particularly relevant in enabling designers to uncover a lot of problems that they had previously overlooked when using their full able-bodied capabilities.

The visual simulators were probably the most effective component of the whole toolkit. This is very interesting because these simulators were also the easiest and cheapest to construct, which suggests that even simple simulators can be quite useful.

The reaching and stretching and the locomotion simulators also had a notable impact during the simulation assessments, for instance as previously mentioned by a designer struggling to bend down and reach the socket on the wall. They were fundamental in the identification of problems missed by the designers during their self-observation evaluations.

Simulation as a Supplementary Assessment Tool

The aim of using simulators during the design process is to explore alternative and engaging ways of assessing the ease of use of everyday interactions. However, it is important to bear in mind that this is a supplementary technique to designers' self-observation and not a replacement for the way they work. Using simulation as the only method of assessing a device's ease of use could induce designers to focus only on the physical capability loss being simulated. This could lead designers to overlook other important aspects of the interaction. The end result could be that designers would rely excessively on the use of this tool and miss certain design shortcomings that could have been uncovered during typical self-observation evaluations, or even more importantly during user trials.

For instance, when assessing the ease of use of three electrical kettles, some of the designers pointed out during self-observation that the surface of two of the kettles got dangerously hot after boiling. They also said that the hot steam would come towards the handle when pouring water from the first kettle. These same problems were not mentioned again by these same designers during simulation assessments. It is possible that the gloves simulating dexterity limitations (which were an earlier version of the latest simulators) unintentionally protected their hands against the high temperatures. These restrainers have since been redesigned to avoid situations like these. Nevertheless, in real design practice it would be more appropriate to resort to simulation as a supplementary approach to self-observation. Considering the results from the two methods together will increase the chances of uncovering a wider range of design problems.

Simulating the 'Right' Capability Losses

Despite the efforts involved in calibrating the existing capability loss simulators, these were not accurately calibrated against the real impairments that the users exhibited. Instead, the simulators were calibrated against the descriptions of the users' level of disabilities, presented in the population scales mentioned previously. In practice, the different components of the toolkit tried to simulate possible (but not all) capability losses that, ultimately, could have led the designers to experience a series of real disabilities. However, impairment and disability are two distinct concepts. In fact, different impairments can give rise to the same disability. For instance, two entirely different impairments such as: a swelling and stiffness of the joints (typically generalised as 'arthritis'); and a breakdown of the muscled fibres leading to weak and wasted muscles (muscular dystrophy), could both result in the same disability of not being able to turn knobs on a microwave, if these were too stiff to rotate. Until this date, it has not been feasible to incorporate all the possible symptoms of impairments described by the survey used into the simulators developed. This was due to a lack of information about the specific impairments behind the disabilities described on the survey and also to technical limitations in achieving a completely accurate simulation toolkit.

Another important aspect of the toolkit that ought to be considered is the fact that any restriction placed upon the wearers' capabilities is applied externally. The toolkit components consist of physical wearables that are placed over different parts of the body to reduce the wearer's capabilities. However, most real capability losses are likely to be caused by different and usually complex internal dysfunctions, such as swelling of the joints, muscle breakdown, or clouding of the eye lenses. Hence the toolkit's limitation in *simulating* rather than *replicating* particular behaviours.

An equally critical issue is the fact that the simulators were not designed to cause any pain or suffering, but instead to reduce the designers' motor and sensorial capabilities. Real users may, for instance, experience varying levels of pain while using their hands (for example caused by rheumatoid arthritis of the hand), which may result in capability losses not being simulated by the toolkit. However, causing exceeding levels of discomfort or even inflicting pain upon designers was considered unethical, and thus efforts were made to avoid such occurrences. This will inevitably lead to simulations that do not reproduce all the real symptoms of impairments that users exhibit. For instance, the majority of disorders related to some form of arthritis present pain and stiffness as the main impairment, which prevents people from moving different parts of their bodies comfortably. Yet in terms of capability loss simulation, externally stiffening a joint to limit range of movement is probably one of the few things that can be 'ethically' simulated, since it can be achieved without causing any pain.

Therefore, in spite of the physical restrainers enabling designers to identify a wide range of problems that users also experienced with the different devices, the simulators should be used cautiously. They are meant to provide designers with insights into the types of capability limitations that some people may exhibit and, consequently, into some of the disabilities they experience. However, designers should not rely exclusively on what the simulators enable them to experience, but rather supplement the usefulness of this tool with other assessment techniques.

Summary

Despite the existing limitations in developing a simulation toolkit that is accurate and truly representative of the real end-users, the concept of using capability loss simulators during the design process is popular among designers. Simulation offers the benefits of supplementing time-consuming and expensive user trials with the additional bonus that designers can experience a wide range of difficulties faced by users with physical limitations. Experiencing disabilities in such a tangible manner helps designers to cope with the complexity of interpreting particular impairments, or trying to guess the physical challenges that older adult or disabled people may encounter. This kind of information is potentially easier to understand and to incorporate into design decisions. However, knowing about the potential of such a tool is as important as being aware of its limitations.

This chapter discussed how the calibration of the capability loss simulators could be approached to develop a tool that enables designers to objectively quantify the difficulties imposed by particular product features. The major shortcomings of the toolkit developed have also been acknowledged and identified. They were mainly related to the lack of a complete and consistent data source on impairments and capability loss. In everyday design practice it is expected that the simulators would have a greater impact (and thus be more useful) for design practitioners who are not particularly familiar with the issues pertinent to inclusive design.

The existing simulation toolkit has now been used by a few design companies in several accessibility assessments of different everyday products. Preliminary interviews with these companies showed that the toolkit was particularly useful to identify a series of accessibility problems not predicted by the designers. In addition, feedback from these practitioners also suggested that the simulators can play an important role in facilitating the communication of ideas between the designers and their clients. This is particularly the case in raising the client's awareness regarding the levels of avoidable exclusion of 'non-mainstream' users (such as older and disabled people), caused by particular product features.

The toolkit has been further redesigned, increasing its potential to provide design practitioners with a design tool that is visually and physically powerful at conveying the need and opportunity for more inclusive design approaches. This will ultimately raise awareness and help designers to improve quality of life through the design of products, services and workplaces that promote independence and social inclusion.

References

Cardoso, C. (2005), 'Design for Inclusivity: Assessing the Accessibility of Everyday Products'. PhD dissertation, (Cambridge: Cambridge University).

Coleman, R., Lebbon, C. and Myerson, J. (2003), 'Design and empathy' In *Inclusive Design: Design for the Whole Population*, Clarkson, P.J., Coleman, R., Keates, S. and Lebbon, C. (eds.) (London: Springer-Verlag).

Grundy, E., Ahlburg, D., Ali, M., Breeze, E. and Sloggett, A. (1999), *Disability in Great Britain* (London: Department of Social Security, Corporate Document Services).

Hasdogan, G. (1996), 'The Role of User Models in Product Design for Assessment of User Needs', *Design Studies*, 17, pp. 19–33. [DOI: 10.1016/0142-694X%2895%2900007-E]

Hitchcock, D. and Taylor, A. (2003), 'Simulation for inclusion... true user-centred design?' Proceedings of *International Conference on Inclusive Design*, Royal College of Art, London.

Hitchcock, D., Lockyer, S., Cook, S. and Quigley, C. (2001), 'Third Age Usability and Safety: and Ergonomics Contribution to Design', *International Journal of Human-Computer Studies*, 55, pp. 635–643. [DOI: 10.1006/ijhc.2001.0484]

Nicolle, C. and Maguire, M. (2003), 'Empathic modelling in reaching design for all' In *Universal Access in HCI: Inclusive Design in the Information Society*, Stephanidis, C. (ed.) (London: Lawrence Erlbaum Associates).

Pastalan, L.A., Mautz, R.K. and Merrill, J. (1973), 'The simulation of age related sensory losses: a new approach to the study of environmental barriers' Proceedings of *International Edra Conference*, Stroudsburg, PA.

Poulson, D., Ashby, M. and Richardson, S. (eds.) (1996), *USERfit −A Practical Handbook on User-Centred Design for Assistive Technology* (Brussels: ECSC-EC-East Asian Economic Caucus). Available at: www2.stakes.fi/include and www.education.edean.org

Where Do We Find Out?

Cherie Lebbon and Susan Hewer

CHAPTER

14

Introduction

The motivations for researching the inclusive design field will be many but users can be broken down into three broad communities: business, design professionals and design education.

Each of these communities will have their own questions about inclusive design. For instance a company manager might be looking for data on the ageing population and its impact on the market place. A design consultant may need to support her argument to persuade a client that inclusive design is the right approach. On the other hand, a student might be trying to meet a project brief in which an understanding of inclusive design needs to be demonstrated.

Most of the key inclusive design websites are linked, allowing the user to make a journey around the worldwide expertise in inclusive design. However, it is not easy to navigate through the mass of references that a search produces. For instance, making a search using a common phrase such as 'Inclusive Design' brings up about 6,000,000 potential links to a huge number of sites; for 'Universal Design' this number rises to a staggering 19,600,000. This is further complicated by the fact that the results can change every time a search is made. Such abundance can be overwhelming, so where can users find reliable accessible information to support their work?

This chapter lists key resources to help users find the start point of their searching journey. It makes specific recommendations to business managers, design professionals and design students. For the main target audience of this book, that is design educators and design students, it provides case studies from the RSA (Royal Society for the encouragement of Arts, Manufactures and Commerce), illustrating what students can achieve by participating in a major design competition, Design Directions, in the UK.

Key Resources

After consulting a number of UK experts in inclusive design, we drew up a list of inclusive design 'top tens': top ten websites, books, conferences and journals. They are listed here as key, general resources. This is by no means a complete list; however, it will offer you a straightforward route map for information about inclusive design.

Top Ten Websites

DESIGN COUNCIL: ABOUT DESIGN (www.designcouncil.org.uk/en/ About-Design/Design-Techniques/Inclusive-design)

A comprehensive knowledge-base covering key aspects of design. Accessible from the UK Design Council home page by clicking on the About Design link on the left hand side bar.

ADAPTIVE ENVIRONMENTS: HUMAN CENTRED DESIGN (www.adaptiveenvironments.org)

A comprehensive, searchable collection of worldwide resources.

HELEN HAMLYN CENTRE: CENTRE FOR INCLUSIVE DESIGN (www. hhc.rca.ac.uk)

A UK-based website, focusing on the research and practice of inclusive design through collaborations with industry, academia and design professionals, in particular through its Research Associate Programme and annual competitions.

CAMBRIDGE ENGINEERING DESIGN CENTRE (www-edc.eng.cam.ac.uk)

A project-based research website for inclusive design, with a tutorial for inclusive design available from www.eng.cam.ac.uk/inclusivedesign

INCLUSIVE DESIGN SURVEY www.eng.cam.ac.uk/inclusivedesign/ dtisurvey (also accessible at www.betterdesign.org)

Inclusive design business survey, business case and card sets on inclusive design.

RSA INCLUSIVE DESIGN (NOW EDEAN DESIGN FOR ALL EDUCATION AND TRAINING) (www.education.edean.org)

A 'one-stop' website bringing together new and existing information about inclusive design, suitable for newcomers as well as practitioners. Developed by Helen Hamlyn Centre and the RSA as part of the Engineering and Physical Science Research Council-funded i~design 1 programme. This web resource has now been taken on by the European Design for e-Accessibility Network (EDeAN). EDeAN is an EU-funded network of 160 organisations in European Union member states. The goal of the network is to support all citizens' access to the Information Society.

EUROPEAN INSTITUTE FOR DESIGN AND DISABILITY (www.design-for-all.org)

A communication platform with links to a number of European Institutes promoting inclusive design. Lots of news relating to design and disability.

TRACE RESEARCH AND DEVELOPMENT CENTER: DESIGNING A MORE USABLE WORLD – FOR ALL (http://trace.wisc.edu)

A US-based website providing general information, standards, guidelines and specific tools and resources, with a focus on ICT products.

CENTER FOR UNIVERSAL DESIGN: ENVIRONMENTS AND PRODUCTS FOR ALL PEOPLE (www.ncsu.edu/www/ncsu/design/sod5/cud)

Seven principles of universal design and case studies, with a focus on housing, public and commercial facilities.

CENTER FOR INCLUSIVE DESIGN AND ENVIRONMENTAL ACCESS, UNIVERSITY OF BUFFALO (IDEA) (www.ap.buffalo.edu/architecture/research/idea.asp)

This website supports educators and students in teaching and studying inclusive design.

RICABILITY (PRODUCT DESIGN) (www.ricability.org.uk)

A consumer-research agency with expertise in product evaluation for older and disabled people. Many reports on product evaluation by specialist user panels and usability experts. Publishes unbiased guides for older and disabled consumers.

For environmental designers, it is worthwhile referring to:

CENTRE FOR ACCESSIBLE ENVIRONMENTS (www.cae.org.uk)

Practicalities of inclusive design in the built environment: information, design guidance, training and useful links to a number of access-related website.

Top Ten Books

UNIVERSAL DESIGN HANDBOOK

W. Preiser and E. Ostroff (eds.), McGraw Hill, New York, 2000, ISBN 0071376054.

A comprehensive reference book of great breadth, bringing together selected papers from two 'Design for the 21st Century' conferences on universal design (1998, 2000).

INCLUSIVE DESIGN: DESIGN FOR THE WHOLE POPULATION

J. Clarkson, R. Coleman, S. Keates and C. Lebbon (eds.), Springer-Verlag, London, 2003, ISBN 1852337001.

Comprehensive, international and authoritative coverage of all aspects of inclusive design.

COUNTERING DESIGN EXCLUSION: AN INTRODUCTION TO INCLUSIVE DESIGN

S. Keates and J. Clarkson, Springer-Verlag, London, 2003, ISBN 1852336994.

A text book describing methods for measuring and quantifying design exclusion based on UK population data.

APPLIED ERGONOMICS, 24(1), 1993

Seminal special issue on designing for our future selves, with an overview on ageing process, design strategies and evaluation methods.

TRANSGENERATIONAL DESIGN: PRODUCTS FOR AN AGING POPULATION

J.J. Pirkl, R. Van Nostrand, New York, 1994.

An excellent book written by an industrial design educator, with many case studies and illustrations.

LIVING LONGER: THE NEW CONTEXT FOR DESIGN

R. Coleman, Design Council, London, UK, 2001.

A 56-page online booklet describing the context of inclusive design in a simple and straightforward way.

THE UNIVERSAL DESIGN FILE: DESIGNING FOR PEOPLE OF ALL AGES AND ABILITIES

M.F. Story, J.L. Mueller, and R.L Mace, 1998, The Center for Universal Design, NC State University.

A guide for studying and evaluating universal design. Introduces Seven Principles of Universal Design. Available online : www.design.ncsu.edu/cud/pubs/_p/docs/UDPMD.pdf.

USERFIT –A PRACTICAL HANDBOOK ON USER-CENTRED DESIGN FOR ASSISTIVE TECHNOLOGY

D. Poulson, M. Ashby and S. Richardson (eds.), Brussels, Luxemburg: ECSC-EC-EAEC. 1996.

A useful collection of user research methods for Assistive Technology, many of which can be applied to inclusive design. Out of print, but worth seeking out.

ACCESS BY DESIGN (INTERIOR DESIGN)

G. Covington, and B. Hannah, John Wiley & Sons Inc., and Van Nostrand Reinhold, 1997.

Jointly written by a former Special Assistant for disability to the Vice President of the USA and an award winning industrial designer, this book describes access issues with a number of useful checklists.

INNOVATE: THE JOURNAL OF THE SMALL BUSINESS PROGRAMME OF THE HELEN HAMLYN CENTRE

J. Cassim (ed.), The Helen Hamlyn Centre, Royal College of Art.

A collection of case studies from a UK inclusive design competition organised jointly by the HHC and the Design Business Association. Published twice a year from 2001 to 2004, and superseded in 2005 by *Challenge: Giving disabled people a voice in the design process*, both available from www.HHC.rca.ac.uk/resources/publications.

Top Ten Conferences

INCLUDE (www.hhc.rca.ac.uk/kt/include/2007/index.html)

A biennial international conference on inclusive design, hosted by the Helen Hamlyn Centre, Royal College of Art. Proceedings in CD-ROM format.

DESIGNING FOR THE 21ST CENTURY (www.designfor21st.org)

A biennial or triennial international conference on universal design, hosted by the Adaptive Environments. Proceedings in CD-ROM format and also available online.

CWUAAT (http://rehab-www.eng.cam.ac.uk/cwuaat)

A biennial workshop on Universal Access and Assistive Technology, hosted by the Engineering Design Centre, University of Cambridge. Proceedings in book format by Springer-Verlag.

INTERNATIONAL CONFERENCE FOR UNIVERSAL DESIGN (http://ud2006.iaud.net)

The conference is hosted by the International Association for Universal Design in Japan.

ERCIM WORKSHOP: 'USER INTERFACES FOR ALL' (http://ui4all.ics.forth.gr/workshop2006/)

A biennial workshop on the topic of User Interfaces for All each year since its establishment in 1995.

ERGONOMIC SOCIETY CONFERENCES (www.ergonomics.org/index.htm)

An annual conference covers all areas of ergonomics research, including inclusive design. Proceedings in book form published by Taylor & Francis Ltd.

ESDA (www.lamp.polito.it/esda2006)

A biennial ASME Conference on Engineering Systems Design and Analysis with topics relating to inclusive design.

RESNA (www.resna.org/Conference/Conference.php)

An annual conference of the Rehabilitation Engineering and Assistive Technology Society of North America.

ASSETS (www.acm.org/sigaccess/assets06)

A biennial conference on computers and accessibility.

CHI (www.chi2008.org)

An annual premier international conference for human-computer interaction covering a wide range of interaction design topics.

Top Ten Journals

THE DESIGN JOURNAL (www.ashgate.com/subject_area/art_history/art_journals.htm)

International journal for all aspects of design. Readership includes design professionals, researchers, educators and managers.

APPLIED ERGONOMICS (www.elsevier.com/wps/find/journaldescription.cws_home/30389/description#description)

An international journal, covers ergonomics applications in the office, industry, consumer products, information technology and military design. Readership includes ergonomists, designers, industrial engineers, health and safety specialists, systems engineers, design engineers, organisational psychologists, occupational health specialists and human-computer interaction specialists.

DESIGN STUDIES (www.elsevier.com/wps/find/journaldescription.cws_home/30409/description#description)

The only journal to cover all design domains, including design management, design methods, participation in planning and design, design education, AI and computer aids in design, design in engineering, theoretical aspects of design, design in architecture, design and manufacturing, innovation in industry and design and society.

GERONTECHNOLOGY (www.gerontechnology.info/Journal)

International journal on technology for the ageing society. It reflects the broad categories of interest in the field: health, housing, mobility, communication, leisure, and work.

UNIVERSAL ACCESS IN THE INFORMATION SOCIETY

International journal publishes research work on the design, development, evaluation, use, and impact of Information Society Technologies, as well as on standardisation, policy, and other non-technological issues that facilitate and promote universal access. Coverage includes theories, methods, tools, empirical results, reviews, case studies, and best practice examples with a focus on universal access. www.springerlink.com.

DESIGN MANAGEMENT REVIEW (www.dmi.org/dmi/html/publications/ journal/journal_d.jsp)

Formerly the Design Management Journal, devoted to articles and case studies exploring how design – in products, communication, and environments – is an essential resource, a component of every organization that can be effectively managed to make important contributions to the bottom line and to long-term success.

THE INTERNATIONAL JOURNAL OF ART & DESIGN EDUCATION (www.blackwellpublishing.com/journal.asp?ref=1476-8062)

A primary source for articles about art and design education at all levels.

DIVERSITY IN DESIGN: THE JOURNAL OF INCLUSIVE DESIGN EDUCATION (www.ap.buffalo.edu/idea/diversityindesign)

A new electronic journal that examines diversity issues in design education. It encourages a global community of designers and educators to create new knowledge, partnerships, and gateways to inclusive design education.

BEHAVIOUR AND INFORMATION TECHNOLOGY (www.ingentaconnect. com/content/tandf/tbit)

An electronic journal published by Taylor and Francis. Subjects include Computer Science, Information Technology, Health Science, Human Factors and Ergonomics.

JOURNAL OF DESIGN RESEARCH (published by Inderscience – www. inderscience.com)

An electronic interdisciplinary journal, emphasising human aspects as a central issue of design through integrative studies of social sciences and design disciplines.

Three Paths

The 'top ten' list serves as a general resource of inclusive design. Different users may require different types of information. This section points out three paths for business managers, design professionals and design educators/students. To ease information search, a key start point for each path is given. Typical questions of potential users are listed, all of which can be answered by starting at the suggested website.

A BUSINESS PATH

The best start point for a business path is the 'About Design' section of the UK Design Council site (see Figure 14.1).

Figure 14.1 Design Council's Inclusive Design website

BUSINESS/DESIGN MANAGER QUESTIONS AND START POINTS

- What is the business case for inclusive design?

- Are there any management standards relating to inclusive design?

- Is there any legislation that might affect my business?

A DESIGN PATH

The best start point of a design path is the RSA (Now EDeAN) Inclusive design resource (see Figure 14.2).

DESIGN CONSULTANCY QUESTIONS AND START POINTS

- Do any of the disability related organisations offer any design guidance?

- Is there training available on inclusive design practice?

- Where do I find out about inclusive design research methods?

A DESIGN EDUCATION PATH

The best start points of a design education path are the Universal Design Network website and the Design Council inclusive design education resource at www.designcouncil.info/inclusivedesignresource (see Figure 14.3).

Figure 14.2 The RSA Inclusive Design Resource website

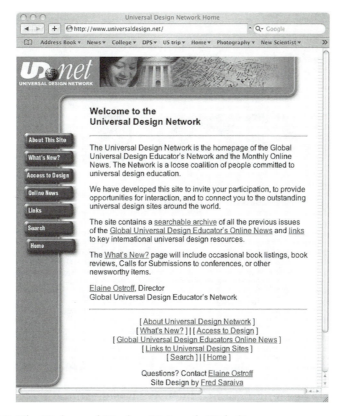

Figure 14.3 The Universal Design Network Website

DESIGN TUTOR QUESTIONS AND START POINTS

- Can I get support materials for teaching?

- Are there any case studies available?

- Can I share teaching experience with others?

DESIGN STUDENT QUESTIONS AND START POINTS

- What have other designers done?

- Is there an opportunity for postgraduate study in the UK?

Organisations are regularly updating their websites and new knowledge is entering the public domain constantly, so these resources should be regarded as active and dynamic and revisited on a regular basis rather than just mined once for information.

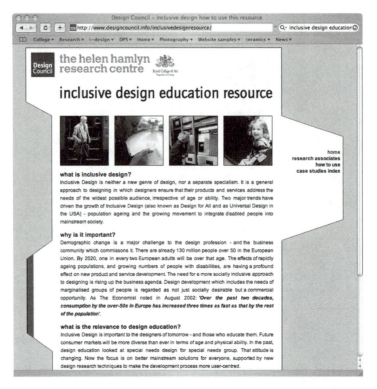

Figure 14.4 The Design Council Inclusive Design education resource

Learning by Doing

For practising designers and design students an exciting and more immediate way of becoming involved in inclusive design is to participate in design competitions. Direct action, or learning by doing, has proved to be a powerful way of building up exemplar design practice and solutions. Chapter 8 has illustrated case studies of inclusive design competitions for practising designers. In this section, we shall focus on case studies involving design students. For many of these students, the experience of engaging with inclusive design challenges and working with older and disabled users has been a life-changing experience and one that has shaped and guided future careers. It has also brought a sense of purpose and commitment to their work and demonstrated that through good design we really can make the world a better place.

RSA Design Directions

The Royal Society for the encouragement of Arts, Manufactures and Commerce (RSA) has been engaged in promoting inclusive design in the UK since

1986. That year witnessed Helen Hamlyn's groundbreaking 'New Design for Old' exhibition at the Victoria & Albert Museum, which alerted industry and design to the urgent need for better, age-friendly design in an era of demographic change. Emerging from this exhibition came the first student-focused competition when Helen Hamlyn initiated the RSA's New Design for Old project in 1986. The Mercers' Company has also helped to develop the scheme, allowing the RSA to offer specific prizes; for example, for an entry which has demonstrably sought opinions from users. In fact, this competition places action research and iterative user evaluation at its heart and many of its 'alumni' have gone on to

Figure 14.5 The New Design for Old exhibition catalogue designed by Vignelli Associates

set up user groups for large companies or have become academics running design courses with strong inclusive design input. The case studies that follow demonstrate the breadth of work and strength of purpose that has been stimulated by this major design competition.

Take Jeremy Lindley, for example. Now Category Development Director – Design at Diageo with responsibility for driving packaging design (this following a number of years as Head of Design for Tesco Stores), his RSA winning design for an inclusive, easy-to-use gas pre-payment meter with heating control led him to develop his interest in the principles of inclusive design in his professional life. This has resulted in a number of innovations in retail, including the classic 'shallow-trolley' for Tesco. This is an example of a product designed originally for older people with restricted movement to cope with the standard deep trolleys, but which now has a universal appeal.

Figure 14.6 Gas meter for Student Design Awards by Jeremy Lindley

Figure 14.7 Shallow-trolley for Tesco

Moving to Inclusive Worlds

The New Design for Old project was extraordinarily successful and influential in harnessing support and enthusiasm for the subject from both tutors and students, but in 2002 the RSA moved the project to another level in order to ensure that the needs of the whole population were addressed through mainstream design. Thus, in 2003, a new design challenge was launched – Inclusive Worlds. This project aims to address these wider issues through briefs that seek inclusive approaches to design. By introducing students to this methodology at an early stage in their careers, the intention is that designing inclusively will become the norm and will thus form an integral part of future professional life.

The Inclusive Worlds brief asks candidates to respond to one of five challenges:

1. How can we make domestic and public environments more inclusive?

2. How can access to information limit exclusion?

3. How can smart wearables change lives?

4. How can the design of products and the environment make life more fun?

5. How can we make things better?

From the beginning there was a clear need to provide both tutors and students with easily accessible tools and information about the subject and that was why the RSA launched the online Inclusive Design Resource: www.inclusivedesign.org.uk in July 2004 (now at www.education.edean.org). The resource has been developed to introduce newcomers to key concepts, examples and design/research methods and to support practitioners in gathering together their own tools and methods.

Allan Sinclair benefited from the competition and resource, having been an Inclusive Worlds winner in 2004 and 2005 and he has certainly changed his career path since he became involved with inclusive design. The first award was for 'Motigait' – a rehabilitation product which helps disabled children to walk and adults to recover after illness such as stroke – and secondly, for 'tennis sensation' a virtual game designed for all types of user but enabling visually impaired people to compete equally. Both designs have a broader mainstream use while being targeted at specific users with certain impairments. Since then Allan has been working on an inclusive consumer product for the company Sagentia in Cambridge prior to starting a postgraduate course at the University of Cambridge.

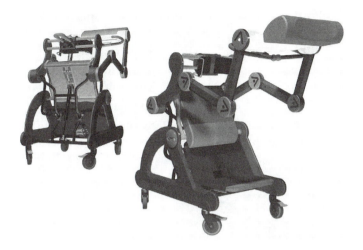

Figure 14.8 Motogait – a rehabilitation product for people of all ages

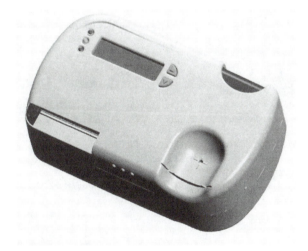

Figure 14.9 Lancitor – a blood analysis monitor

Natalie Scott was the Inclusive Worlds Winner in 2003. By tackling some problems that are faced by diabetics, a growing group within the population, Natalie took a truly inclusive approach. The 'Lancitor' is a blood analysis monitor, combining lancet and monitor in one product, which is especially useful for visually impaired diabetics yet equally beneficial to other users. The product pricks the finger with one touch of a button while another winds on the pre-loaded test strip roll for the next use. The roll is replaced like a camera film by slotting it into the product. Natalie, who has since completed a postgraduate course in Design, Manufacture and Management at the University of Cambridge, has taken out a patent on this design.

Richard Telford was an Inclusive Worlds project winner in 2004. He worked with users from the very start of the project and identified specific problems which older people encountered when using microwaveable ready meals. He found these meals offered an appropriate solution to the needs of older people (and, indeed, to many people of any age), but the packaging left much to be desired. Richard addressed each of the problems and presented solutions – from print instructions through to stay-cool handles. The results were much more user-friendly, safer and would benefit any user, regardless of capability.

Figure 14.10   Microwavable packaging

Information about how to enter the Inclusive Worlds competition can be found via the RSA website, www.rsadesigndirections.org.

In addition to the Inclusive Design Resource, the RSA has produced other, printed, materials to help both tutors and students get started and develop their knowledge of this area. *The DAN* (Design for Ageing Network) *Teaching Pack* for instance, was a resource produced in 1995 to assist in incorporating age-related issues into design courses. Aimed at tutors teaching on undergraduate design courses in universities, it contained an overview of design strategies, design guidelines, professional and student case studies and all supplemented by slides.

Figure 14.11   The DAN Teaching Pack

Moving Forward – New Design for Old, was a publication produced in 2000, which looked back at winning designs from the New Design for Old student project and demonstrated the influence of the scheme. [Copies of this are still available from the RSA].

Finally, *Inclusive Worlds – How to...* produced in 2003 to support the Inclusive Worlds project, provides tips and perspectives for students, from tutors and practitioners, to assist them in designing inclusively. [Copies available from the RSA, free of charge].

The ultimate aim of the competition, of course, is to encourage all students – not just those already motivated and who therefore take part in Inclusive Worlds – to apply inclusive design principles, no matter what the project they are undertaking. The RSA's aim is to encourage students to take account of broader economic, social and ethical issues and to consider these when developing their solutions. For example, do the solutions they

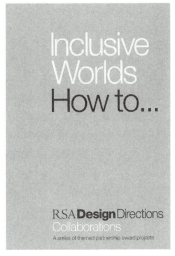

Figure 14.12   'How to Design Inclusively' booklet

propose contribute to the inclusion of all members of society? Do they take account of the need to be accessible? Designers have an important role to play in achieving a fair and equitable world and so it is appropriate that they are asked to take account of these issues in responding to any Design Directions project.

Conclusion

The exploration of resources in this chapter demonstrates the breadth of information and support available to anyone: from those looking to gain a general understanding of how inclusive design affects their business to those working on specific design projects. We hope more and more business managers, practising designers and design educators will become familiar with principles of inclusive design. The aspiration is that, in the future, there will no longer be the need for a project or competition that encourages a more inclusive approach to design – people will automatically apply the principles.

Towards Inclusion: Future Challenges

*Julia Cassim, Roger Coleman,
John Clarkson and Hua Dong*

Raising the Bar

This book has not only covered the how and why of inclusive design; each of our authors has given some thought to what has been achieved and what remains to be done, along with continuing challenges, and it is well worth gathering those insights together in thinking about where best to concentrate our energies in the future.

On the positive side, what is clear is that a raft of practice and process models has been developed and considerable resources created in the form of publications, websites, conferences and design exemplars. The inclusive design knowledge base has achieved a degree of maturity in recent years, and the current goal must be to ramp up the level of knowledge transfer to industry. The publication of BS 7000-6 has delivered a driver for industrial uptake, but the pace of that will depend very much on the support available to industry and the level of knowledge transfer achieved. The inclusive design website commissioned by BT (http://www.inclusivedesigntoolkit.com/) and made publicly available through the company's Corporate Social Responsibility programme is a big step forward in this regard. In tandem with BS 7000-6 and the Design Council web resource on inclusive design (see page 212, we can see the foundations of a public knowledge base that can be added to by the research community and built on by companies that recognise the potential for competitive advantage through inclusive design.

We are well placed for the future and can face it with confidence, but must not slip into complacency. There remains a need for constant vigilance, to ensure that standards do not slip. It will take some time before designing for inclusion becomes the norm and is recognised as an essential component of good design. One way of achieving this is through more robust consumer pressure on manufacturers and suppliers, to ensure that gains in inclusivity are not watered down or lost in the next generation of products and services. This is a challenge for the voluntary sector and representative organisations of older and disabled people, and could be a spur for direct consumer action. It is also a challenge to commercial organisations to ensure that they encourage and sustain a dialogue with consumers and engage them in rigorous evaluation of what is on offer. This in turn requires a change in attitude within marketing and advertising, a greater emphasis on fitness for purpose in products and services, and a focus on consumer benefit rather than promotional gimmickry.

Another way of achieving this is to develop and nurture a generation of aware and well-equipped young designers, with a vision of a more equitable world, and this is an important challenge for design education. Luckily, many young people have an instinct and desire to make the world a better place, and inclusive design can offer them a way to do that. But we must also remember that inclusive design has its own very clear limitations. It is essentially about making public environments and consumer products and services more accessible, usable and desirable. The better we do that, the fewer people will be excluded from participation in the mainstream of society, but we will never be completely successful in this endeavour. The practical limitations and economics of production and distribution processes, technologies and design innovation will mean that a small, but significant minority will be excluded, even if we are most careful to ensure that the implementation of new technologies – such as the set top box for digital television discussed in Chapter 11 – does not unnecessarily exclude vulnerable groups.

Working at the Margins

There will be a continuing and important need to work at the remaining margins of the capability curve, where the usability challenges are the greatest. There is good reason to believe that innovations in this area will deliver important usability gains in the future. For example, predictive (or disambiguating) text technology was developed as an aid to communication for disabled people before it found its ubiquitous application in mobile phones. Importantly, we need to see the field of assistive technology and universal access as a precursor to inclusive solutions in the mainstream and invest in it accordingly. We also need to see a high quality design input, to ensure consumer adoption beyond the immediate target group, where mere functional advantage will present a real benefit. That suggests collaborations between designers and those working in assistive technology and is something that the research councils and the charities and other bodies funding such work should take note of and encourage.

Managing Design

If inclusive design is to be seriously adopted by business, and there is growing evidence that things are moving in this direction, then there will be a continuing need for the sort of tools, guidance and resources described in section three of this book that can support that endeavour. Much has been done in this area, but a big gap remains in our understanding of how best to implement and manage inclusive design. The new British Standard sets out a framework for this, and offers tools and techniques for achieving it, but there is a dearth of real life experience of introducing the level of cultural change required within organisations, of promoting the benefits of inclusive products and services, and of sustaining them in the marketplace. Given that this is a very new approach for many companies, there is a need and an opportunity to study the uptake and implementation of inclusive design in its early phases, and to learn lessons and generalise them through business and management studies.

Case studies of successful and less successful designs, and how they were arrived at and commercialised, will help advance understanding in this area. So too will case studies of the companies such as OXO Good Grips that have succeeded in taking inclusive products to the marketplace. Understanding market advantage and how to maximise it is a crucial part of the business case for inclusive design, and a further fleshing out of that case is urgently required to convince companies that an inclusive approach and ethos outweighs the perceived risks involved. In an era of early commercial adoption of inclusive design, gathering these case studies is not easy, but remains of vital importance.

Engaging with Users

One of the major success areas of inclusive design has been the encouragement of user involvement in design, and the development of models and exemplars of how to achieve this. The Challenge Model, as described in Chapter 7, has proved particularly influential in changing the attitudes of professional designers, largely because they have seen it as a way of driving innovation and creativity. For them, direct user engagement is more effective than guidelines, which are perceived as inhibiting by the creative industries. This is not the case in engineering, town planning and construction, where guidelines and regulations are welcomed as a way of simplifying and clarifying often complex decision-making processes, and of creating level playing fields in terms of expectations and cost implications.

The advantage of guidelines and legislation is that they are readily available as publications. The problems of direct engagement with users are many, from time and cost to recruitment, and importantly in the process area itself – in how to do it. Here there is a real need to develop either a nation-wide resource, or a network of local resources and expertise that designers and companies can tap into. There is an equivalent need in education at degree and post-graduate level, but also in schools. Inspiring and nurturing a new generation of inclusive designers will be crucial for the future, and the most effective way of doing this is to encourage young people to think about people other than themselves. Ensuring that young people have meaningful contact with older and disabled people is pivotal in this regard; not an easy thing to organise, but a challenge that could be taken on by appropriate voluntary sector organisations.

From Product to Service

While much of this book is inevitably concerned with the design and development of products and systems, and there is no doubt that older and disabled users will benefit greatly from more inclusively designed products and accessible interfaces, the biggest gains are now likely to be made in the area of information technology and associated services. Indeed, products of the future are most likely to be component parts of larger services to which they function as access points. Mobile phones are a good example, along with PDAs, the Blackberry, and of course personal computers. As intelligence is increasingly embedded in products this trend will gain momentum and we will move nearer to the illusive 'smart' home and other 'smart' environments.

Ensuring that these new developments deliver the potential benefit to the widest possible range of users will not be easy. The discussion of the rapid introduction of set top boxes discussed in Chapter 10 illustrates some of the challenges involved. At the core of this is the need to really understand different users and the different ways in which they are likely to access and use services. As is pointed out in Chapter 8, 'Usability is only possible, and actually only definable, with regard to a particular user group, doing a particular task in a particular context.' Given that as new technologies are introduced people find uses for them that were not initially envisaged, 'texting' on mobile phones being a good example, this is likely to remain a central challenge for the foreseeable future. Just as the Disability Discrimination Act and Part M of the Building Regulations have created a need for specialist accessibility consultants, so there is likely to be a significant demand for user research specialists to ensure that new technological applications are implemented in inclusive ways.

Not only will this have implications for the introduction of new technologies, such as digital television, and the convergence of other information technologies around those access points; it is also likely to drive the development of more user-specific and customisable forms of interface and access devices. As we move closer to the personalisation of 'smart' devices and environments, there will be a growing need to set up and customise them, either through the support of experts, as we see in computing, where most offices and businesses have some form of in-house or on-line IT support, or more expert and readily customisable systems that can remember the preferences of multiple users. Getting this process right, and ensuring that a 'smart' future is genuinely user-friendly and inclusive is perhaps one of the biggest challenges we face. As Newell and Monk say in Chapter 8, 'The inclusive design of software and services is not a matter of designing for the maximum possible proportion of the general population. It is about defining and understanding your target users, what they want to do and the context in which they do it, and then and only then, making sure that the real needs and wants of this user population are catered for.' How successfully we achieve this, for example through customisable interfaces and access devices that enable individual users to navigate multiple option services, such as those envisaged for digital television platforms, will determine how inclusive or exclusive the 'smart' future will be.

Importantly, as we move into an era of 'smart' environments, where information is shared and exchanged between people, products, buildings, roads and the services and systems within which such elements function, we will see a convergence of people, products, interfaces and place which will raise new issues for inclusive design. If earlier approaches were very much focused on removing and eliminating physical barriers to access, for example for wheelchair users, ensuring that all are treated equally and ethically in the information rich environments of the future will challenge many of our assumptions about ownership and control of information and about privacy and personal rights. As our environment becomes more 'aware' of our presence – of who we are, of our capabilities, preferences, networks and histories – the potential for inclusion will grow, but along with it the potential for considered and unconsidered exclusion will grow too. The challenge of social inclusion will take on new dimensions in the near future, and as in the past, while some of these will be practical and amenable to design thinking, others will be profoundly political and impact on human rights in new ways.

Better Data

In Chapters 11, 12 and 13, the authors discuss ways of assessing, measuring and simulating design exclusion. Some of the methods described are relatively 'rule of thumb' and designed to give people working in design and development simple tools to help them understand and assess levels of inclusion and exclusion. In essence, these tools are user-friendly representations of complex population data, and the effectiveness of the tools is dependent on the quality of the underlying data. For example, simulators, such as the 'Third Age Suit' developed at Loughborough University and used in the design of the Ford Focus, can give designers both practical and empathic insight into the capabilities of older users, but only recently have attempts been made to 'calibrate' simulators to accurately represent specific sets and sub-sets of users.

The accuracy of this calibration depends on the availability of good data, as does its usefulness to industry and in particular marketing and business decision-making. The team at the University of Cambridge responsible for developing these calibrated simulators is well aware of the limitations of currently available data sets, such as the OPCS surveys of disability in Great Britain. An immediate challenge is to first design, and then undertake a new national survey of sufficient size to give the required data set that can underpin a generation of better and more accurate tools for assessment and evaluation of designs and also be employed in the design and development process.

There is no doubt that the 'Third Age Suit' made a significant contribution to the success and accessibility of the Ford Focus, an early example of inclusive design in action, and it is important not to undervalue the contribution that existing tools and techniques can make in design. However, the certainty that would come from a truly representative national survey is likely to be a powerful driver for industry uptake of inclusive design. That survey should be designed to better understand the spread of capabilities across the nation and their impact on everyday life in terms of common activities, social participation, independence and well being, and how capability impacts on the use of everyday products, services, environments and interfaces.

Making the Social Case

Better data would also support the making of a convincing 'social case' for inclusive design. Population ageing is now well understood, and the design implications of an ageing population have been set out in a publication by the UK Design Council and also by the DTI Foresight Ageing Population Panel in its reports. Extending active independence is the major goal in this area, and a crucial economic driver is the dramatic shift in the potential support ratio (the number of people of working age relative to one older person above retirement age) as the population ages and birth rates remain low. Encouraging people to work longer is a further goal, and the raising of the UK pensionable age to 67 has been proposed as an additional measure to reinforce this.

While there is a clear general case for lifetime homes and age-friendly products and services, the economic and social benefits of adopting inclusive design as a national goal have not been spelled out. Making that case effectively could go a long way towards triggering government support for a drive towards inclusive design and focusing the DTI on encouraging and supporting UK business and industry in that endeavour.

Living Longer – Working Longer

If increasing longevity and a reducing support ratio mean that we will all have to work longer, then work and the working environment will have to become more appealing to older people. Just as youthful companies like Google seek to make the work environment attractive, with relaxation areas and an opportunity for employees to develop their own ideas and contribute to the company's success, established organisations are going to have to ensure that the work environment is age-friendly, and that the design of equipment and technology accommodates the older worker. Job design will also have to change, as part-time working and working from home become increasingly important to retain an ageing workforce. This near virgin territory is a real research and design challenge, and a significant commercial opportunity both for employers and for companies supplying the buildings, equipment and facilities to house and support the multi-generational workforce of the future.

It will require an extension of access consultancy and auditing from its current focus on disability and wheelchair access, to encompass the needs of older people in the workplace and ensure that public buildings and transport systems are equally age-friendly.

Research Challenges

As industrial uptake of inclusive design becomes a reality, we can add to the well-understood and continuing research challenges of understanding consumers, understanding designers, and understanding business needs, more specific challenges in the practical area of implementing inclusive design. There is now an urgent need to focus on the effective managing, validating and evaluating of inclusive design.

How do we commit an organisation to inclusive design, how do we decide what it is we need to do: what makes a product or service inclusive, how and for whom? How do we manage the design and development process towards that goal, how do we determine that we have achieved what we set out to achieve, that the product, service or interface performs as it was meant to? And how do we advertise, promote and sustain it in the market place? It is clear from the chapters covering these subjects, that although good progress has been made there is still much to understand and a paucity of best practice exemplars and case studies.

Understanding how to make inclusive design work for industry and building up the case study knowledge base in this area is probably the most pressing task and challenge for the inclusive design research community.

Are We Making Progress?

There are important tasks and challenges ahead, but it is also worth reflecting on some of the progress made by the inclusive design community over the past few years. In 2001, the Design Council, through its publication *Living Longer: The New Context for Design* set out a series of 15 recommendations, primarily for government and DTI for action, but with more general implications for business, education and design. These were grouped under 5 main headings:

- champions for inclusive design
- getting business on board
- plugging the knowledge gap
- involving the older consumer
- building the skills base.

Although these recommendations related to older people, the delivery mechanism was seen to be inclusive design. Consequently, they offer us a good datum point against which to measure achievements since 2001.

CHAMPIONS FOR INCLUSIVE DESIGN

The publication suggested that these be appointed at national and local government level, and there has been little or no progress on this front. The implication is that government has not seen a strong economic and social incentive to put its weight behind inclusive design. Clearly national recognition for inclusive design and monitoring of progress would provide a powerful incentive for business and the voluntary sector, while establishing inclusive criteria for purchasing at local and national government levels would further reinforce that incentive. There is much that needs to be done in terms of bringing government on board, in particular in setting out the economic and social case in convincing terms that reveal the potential impact of inclusive design in extending independence and well being, and effectively reducing the need for expensive care in the home.

GETTING BUSINESS ON BOARD

Significant progress has been made in this regard, although not necessarily through the DTI, as suggested. Market leaders have been brought on board, the design industry has been solidly engaged, young designers have been well targeted with some exceptional successes. Less progress has been made on the promotion of inclusive design, but importantly, a new British Standard is in place, directly addressing recommendation 7, and there is growing understanding of the issues within industry.

Excellent progress has been made in this area. Although there are still significant gaps to fill, the inclusive design knowledge base has expanded dramatically over the past 6 years and is now in a very healthy state. Not only that, it has become increasingly available and accessible, in particular through its presence on the Internet, and most recently through the BT Inclusive Design Toolkit website that was made publicly available in July 2007.

INVOLVING THE OLDER CONSUMER

Some good progress has been made in terms of engaging with older and disabled consumers and their representative organisations. The cerebral palsy charity SCOPE, the Royal National Institute for the Blind and the Royal National Institute for Deaf and Hard of Hearing, the car scheme for disabled people Motability, the Research Centre Institute for Consumer Affairs Ricability and the major age charities have all taken an interest in and played a part in promoting the value of inclusive design both to the communities they represent and nationally, to the general public.

BUILDING THE SKILLS BASE

With regard to curriculum development and incentivising students and tutors through awards schemes, educational programmes and professional training, considerable progress has been made. The establishment of a European network on e-accessibility (EDeAN) will ensure that inclusive design is embedded in educational curriculum through its 160 member organisations. The RSA has created an Inclusive Worlds section within its new 'Design Directions' awards scheme (described in Chapter 14), and the Inclusive Design Challenge hosted by the UK Design Business Association (as described in Chapter 7) has been successfully exported by the Helen Hamlyn Centre to Japan, Israel, Korea and China.

Progress is less evident in business and management studies, which is disappointing, as informed business decision making and purchasing have the potential to complete a virtuous circle of consumer pull and design push, and it is worth considering why this has not taken place in the UK. Here there is an interesting international comparison. In Japan, inclusive design is driven by interest at senior management level, and by committed designers working within industry. The Japanese business model allows a degree of collective action and commitment that is not paralleled in the UK. This suggests an important role for the DTI in encouraging and supporting the uptake of inclusive design by individual companies, which, ironically, is exactly where there has been least progress on the 'Living Longer' recommendations.

Design has a central role to play in the drive for a more inclusive society. So much has been achieved in recent years, and the adoption of inclusive design thinking by design professionals in the UK, Europe, Japan, the US, and elsewhere is impressive. Business is coming on board, and what is now needed is a focused lobbying campaign to communicate the potential benefits to decision-makers in government and industry, and ensure that design for inclusion features high on the political and commercial agenda.

References

BS 7000-6 (2005), *Guide to Managing Inclusive Design* (London: British Standards Institution).

Design Council (2001), *Living Longer: The New Context for Design* (London: Design Council).

Grundy, E., Ahlburg, D., Ali, M., Breeze, E. and Sloggett, A. (1999), *Disability in Great Britain* (London: Department of Social Security, Corporate Document Services).

Martin, J., Meltzer, H. and Elliot, D. (1988), *OPCS Surveys of Disability in Great Britain (Report 1): The Prevalence of Disability Among Adults* (London: Her Majesty's Stationery Office).

Index